Radical Wisdom

Radical Wisdom

A Feminist Mystical Theology

Beverly J. Lanzetta

Fortress Press
Minneapolis

Cover art: *Woman Walking*, colored glass collage, © Shoji Sato/Photonica. Used by permission.
Cover design: Laurie Ingram
Book design: Beth Wright

Unless otherwise noted, scripture quotations are from *The New Jerusalem Bible*, copyright © 1985 by Darton, Longman and Todd, Ltd., and Doubleday, a division of Bantam Doubleday Dell Publishing Group, Inc. Reprinted by permission.

Library of Congress Cataloging-in-Publication Data
Lanzetta, Beverly.
  Radical wisdom : a feminist mystical theology / Beverly J. Lanzetta.
    p. cm.
  ISBN 0-8006-3698-8 (alk. paper)
  1. Feminist theology—History. 2. Women mystics. 3. Mysticism—History. I. Title.
  BT83.55.L36 2005
  248.2'2'082—dc22
                          2004025450

Manufactured in the U.S.A.
09   08   07   06   05   1   2   3   4   5   6   7   8   9   10

In memory of
my maternal grandmother
Gilda Annucci Acampora
1899–1958

and

in honor of
the many women who have graced my life by sharing their soul wounds
and spiritual strengths, and the countless women who nourish and sustain
life

I dedicate this book with deepest gratitude and respect.

Contents

Acknowledgments

I wish to thank the Association for Religion and Intellectual Life for awarding me a Time-Out Fellowship to attend Studium at St. Benedict's Monastery in St. Joseph, Minnesota, where major portions of the book were first conceived and written. I especially want to acknowledge the spiritual support and generous welcome I received from all the women of Studium—in particular Srs. Theresa Schumacher, Linda Kulzer, and Dolores Super—who provided an atmosphere of loving silence and lively friendship. Through their commitment to this project, Studium granted me an additional fellowship, which allowed me to return to St. Benedict's for another extended period of research and writing. Equally important, without the academic resources of the Southwest Institute for Research on Women (SIROW) I never would have been able to complete this book. I am, thus, deeply appreciative of the commitment Janice Monk, Sally Stevens, and all the faculty and staff at SIROW make in support of women's scholarship.

In the rocky shoals of life, much can be accomplished when we do not travel alone. Over these years of writing and teaching, three women have remained life-long companions on the journey. I am most grateful to Sarah Stein, Margaret Riordan, and Patricia Kilcullen for their generosity in reading and commenting on major portions of the text. Their indomitable love and anarchic humor have kept me going. In addition, I would like to thank Patricia for her faithful rendering in graphic design of my original sketch of the seven dwelling places (*moradas*) in St. Teresa of Avila's *The Interior Castle*, which appears in chapter 6.

Writing is one endeavor that consumes the whole person. But having to publish what one writes is its own particular kind of angst. It is the calm presence and kind heart of my dear friend and acting agent, Charles Roth, who has guided me through the sometimes bewildering decisions that accompany the publishing enterprise. I could not be happier that Charles brought my manuscript to Michael West, editor-in-chief of Fortress Press. It is a distinct pleasure to collaborate with Michael, whose gracious enthusiasm for *Radical Wisdom*, along with his depth of knowledge about theological issues, has inspired and encouraged me. I must also extend my highest praise to all the professionals at Fortress Press for their dedication and for the extraordinary efforts they make to bring vital religious issues into the public domain.

All of this would not be possible without the great weaving cloth in which I am held and nurtured by family. They inhabit the text, reminding me to write from my heart about things that matter to life, here and now. It is my mothering responsibility to Maya, Gina, Tobin, and Shana—now all adult professionals in their own right—that gives me the courage and the faith to form words in the dark. Their unconditional love sustains me through all that life gives and takes away. It is my daughtering gratitude that, unbeknownst to my conscious mind, finds the strength of my mother, Evelyn, and the gentleness of my father, William, at play among the marks on the page. It is my sisterly bonding to Carol that has taught me that every woman's struggle is enshrined in the textual silence where there is an absence of words. And it is my spousal commitment that inscribes the unity of bodies and souls into language, so that the text itself traces a claim of reverence for the beloved. It is through my husband, Bill Walton, that I am continually encouraged to interweave the impossible and the possible into a seamless garment of praise. Without them, there would be no text, no breath, no vision; without them, there would be an impoverishment of love.

Prologue

Low Places Where Grace Flows In

In our various forms of contemporary analysis, we have yet to take a serious look at the spiritual dimensions of women's oppression. Violence against and subjugation of women—as well as the more subtle forms of gender disparity that wound and debase—are still practiced with painful repetitiveness around the world. As a global community, we cannot claim victory over this failure of the human heart to face and heal an ancient distortion that re-inscribes on a daily basis the inequality of females. Nor can we offer restitution to the endless stream of female bodies and souls who have courageously given themselves to the procreation of all human life, or who have been forcibly taken as fodder for every imaginable and unimaginable act of outrage, humiliation, and contempt.

Sustained and urgent efforts continue to be made to address the status of women by feminism, human rights, civil rights, and a host of governmental and nongovernmental agencies. Not only do women constitute 70 percent of the world's poor, the United Nations' Fourth World Conference on Women concluded in 1995 that there is still "no country in the world where men and women enjoy complete equality."[1] These worldwide efforts to name, alleviate, and transform the inferior status of women and girls have made inroads into changing attitudes that support and institutionalize inequality in the material and religious conditions of their lives. Yet attempts to uncover the causes of women's oppression, or to uproot deeply held misogynist beliefs that reinforce the status of females as defective or "misbegotten" males, have been less effective. While feminism has awakened women to the structural components that generate violence, it has been less successful in analyzing the deeper spiritual causes and consequences that underlie dominating behaviors and subjugating forms of consciousness.

The perspective I offer in this book is a different one. It begins from the premise that we must look to women's souls for a remedy to this global history of suffering and shame. It suggests that by turning inward to their mystical core, women tap into deep spiritual reserves that identify and heal the roots of their oppression; in turn, this feminist mystical awareness becomes a prophetic witness empowering women in our world. In referring to the spiritual dimension, it is natural to think in formal religious terms. The suppression of women by religious institutions, theologies, and philosophies is one aspect of the problem. But spiritual oppression goes beyond external evidence of social and cultural forms of violence to wound and harm a woman's interiority—her connection to her true self. I thus use the modifier "spiritual"—and its related terms "mysticism" and "contemplation"—when speaking about oppression to highlight that violence against a woman is directed first and foremost to the core of her nature—to her unique embodiment of the divine in this world. What harms a woman's soul reverberates in her physical, emotional, and mental spheres, generating suffering in every area of her life. At the same time, violations of a woman in the material realm have a direct impact on women's integrity, health, and moral agency. To get to the causes of women's oppression we have to study the dynamics of women's soul suffering and the spiritual techniques used to confront and alleviate the misogyny that inhabits their consciousness.

Radical Wisdom: A Feminist Mystical Theology charts a way to God that recognizes and transforms the devastation to women's souls and to our world that millennia of oppression have wrought. It joins the resources of feminist theological scholarship with the contemplative processes and spiritual practices found in women's medieval mystical texts. Drawing on the mysticism of Julian of Norwich and Teresa of Avila, along with other supporting voices, *Radical Wisdom* studies the spiritual dimensions of violence against women and the contemplative techniques used by women spiritual masters to achieve their highest spiritual potential. It traces a mystical path to women's liberation from all forms of oppression by exploring the implications of gender in the spiritual life. It studies the mystical or contemplative process medieval women mystics used to name, eliminate, and transform their soul suffering, and to dignify and empower themselves as women.

In re-reading mystical theology from a feminist angle, *Radical Wisdom* follows a path of negation or "un-saying," defined in Western spiritualities as the process or tool of destabilizing and deconstructing concepts and identities in order to open a space in which to experience something—God, self, or other—in its original nature. Applied to women, negative or apophatic mysticism traces an intense spiritual process that takes apart all that defines "woman" as the lesser or inferior product or object of male-dominated cultures. In so doing, it develops for our times a systematic feminist mystical theology that constructs a new and freeing vision of women's divine personhood, moral agency, and spiritual strength.

While the impetus for this book arises from women's particular spiritual concerns, it is directed to a wider audience of men and women who desire to learn about and rectify the injustices that have marred the hearts, minds, and souls of humans throughout these many centuries. Standing on the precipice of new thought and new religious foundations, many men I know share feminist concerns and also struggle to find ways to integrate and heal the masculine and feminine within. They, too, are aware that we must bring together and mend the divisions between us so that—as Thomas Merton so prophetically realized—"by healing the divisions in [ourselves we] would help the divisions of the whole world."[2] Thus, for the first time in recorded history we would breathe free of the spiritual superiority and theological exclusion that have injured, violated, and denied the inseparable and interdependent dignity of women, men, and all sentient beings so vital to healing and restoring our planet.

Part One

Theory and Historical Background

chapter one

Via Feminina and the Un-saying of "Woman"

Women today stand on the borders of a new country, mapmakers of uncharted spiritual territory. It is through them that new visions of the divine enter our world, and new spiritual pathways organically form. Having been drawn by a force greater than faith to a "place" in their own soul that is beyond the name "woman"—and even beyond religion—women live between realities. Unable to go back to damaged self-images and classical views of God that subordinate them, women are breaking through inherited cultural patterns and religious systems into new revelatory landscapes that transform the whole of life. Enclosed in a cocoon of their own divine becoming, women give away the known for the unknown, as the experience of crisis, restlessness, and hopelessness that marks the spiritual journey of many women "is the crucible in which our God images are transformed and a feminine value system and social fabric generated."[1]

In the last forty years, much has been written about women's spirituality and feminist theology. Since the groundbreaking scholarship of the 1960s and 1970s, feminist spirituality has expanded from a primary focus on personal experience to include a wide range of studies in women's mysticism, among these the role of medieval women monastics, the function of the body in constructing mystical piety, and the exploration of women's styles of language and ways of knowing. Central to many of these discussions is the voiced need to replace patriarchal religions based on transcendent deities and life-denying theologies with a more affirming, embodied, and holistic view of the cosmos and humans' place in it. Yet, very few of these studies move beyond theory to show us how to transform spiritually the violence women internalize or how to achieve this revolutionary shift in consciousness that is having an impact on women and men from all walks of life and religious persuasions.

This book addresses this need by focusing on the mysticism of women's journey from oppression to liberation and the importance of gender in the spiritual life. In this study of a feminist mystical theology, I explore how gender differentiates the spiritual process in significant ways, playing a role in both the structure and content of mystical consciousness, as well as serving as an interpretive lens through which women negotiate the sacred. Both socially engaged and deeply embodied, this feminist mystical process reforms our understanding of the spiritual life and highlights the depth and complexity of women's quest for wholeness. It concentrates on the contemplative practices, methods of interpretation, stages of growth, and visions of divinity that lead us to discover, by and through women, new spiritual lineages and revelatory traditions.

It also investigates how unjust social and political conditions afflict women's souls, and the spiritual disciplines women use to transform centuries-old structures of consciousness that are fundamentally damaging to the human spirit and to creation as a whole. It asks what kinds of spiritual struggles and liberating experiences happen in the soul of a woman undergoing life-changing shifts of consciousness and self-identity. How do unequal power relationships impact women's spiritual development and maturity, and how do they appropriate and live out these oppressions at deep levels of consciousness? What metaphors, symbols, and images of God do women see, unite with, and reveal if they travel by way of the feminine? What wisdom can be gleaned from medieval women mystics on the geography of the soul, and on those interior processes that strengthened them to develop new spiritual visions, and brought them to dignity and empowerment?

Contextualizing the Journey

In the last decade there has been a more vocal critique of feminism and the women's movement in general. The extent of this discomfort was evident in a recent class I taught on women and spirituality. The main point of my talk was the need for spiritual directors to be aware of the specific types of soul wounds women sustain. One of the male clergy in attendance expressed a deep resentment of women's continued need to speak about these issues. He felt the problem was overblown, as women today have the freedom to create new theologies, participate in ministry as never before, and be on the forefront of exciting thought. There are gender-inclusive Bibles, he reminded us, and scores of books by and about women on the spiritual life. He raised an important question: Was I further victimizing women, and taking away their dignity and power, by asserting that women are still not free?

A surprising number of people I interact with in college classes, spiritual direction sessions, or daily life situations would agree with my clergy friend. Many Americans assume that the advances made by women in the work force, the political arena, and civil rights have resolved the "women's issue," and make women's liberation no longer necessary or obsolete. We need only glance at one of the many popular magazines to find articles in support of this view, which ridicule the women's movement and the strides made by feminists. These various responses reflect a tacit assumption in American culture that well-being and value can be measured exclusively on an intellectual, social, or economic level.

In Western cultures, there are certainly signs of educational, political, and economic gains by women that were unheard of even twenty-five years ago. Women's advancement in the material dimension of life has been invaluable in raising awareness of society's role in upholding the dignity and rights of more than half the human race. While American women are considered to be among the most liberated in the world, many women I see in the classroom or for spiritual direction still struggle with profound inner battles of the spirit. The perceptions of inferiority, despair, and anger expressed by many women are not immediately recognized as symptoms of a deeper soul suffering and are not outwardly distinct from similar feelings experienced by men. Yet, in listening to women's spiritual lives I have come to understand that there is a continual and subtle form of violence directed against them that is difficult to name. Part of this difficulty has to do with the interior level on which these wounds take place, in which what is most vulnerable and intimate about a person is subjected to forms of oppression outside the bounds of accepted social discourse.

Another fact that impedes women's recognition of interior suffering has to do with a cultural tendency, peculiar to Western civilization, to separate the spiritual from the material life and a kind of American pragmatism that dismisses probing into spiritual things in order to avoid that which is too hidden or deep. Yet, in the mystical writings of the great medieval women mystics—Teresa of Avila, Julian of Norwich, and Gertrude of Helfta to name a few—we find a profound interrelationship between a woman's social and spiritual status and the suffering of her soul. Women's inner life mirrors in certain measure the outer conditions of women's personal and collective health. If this interior level of interpretation is ignored or trivialized, one of the most significant dimensions of effective analysis and social change is overlooked. Women's dignity and autonomy cannot be segregated from the exterior state of our global community where women are still among the most oppressed of oppressed groups, lagging behind men in education, reproductive rights, civil rights, and economic independence. "While women have made significant advances in many societies," summarized Boutros Boutros-Ghali at the United Nations' Fourth World Conference on Women held in Beijing, "women [still] constitute 70 percent of the world's poor. . . . In 1995 there is no country in the world where men and women enjoy complete equality."[2] Every day, violence against females is exposed as a tragedy and a failure of the human heart in which thousands of women and girls all over the world are raped, murdered, sold into the slave trade, and conscripted into lives of poverty, brutality, and neglect.

The disparity between lived experience and social indicators of women's health shows that the material dimension does not tell the whole story. Beneath the cultural, economic, and political aspects of change, and the important strides feminism has made in equalizing the dignity of all persons, there continues to exist a spiritual wound that requires recognition, healing, and transformation. The effect of this split in consciousness continues to have enormous ramifications not only in a woman's personal and social life, but also in the depths of her soul. This soul fracture blocks women's ability to claim and name themselves as subjects in their own right apart from structures of consciousness that oppress them. Further, it prohibits men from finding their true freedom, a freedom that is not dependent on the subjugation of women or feminine consciousness. "The evolutionary imperative for the masculine," writes Richard Tarnas, "is to see through and overcome its hubris and one-sidedness . . . [and] to choose [to transcend itself and] enter into a fundamentally new relationship of mutuality with the feminine in all its forms."[3]

Acknowledging these soul wounds allows us a unique opportunity to reconcile in ourselves the divisions and anxieties that afflict our fellow humans, and to mend the fracture between the spiritual traditions and secular culture. For much of recorded human history women have been representative of two poles of a paradox—as temptresses to be feared and suppressed, and as immaculate virgins of divine purity and beauty. Even the greatest mystics were not exempt from cultural stereotypes that assailed women's dignity and, at the same time, glorified their sanctity. In naming and healing this split through the experience of women, we unite an ancient division in intellectual history between body and soul, matter and spirit, human and divine, and humanity and the natural world. This great divide in the soul of humanity perpetuates violence against and oppression of women and other subjugated groups as persons and as representative of divinity, and is at the core of our cultural pathology. Through the recognition of the soul wounds and contemplative processes that compel women toward liberation, we discover a new integration of male and female that transforms the quality of our humanness and restores the heart of creation.

In speaking about the suffering of a soul and the emergence of new visions of reality, it is necessary to make reference to the mystical life and to those interior states of consciousness that are termed "spiritual," "contemplative," and the like. Mysticism, as an ancient subject of human inquiry, retains its own language and method of interpretation. It has been called by some of the greatest thinkers the science of "loving knowledge," of learning through compassion, which is, at the same time, more exacting and penetrating than cognitive or intellectual knowing. Relegated to a marginalized place in Western discourse through centuries of suppression, mystical knowledge has been effectively trumped by rationalism and its demand for material evidence as justification of truth claims. With its emphasis on the inherent dignity and freedom of the person, and on prayer, silence, and the "unseen," mysticism challenges our cultural preoccupation with the merely physical—that is, the material as an end in itself. Further, mystics often subvert authority, whether of church or state, exposing its dependence on money, power, and war. Those most vulnerable to the violence of authority—women, children, and marginalized men—bear the greatest burden of its sin.

It is thus instructive that scholars explicitly associate the suppression of mysticism and contemplation in Western thought with the oppression of women in medieval culture. Constance FitzGerald traces the condemnation of quietism—a movement that emphasized a withdrawal of the mind from worldly interests and a passive contemplation of God—in 1699 with the muffling of the tradition of mysticism and women. The marginalization of the language of mysticism "has a symbolic affinity," she writes, "with the marginalization of women and the neglect of the Spirit. Have no doubt that the muting of contemplation was/is directly related to the place of women in society, the role of conscience in religion and politics, the fear of direct inspiration of the Spirit, and the transformative and therefore seditious character of contemplative prayer."[4]

While Christianity has preserved the accounts of a number of women mystics who sought and achieved the highest reaches of contemplative perfection, there is nonetheless a disturbing tradition within Western spirituality that forcefully denies women's capacity for becoming divine. This negation penetrates women's consciousness at a level that is difficult to name and to see, because it defines the core of a woman's being as lacking and inferior to a man's, dictating her primary relationship with the world, the morals of her own conscience, and her relationship with God. Feminists who explored mysticism as a higher ground upon which they could rise above the narrow expectations and petty rivalries of patriarchal exclusion soon discovered that even the mystical life is not free from sexism and gender bias. Grace Jantzen, for instance, insists that this centuries-old subjugation has infiltrated women's imaginations and robbed them of their ability to discover themselves as subjects in their own right apart from the invasion of male-dominated culture.[5] Recognizing that it is naïve and dangerous to assume that spirituality somehow escapes the interpretive limits that are suspect in every use of symbol, language, and ideology, one of the great insights of feminism is that the spiritual life itself is susceptible to the whims of the human heart, and that it too is vulnerable to corruption, co-optation, and distortion. Women cannot simply retrieve or re-appropriate tradition. They must find a deeper spirituality, a new mysticism.

On closer examination we discover that the subject that informs mysticism, namely the quest for one's self and one's relationship with divinity, is an ancient and revered part of women's journey. Understood in a contemporary context, a redefined and critically aware mysticism is intrinsic to feminism and women's concerns. In tracing the liberation of the self and the inseparable unity of divine and human, mystical feminism affirms the power and beauty of difference—gender, religion, age, race, culture, or belief—while simultaneously recognizing in them a new unity. This confrontation with women's spiritual wounds, mapping the geography of their souls, and naming women's mystical paths to the divine constitutes the next phase of women's claim of dignity and empowerment. It is in the area of mysticism and contemplation that the deeper, more hidden layers of violence against women are found and ultimately overcome. Thus, it is also through feminist mystical consciousness that women are healed of the wounds of inequality and subordination, and find the strength to claim themselves as spiritual authorities in their own right.

Via Feminina and the Classical Spiritual Journey

Several years before I began formal work on this book, the phrase *via feminina* came to mind. At the time I was teaching a class on medieval women's mysticism. In describing two Christian paths of union with God—*via posi-tiva* and *via negativa*—I found myself saying that there was a third way—the way of the feminine, or the feminine way—*via feminina*. I was immediately struck by the power of the phrase because it evoked the classical spiritual paths and situated the feminine within the lineage of revelation and pro-phetic history. Within its historical context, the all-important Latin word *via*, meaning "road" or "way," signifies the spiritual journey we take toward union with God. Having chosen the word *feminina*, instead of the more familiar Latin term *femina* (woman) or *feminae* (women or of the woman), I wanted to convey a quality of consciousness and a mystical path that include but are not confined to categories of biological sex or attributes of gender construction.[6] The way of the feminine is present in both women and men; nevertheless, I hold that feminine consciousness is embodied and expressed differently in females than in males.

Via feminina is a linguistic expression that affirms the revelatory and pro-phetic in women's experience. It is revelatory because it is that period when the Feminine Divine breaks into history and calls us to listen to women's prophetic voice and gaze again on Wisdom's suffering face. It is feminist revelation because it is Her gift of unveiling what women have longed for and dared not hope: the feminine heart of divinity and the spiritual equality of women. It is feminist prophecy because it emerges from an unrelieved distress over the violation of women and of the feminine in our world. Undertaking a feminist reading of women's mystical theology, *via feminina* represents the contemplative paths and processes that break through and transform the historical denigration of women encoded in patriarchal cul-tures. As a new spiritual path with ancient roots in women's experience, it experiments with a particular type of mystical experience—the apophatic or negative—to find the tools women need to pull up the sources of misog-yny imbedded in their souls. It also exposes the depth of women's struggle for spiritual equality, and the profound efforts women make today to trans-form and heal the ancient fracture in consciousness that distorts females and the feminine. Further, this feminist mystical process has efficacy not only for women, but also for men who have been wounded by an excessive mascu-linity, are marginalized as "outsider" males, or desire to mend in their own hearts the painful suppression of their feminine nature.

To understand the significance of *via feminina* as a category of religious consciousness and a mystical path to God, it is helpful to review the classical traditions out of which *via positiva* and *via negativa* emerge. Although these concepts were present in theological circles during the first centuries of the Christian church, they were not explicitly distinguished and clarified until Pseudo-Dionysius, an anonymous sixth-century monk, did so. In describing how the soul progresses in union toward God, Dionysius names two types of contemplative consciousness—the positive and negative theologies—and claims they are intermingled in each person's spiritual journey. We ascend to God, Dionysius wrote, through praising the "affirmative theology" and the conceptual names, symbols, images, activities, and emotions of God. And yet, as we rise from the things of this world up to God, we leave behind language and names because everything we *know* about God pales in comparison to what God *is*. Only one dimension of the journey, affirmation will cede to the higher and more holy negation, the pathless path of contemplating God in its mode of nothingness.

In relation to these two classical pathways, Dionysius also is credited with placing a particular style of linguistic negation—called apophatic discourse—centrally within the Christian tradition. From the Greek word *apophasis* (to un-say or speak-away), apophatic discourse is a language of negation based on the dilemma posed by attempting to name the transcendent. It is usually found paired with its opposite term *kataphasis* (to say, speak-with), and the language of affirmation.[7] If *kataphasis* expresses Divine Word, *apophasis* is Divine Silence. Leaving behind our ideas of God, the more the soul climbs toward God "the more language falters, and when it has passed up and beyond the ascent," cautions Dionysius, "it will turn silent completely, since it will finally be at one with him who is indescribable."[8] The result is a language of paradox and the denial of names. Only a language that continually erases itself can capture the unknown divinity.

In terms of a person's spiritual development, affirmation is associated with the beginning stages of the spiritual journey, when we rely on religious tradition, accepted names for God, and historically transmitted prayer forms and contemplative techniques. But the journey of faith moves away from known into unknown, from belief into doubt, and from intellect into mysticism. This shift from affirmation to negation involves the whole person and everything that one has—up until now—accepted as true or real about self, God, or the world. While articulated in a Christian context, this movement from affirmation to negation as a discourse or a method of spiritual advancement is evident in the world's spiritual traditions. Mystics from traditions as different in their metaphysical orientations as Buddhism, Islam, and Judaism tell us that it is in this radical ambiguity—or nothingness—of being that we are open to Reality in itself. As the fuel of self-emptying, negation takes apart all that is constructed, all that is not immediately present, dynamic, apparent, or real. It functions as a disruptive element in the spiritual life, designed to break down its linguistic coherence and structural logic, and thereby to shock the person outside conventional notions of reality into another plane of existence.

In a deeper spiritual sense, apophasis reflects the transformation of a person's core identity, performing in language the task that the mystic performs in the dark night or great death experience, when a person's false identity is finally given away. The corollary to the negation of concepts is the unsaying, undoing, and unwilling of the "lower self"—that entity defined by the world of attraction, ego demand, and economy—to find the one thing necessary, the true self. Described in the world's religions by terms that evoke images of shock, bewilderment, or loss, negative theology quenches our fundamental thirst to be separate. Breaking through the foundations upon which all that is false has been erected, it heals us of illusions that separate us from our ultimate source.

Dionysius held that the discourse of *kataphasis* and *apophasis* and its attendant theologies of *via positiva* and *via negativa* are stamped into our natures and we follow their ancient methodology, often unknown to our conscious minds, to the divine nature itself. They are not merely conceptual categories but represent complementary paths to, and expressions of, ultimate reality; as such, each refers to distinctive orientations to the world, techniques of prayer and contemplation, images and structures of language, ways of knowing, and views of the inner life of God.[9] Incorporated into each person's journey, consciously or latently, they represent the method and structure, and way and goal, of the spiritual life. Without maintaining the dialectic of naming and un-naming, illumination and darkness, revealed and hidden, our spiritual life would cease to grow toward integration and wholeness. Yet, he also cautions us to "not conclude that the negations are simply the opposites of the affirmations, but rather that the cause of all is considerably prior to this, beyond privations, beyond every denial, beyond every assertion."[10] Brought into Latin Christianity by John Scotus Eriugena and other ninth-century translators of Dionysius, the positive and negative ways are transposed from Greek into the Latin terms *via positiva* (positive way, way of affirmation) and *via negativa* (negative way, way of negation).

From this brief historical review, we begin to glimpse the all-pervading way in which the classical stages of the soul's journey and the positive and negative theologies have captured the Western religious imagination. Organic representations of an unending process of spiritual maturation, they continue to be relevant to the lives of people today. However, many feminist scholars and spiritual women contend that the classical mystical traditions do not perfectly depict the fullness of their lives or the process women and men are taking to touch and live out new dimensions of the sacred. We cannot assume that traditional maps of the soul's journey and positive and negative discourses perform in contemporary women in a similar way and with a similar spiritual process as their medieval counterparts; or that they are effective for women, actually leading them to the desired freedom and divine union. Further, we need to examine more closely whether there are distinctive patterns of consciousness particular to women's historical treatment as a perpetual underclass that provide us with a new understanding of women's liberation and require a new interpretation of such historically embedded concepts as enlightenment, salvation, mystical union, and similar terms. This disjunction between semantic descriptions of spiritual life and women's actual experience needs to be acknowledged, questioned, and explored. If mysticism traces the journey to freedom, and if the God of the mystics is a God of freedom, then women cannot achieve their full spiritual potential without confronting the injustice and violence within which the terms *female-feminine-woman* have been inscribed throughout recorded human history.

Via Feminina as Radical Mysticism

The concept *via feminina*—the feminine way—is instrumental in helping us to think differently. As representative of a feminist mystical path to God and to personal freedom, it appropriates and goes beyond the function of the apophatic, or negative, journey as situated within its Western, primarily Christian, theological context. As a constructed phrase, *via feminina* is related to the pathways, structures of language, and positive and negative theologies inspired by or inscribed within its classical traditions; but it also disturbs and transgresses them. Standing outside or beyond the logic that formed their language, spirituality, and theology, the radical mysticism of *via feminina* functions as a continual un-saying, a continual disruption of the previous thousands of years of "saying" by patriarchal cultures and religions. Applying a feminist re-reading to the mystical journey, *via feminina* extends the apophatic process not only to language and conceptual ideas about God, but also to the gender disparity codified within its spiritual practices and contemplative paths. It thus involves a radical type of ontological negation that pulls up the roots of misogyny and seeds of oppression that have been handed down from generation to generation and planted in our souls.

As another product of patriarchy, mysticism must be critically evaluated and reassessed. Formed within the same symbolic system women seek to escape, classical mysticism is not free from the underlying logic of Western theisms and can provide guidance along the path only so far. The point at which a woman confronts her liberation as "woman" is where she also discovers the great lie about the "feminine" and her *spiritual* suppression and marginalization as a representative of the lesser sex.

There comes a time in a woman's journey when she may feel that her religion of birth or her spiritual practice can only domesticate and frustrate her search for her authentic "wholly other" divine self. It is at this point that a woman's spiritual life moves from affirmation to negation, and then into a deeper negation—what I term the "dark night of the feminine," discussed in subsequent chapters—in order to "un-say" and "un-become" the internalized inferiority that oppresses or denigrates her soul. Most significant is that this mystical process of deconstruction not only involves a woman's personal feelings and identities but also includes the whole range of cultural, religious, racial, and social attitudes and structures that participate in and perpetuate worldwide abuses against females. Simultaneously, this feminist path of negation heals women's abused consciousness and restores women's dignity and worth. It thus does not remain in a permanent suspension of unnaming and unknowing but returns to language bearing the fruits of a new self-understanding and a new vision of the sacred.

As one expression of women's lived spirituality, *via feminina* maps out a spiritual path to women's divine humanity. It is represented at every level of religious life: in metaphysics as feminine structures of being; theologically, as the articulation and study of the Feminine Divine; in language, through female metaphors and images; and mystically both as the path that leads to intimacy with God, and as a revelation that heralds a new way of *being* human and a new vision of a transformed world. In creation, *via feminina* is reflected in nature, in our minds and our hearts, and in the abundant fecundity that sustains and nurtures the diversity of life. It offers distinctive languages and ways of knowing, prayer forms and contemplative techniques, and experiences of the inner life of God. It is the spiritual life we discover, experience, and eventually articulate as we travel by way of the feminine.

Via feminina also addresses the historical subservience of women in theological and spiritual circles, and the still-prevalent prohibition against women in the highest spheres of spiritual authority to speak new revelation. I suspect that it is this fact that underlies the still-rampant oppression of women in religious institutions and in all manner of spiritual decision making. Economic and social equality is not as threatening to prevailing power politics as is spiritual authority. For women to experience their lives as the birthplace of revelation requires an act of radical bravery. It is an expression of what the kabbalists call *ayin* (nothing), the opening that is the inscribing of (new) tradition in our body and in the world. Women, oddly, seldom claim the revelatory. Being the womb of its enfoldment, they are erased. Once the blood has been spilled and the umbilicus tied, "woman" is the offering. In women, the mystical, if not reclaimed in its purely feminine mode, if not in fact reinvented outside tradition, can oppress women and stifle their voices beneath the voice of the fathers, the past, and tradition, and to spiritual directors out of touch with women's experience of divinity. By extension, the reviling of the feminine is an oppression of the mystical and helps us to understand why so many mystics, men and women alike, have suffered at the hands of orthodoxy.

Questioning the Term "Feminine"

Central to women's journey is the whole complex of questions surrounding the meaning of the word "feminine." While a full investigation of scholarship in this area is outside the scope of this introduction, the critique of the "feminine" as an invention of patriarchy is fundamental to feminist thought. The main thrust of the feminist position is that as subordinate females in dominant androcentric (male-dominated) cultures, women lack an adequate sense of self. History, philosophy, theology, and literature, as well as legal, social, and political codes, were established and written by men. As daughter, wife, and mother, females were the property of males and gender stratification was maintained through complex economic arrangements, power disparities, and social controls endorsed by church and state. Forced into dependent economic and social positions, and tied to the domestic household, "woman" in patriarchal cultures is the name of she who is defined according to male needs. Feminists contend that, deprived of the resources of education, literacy, and empowerment granted to men, a woman's self is not her own, but the object of others' needs and desires. In fulfilling the demands of this patriarchal feminine—as selfless helpmate, silent procreator, and dependent sexual partner—women lack a voice, unable to conceptualize themselves as subjects separate from distorted and demeaning sexual stereotypes.

Further, feminists assert that since language is intrinsic to culture, and men were the main architects of naming, language reinforces women's oppression within a matrix of meaning that betrays them and from which they struggle to escape. Simone de Beauvoir's *The Second Sex* and Betty Friedan's coining of the term "feminine mystique" stand out as two early attempts within feminist scholarship to probe how women function as the "other" of patriarchy (the rule of the father) and kyriarchy (the rule of the lord and master). This whole "patriarchal imaginary"—as it is often called—fragments a woman's self, placing her identity in the hands of men and denying women the right to experience and name themselves as the subjects of their own lives.[11]

At the core of gender dualism or gender polarity is the question of what constitutes human nature. Thinking in binary terms, gender dualism ascribes to women and men two separate kinds of human nature, each with its own characteristics. Masculine nature is associated with reason, independence, and the ability to analyze, take action, and make judgments, while feminine nature is marked by emotion, receptivity, and the ability to nurture, show compassion, and suffer for love. As representative of the lesser sex, selflessness, sacrifice, and devotion are held up as the highest female attributes. This rigid assigning of sexual identity and social roles based on arbitrary qualities of masculine and feminine works to the detriment of both sexes, undermining the natural integration of these qualities in men and women. Extrapolating from these gendered qualities associated with male and female to the divine nature and to the social sphere, patriarchy elevates sexual difference to an ontological principle, ascribing to God male characteristics and powers. What is considered female or feminine is seldom, if ever, granted full authority or identity within patriarchal languages and theologies—and is infrequently attributed to God itself—but is kept in a helping or subordinate position.[12] Thus, contemporary attempts to incorporate feminine attributes of the divine into Western theologies has come under criticism precisely for the way they *appear* to correct and affirm women while still working from an invisible dualistic anthropology.

Elizabeth Johnson has spelled out this issue at great length in her most recent book on Mary, *Truly Our Sister*. Citing efforts to recognize the force of Marian devotion in Christian culture, Johnson illustrates how the figure of Mary is held up either as the ideal face of women or the maternal face of God. When Mary is held up for women as their ideal, she represents the essential or Eternal Feminine. "Picturing Mary as the most perfect of women," Johnson writes, "the patriarchal marian tradition functions paradoxically to disparage all other women. . . . Mary does not *exemplify* the capacity for God of redeemed humanity including women. Rather, she is the great exception."[13] The disparity between Mary and real women fosters gender stereotyping, Johnson contends, because it imbues "the image of Mary with virtues and roles conducive to women's subservience."[14] However, if Mary represents the maternal face of God, there is also the danger that female images and figures represent the "feminine 'dimension,' 'side,' 'aspects,' or 'traits' of the divine. Theologically speaking, God does not have a feminine dimension, or a masculine dimension," Johnson insists. "God is simple."[15]

Applied to social roles, gender dualism assigns to women rigid expectations and functions, marginalizes them as representatives of holiness and divinity, and contributes to their violation and abuse. Feminist scholarship does not deny the differences between the sexes or the value of recognizing gender and sexual diversity. But it rejects using these differences to justify preassigned characteristics of masculine and feminine, or to contribute to and establish distorted relationships. Women know that by defining the ideal feminine as submissive to the will of God, and as dependent, devoted, and receptive, "inevitably privileges men in terms of social, political, and spiritual power while leaving women themselves to do the daily work that sustains life."[16] "In the theoretical world of gender dualism," Johnson contends, "women do not appear as historical agents in their own right but as rhetorical codes for many other concerns. . . . Constructed as man's 'Other' their feminine nature functions as a stand-in for abstract theological concepts, cosmological powers, or distressing forces in male consciousness. Whether they are placed on a pedestal as a symbol of virtue or blamed as originators of sin and death, however, they are treated as symbolic representatives of male experience rather than as persons in their own right."[17]

Un-saying of "Woman"

Within this historical context of debasement, silencing, and subordination, the idea of mystical emptiness can appear to be another ploy to re-inscribe the inferiority of women, perpetuating their status as a subjected underclass. Similarly, the introduction of a spiritual path with a distinctly gendered title—*via feminina*—may generate concerns that the terms "female," "feminine," and "woman" are again being used to assign gender dualism to God that elevates the male God to the detriment of females, or conversely extols a female or feminine divinity thereby debasing males. In addition, the concept *via feminina* may appear to relegate the feminine once again to a subordinate place as an aspect or spouse of a prior male deity. What I am attempting to do, however, by associating mystical negation with women's liberation is to reform and redefine the spiritual journey from a feminist perspective and to illustrate that a mysticism of feminism takes us by necessity through the pain of gender dualism to healing the historic split in women's and men's consciousness, and then all the way to re-imagining and re-experiencing God as She. In re-reading mystical theology from a feminist angle, *via feminina* traces a path of un-saying, un-doing, and un-being of all that defines women as the product or object of male-dominated cultures, and that ascribes to women and men separate and unequal attributes or roles. In so doing, it gives up the "patriarchal feminine" to rediscover the positive fullness of being female.

Yet, as we have seen, there is a difficulty with adapting the classical understanding of mystical theology to women's quest for freedom, because its logic is already imbedded within dualistic discourses and structures of consciousness that name and map the spiritual path. When applied to women, the relationship of sexism and social violence to their spiritual health and moral agency is ignored because mysticism—at least in the modern, academic use of the term—is often assumed to be universal and normative, transcending differences of sex, culture, and race in a higher or more universal state. Built on the superiority of spirit over matter, the Western mystical tradition always pushes to transcend material reality, including oppressions and abuses of human body, mind, and soul. Further, embedded in the split between mind–body, spirit–matter, and male–female in classical thought, mysticism was seldom, if ever in its long trajectory, associated with issues of gender, or social, cultural, or religious injustices. According to mystical rhetoric, the highest virtue of perfection is to leave behind and detach oneself from the world below, especially that realm inhabited by a woman's body, or female sufferings, needs, and desires.

Taken in its classical forms, the spiritual transformation associated with mystical theology cannot completely free women from these age-old inscriptions that block them from identifying the root causes of women's struggle for equality, and from attaining the highest reaches of mystical awareness. Despite its uplifting languages and paradoxical play of words, mystical theology still operates within what Luce Irigaray calls the "other of the same"—female as the necessary negative of the matrix of meanings that constitute the male subject—and thus cannot break through the patriarchal "imaginary" to go deeper into the roots of women's soul wounds.[18] Women today who attempt to understand their spiritual lives through, for example, Christian mysticism's medieval expression—whether in St. John of the Cross, *Cloud of Unknowing*, St. Bonaventure, or Meister Eckhart—often realize that something of their experience is left out.

The spiritual path of *via feminina* takes a different approach. It places primary importance on the recognition and elimination of all interlocking forms of oppression in a person's journey toward God and self-understanding. Women's spiritual liberation involves an awareness of the simultaneous, interpenetrating, and dynamic interrelationship between embodiment and transcendence—finite and infinite—that constitutes the whole complex of the person. As a spiritual path, it pays particular attention to integrating and incorporating the multiple wisdoms of body, psyche, and soul in order to name and heal what offends, diminishes, or violates women. Its single most distinguishing feature is that as a spiritual path it does not transcend differences—whether of gender, culture, race, or sex—but enters into them directly to experience a deeper unity capable of transforming the underlying causes of soul suffering. Thus in its development of a feminist mystical path, *via feminina* is vigilant about the ways in which the categories that name and define the spiritual life—redemption, salvation, soul, self, God, virtue—as well as the processes or stages of mystical ascent—purgation, dark night, union—repeat subtle forms of gender, racial, or social violence.

Via feminina traces a feminist path of the apophasis—or un-saying—of "woman." In using the term "un-saying" to refer to women's liberation, I intend a mystical path that enters into and moves through a woman's "nothingness"—that is, what diminishes, injures, humiliates, or shames her—to a positive affirmation of her dignity and worth. By negating all that falsely defines her, a woman steps outside the symbolic order of culture, religion, *and* God, giving up and subverting her capacity to be identified by patriarchal cultures. In its historical expression, these socially constructed forms of women's debasement are considered to be unimportant to the quest for transcendence and are ignored. When gender does enter into the discussion, it functions as a negative factor that needs to be controlled or transcended. In this caricature, to *be spiritual* is to *be without* gender, race, culture, or sex. The spiritual aspirant is taught to rise above or go beyond her unique embodiment to experience a superior or higher self. But this advice conceals a deeper and more illusive form of oppression. It suspends difference in order to disrupt the web of meanings that constitute the "generic human"—supposedly unsexed and ungendered, but typically represented by dominant males—while leaving intact a whole range of experiences that arise from precisely those violations, failures, exclusions, fluxes, or uncertainties that make up women's lives.

Tracing the liberation of consciousness from the distortion of gender inequality, *via feminina* uncovers a spiritual path to that as-yet-unnamed "woman" who is outside, beyond, or healed of all binary oppositions. Through the mystical process of letting-go and letting-be, women learn to take off the mask of the patriarchal feminine who endorses women's subordination and uncover the truly "other" feminine subject that is not defined or constrained by the constellations of meanings, values, principles, judgments, and suppositions that potentially make a woman an object of exchange in male-dominated cultures. In this sense, the whole thrust of feminist thought can be seen as the un-saying of "woman," and its activism, discourse, and scholarship as a global process of disruption and subversion of what has named, ruled, defined, or possessed her.[19] In this process of deconstructing and destabilizing, the mysticism of feminism purges and rents the structures and meanings that define women as a product of someone else's imagination. It is a journey that moves by way of negation to arrive at the feminine subject who is truly free and—as Meister Eckhart liked to say about God—is "neither this nor that."

While *via feminina* studies the spiritual processes that lead women away from oppression and toward freedom, a legitimate question arises: Is it suppressing genuine diversity and perpetuating division? Feminist scholarship cautions against its early tendencies to ignore historical concreteness and to project the experiences of white middle-class women to all women, overlooking differences. Writing out of the context of "privileged, educated women, those with a voice in politics or the academy,"[20] and of medieval women mystics from economic and social elites, can a feminist mystical theology legitimately be a spiritual tool for women from differing religions, races, economic classes, ethnicities, or historical periods? Further, does it apply to men? Can men truly achieve liberation while their own feminine natures and women remain abused and oppressed? How do historic conditions of global suffering, environmental devastation, and debilitating power politics afflict the soul and demand new forms of contemplative practice and spiritual awareness? These are provocative and vitally important questions, which must be tested out in concrete and diverse human circumstances. For the present, my reading of the world's spiritual texts and my work with women and men of differing religions, ethnicities, classes, races, gender orientations, and ages leads me to wonder if this introduction of a feminist mystical process that specifically enters into and transforms soul oppression is not implicitly present, even as it has remained unnamed, in the lives and spiritual experiences of a great many mystics and ordinary people today. Perhaps the tracing of a socially-engaged and bodily contemplative practice named *via feminina* will assist in the expansion and refinement of a spirituality that is truly representative of our global, changing, and plural world.

Further research will be necessary to see if this marking of the "unsaying of 'woman'" has applicability across multiple landscapes of experience. For now, I can only write from my own location—as an academic, spiritual director, and American woman of European descent living in a post-industrialized Western context—hoping that this extrapolation does no violence to those who differ or disagree. Requiring of women a spiritual practice and mystical process that moves through a continual process of deconstructing and un-saying all that falsely defines "woman" and "feminine," *via feminina* is suggestive of a possibility: it uncovers the ground or foundation—that is always un-grounding, un-founding—of a woman's self. Women's "ground" is a fluid, creative, and continual process of dying and being born, receptivity and closure, presence and absence. It is an unlimited dynamic that is not the debasing of a woman, but the realization of her holiness and dignity. It affirms a subtler, non-dual, or unifying quality of being that moves from identity to intimacy, ground to un-ground, affirmation to negation, and then beyond all these opposites, paradoxes, and denials to "the unspeakable possibility of God/Woman."[21]

Direction

In the following chapters, I develop a feminist mystical theology along three main lines, dividing the book accordingly. Part 1 is theoretical; the second part is textual and historical, while the third is constructive and contemporary. I continue with the first part's theoretical dimensions in the following three chapters, providing an overview in chapter 2 of the terms "spirituality," "mysticism," and "contemplation," and a survey of current scholarship on mysticism and feminist theory. Chapter 3 on goddesses and Mother Jesus studies the historical development of female metaphors and images in the world's scriptures and mystical texts. It then concentrates on the Christian tradition and on an analysis by feminist scholars of the function of female metaphors and goddess figures in medieval culture and religious practices. Part 1 concludes with chapter 4, which takes up in greater detail the theoretical foundations for an engaged and embodied contemplative feminism. It highlights the important function that naming spiritual oppression occupies in the spiritual journey to eliminate and heal all forms of interlocking violence against women.

In part 2, I turn to the women mystics of medieval Europe for insight into how they understand and map the geography of the soul, and the specific spiritual pathways they practice to travel from subordination to dignity and freedom. Staying close to the writings of Julian of Norwich and Teresa of Avila, along with other supporting voices, chapter 4, "Feminism of the Inner Way," distinguishes a number of themes in women's mysticism, among them the annihilated self, longing and the love of God, and the determination that propels the journey. In "Julian and Teresa as Cartographers of the Soul," chapter 6 follows Julian and Teresa as they map the inner and outer soul, distinguish and transform soul wounds into "honours," assert the inherent unity of God and soul, and juxtapose suffering and exaltation as necessary stages in women's ennoblement. Teresa of Avila is taken up as a case study in "The Soul of Woman and the Dark Night of the Feminine," chapter 7. Here, the pain of gender oppression is identified as a specific contemplative process that is unnamed and unexamined in Christian literature. This addition of the "dark night of the feminine" to our religious vocabulary highlights the depth of women's struggle for spiritual equality. Part 2 culminates with the discussion in chapter 8 of Julian and Teresa's usage of three spiritual powers—resistance, resiliency, and dignification—to dignify women and transform the spiritual environment in which each lived.

While I draw in these chapters from the wisdom of a variety of Christian mystical texts, I concentrate on those uncharted spiritual passages that women travel in isolation away from the mainstream of classical (patriarchal) spirituality, whether within or outside formal religious practice or tradition. In the process, I distinguish a number of differences in women's mysticism from that of the dominant religiosity of their times, being cautious not to "feminize" them in any contemporary sense. Rather, in the spirit that energized their lives and thought, I keep close to their historical context and to one of their central concerns—growth in love of the divine and diminishment of self-interest. The challenge is distinctly integrative—to bring together the uplifting mysticism of medieval Christian women masters with feminist critical theory in order to illuminate the unique contemporary situation in which we find ourselves.

Finally, in part 3, I turn to practical considerations for women today on how to identify, actualize, and live out a spiritual path that is devoid of all forms of violence against women, and that lifts women up to a realized and integrated wholeness. Dialoguing between present feminist concerns and goddess-veneration and other affirmations of the female form, chapter 9, "Women's Body as Mystical Text," explores the metaphor of women's body as God's body. It also proposes a reading of a woman's body as a sacral text and her embodiment as a writing of divinity into the world. Chapter 10, using contemporary research in human rights, develops a category of "spiritual rights" to explore the divine dimension in violations of human dignity. It studies, as well, intimate, or sexual, violence against women and the effect of these violations on women's spirit, emotional health, and moral agency. "Love of the World: An Ethic of Ultimate Concern" is the subject of chapter 11. It develops a contemplative ethic based on bearing three qualities—intimacy, *amor mundi* (love of the world), and divinity—in order to focus on social justice and the indiscriminate love God showers upon us as She labors to sanctify and grace all of creation. The final section of the chapter outlines a "World Ethic of Spiritual Rights." The book concludes with a narrative poem, "Hymn to Hagia Sophia [Holy Wisdom]" in the epilogue.

At the turn of the last century one of its greatest writers, Rainer Maria Rilke, turned his poetic mind to the question of the sexes, and to his own artistic need for solitude. It is fitting to conclude this chapter with his eloquent words; forged as they were in the fire of personal crisis, they are a testament to the shining citadel of a lonely heart.

> Perhaps over all there is a great motherhood, as common longing. . . . And the mother's beauty is ministering motherhood, and in the old woman there is a great remembering. And even in the man there is motherhood, it seems to me, physical and spiritual. . . . And perhaps both sexes are more related than we think, and the great renewal of the world will perhaps consist in this, [that men and women], freed of all false feelings and reluctances, will seek each other not as opposites but as brother and sister, as neighbors, and will come together *as human beings*, in order simply, seriously and patiently to bear in common the difficult sex that has been laid upon them.[22]

chapter two

Feminism and Mysticism

Foundations

> Mary and Martha never fail to work almost together when the soul
> is in this state [mystical marriage]. For in the active—and seemingly
> exterior—work the soul is working interiorly. And when the active
> works rise from this interior root, they become lovely and very fragrant
> flowers. For they proceed from this tree of God's love and are done for
> Him alone, without any self-interest. The fragrance from these flowers
> spreads to the benefit of many. It is a fragrance that lasts, not passing
> quickly, but having great effect.[1]

The poetic way in which Teresa of Avila describes her inner life helps
the contemporary person in understanding the subject of mysticism.
Simultaneously precise and elusive, the inner world has its own language,
method, interpretation, and evaluation. In living the contemplative life,
Teresa becomes a master of the vocabulary of the spirit and is able to name
for others the subtleties of the soul's journey. In the above passage, she
clarifies an issue rooted in the Christian Bible and debated over the centuries concerning the relationship between the active and contemplative lives.
Teresa reminds us that action and contemplation work together, as every
outer gesture is the fruit of a more primary inner communion. Learning to
see the world through the lens of the mystical and becoming fluent in its
language were essential to her maturity and empowerment. No less true for
our times, we require education in the divine pedagogy and benefit from
access to the alphabet and vocabulary of the spirit. It is thus instructive to
become acquainted with the meaning and usage of the terms "spirituality," "mysticism," and "contemplation," and of how the realities to which
they point have intersected with feminist scholarship and contemporary
theology.

Defining Terms

In popular culture today, the terms "spirituality," "mysticism," and "contemplation" are often used interchangeably, and are frequently divorced from association with religious tradition or community. While contemporary persons are aware that each term refers to one's interior life and experience—rather than conceptual knowledge or ideas—of divinity, they often do not have access to the historical context in which its definition and meaning arose. "Spirituality," "mysticism," and "contemplation" are religious terms that refer not only to personal experience, but also to the principles and processes of the inner life, including prayer, spiritual direction, techniques of contemplation, languages of the sacred, images of the divine, and the commitment of the individual to a process of spiritual growth and transformation.

Various words for "spirit" are used in the world's religions, such as the Hebrew *ruah*, and the related Arabic *ruh*, Latin *spiritus*, Greek *pneuma*, and *prana* (breath) in Sanskrit. Many traditions do not have a word for "spirituality" and its usage in the English language is tied to strong Christian roots, since in the Christian Bible "spirit" (*pneuma*) and "spiritual" (*pneumatikos*) are key terms, and the words *spiritualis* and *spiritualitas* were often employed in Latin Christianity. Referring to the force of divine breath, animation, or presence, we can think of spirituality as the all-pervading divine energy and seamless web of oneness intimate to life itself. Creation is not alone, separate from its source, but deeply and mysteriously imbued with spirit in every aspect of mind, soul, and matter.

This notion of the spirit being the binding force of the unity between the inner and outer life takes on further clarity with reference to Judaism and Islam. "Seeking the face of God, striving to live in His presence, and to fashion the life of holiness appropriate to God's presence," writes Arthur Green, "is perhaps as close as one can come to a definition of 'spirituality' that is native to the Jewish tradition and indeed faithful to its Semitic roots."[2] In Islam, "spirituality" is a word of Arabic origin with two distinct connotations: the first is found in the Qur'an in the statement "The Spirit is from the command of my Lord"; the second connotes inwardness, and real as opposed to apparent—"that is, pertaining to a higher level of reality than both the material and the psychic and being directly related to the Divine Reality Itself."[3]

In the preface to a multi-volume series on world spirituality, Ewert Cousins provides a comprehensive definition of spirituality worked out with contributors from representatives of the world's religions.

> The series focuses on that inner dimension of the person called by
> certain traditions "the spirit." This spiritual core is the deepest center
> of the person. It is here that the person is open to the transcendent
> dimension; it is here that the person experiences ultimate reality.[4]

Other studies of the term "spirituality" uphold Cousins's emphasis on the inner relationship of the person to his or her ultimate source,[5] and further emphasize the nondualism that arises from the importance religious traditions place on the central absence of ego-identity in living a spiritually focused life. As Krishna Sivaraman writes out of a Hindu context, "The locus where there is absent a sense of 'I' and 'mine' is the locus of spirit."[6] Sandra Schneiders relates this inner dimension to the unifying of the whole person, defining spirituality as "the experience of consciously striving to integrate one's life in terms not of isolation and self-absorption but of self-transcendence toward the ultimate value one perceives."[7]

Too often in history, spirituality has taken on an unfortunate connotation that suggests an extreme form of otherworldliness, interiority, and opposition to the body. Certainly spirituality requires inner focus, silence, and even, at times, solitude to hear one's God speak. Yet, as these scholars remind us, all authentic spirituality strives toward holiness in this world, however perfectly or imperfectly, and yearns to remember the divine mystery in all one does. The richness of the term is found in the role spirituality plays in unifying the tension between mind and heart, body and soul, and inner and outer life. Spirituality is the awareness of the oneness that underlies duality and difference, as each outward action reveals the interconnected presence of the holy. It is neither partial nor selective, filling each and all. A person may be more or less conscious of the sacred in every day; she or he may even deny or reject it. But spirituality is the primordial stuff of existence and therefore is always present. A feeling of oneness with life, deep empathy and compassion, genuine selfless love, and an abiding trust in the unfolding of reality are marks of a spiritually aware temperament.

When our natural spirituality becomes more mature and focused, and expands beyond an instinctive activity of the heart to turn toward an intensity of desire for God, it is often called mysticism or contemplation. Mysticism, as a category of religious experience, enjoys a long history in human cultures, although there is considerable debate in academic circles concerning the content and context of its modern construction. Variously described as a consciousness of Divine Presence—whether we use the term "God," "Goddess," "Great Spirit," "Tao," "Christ," or "Allah"—this reality is experientially accessible to us in the fully actualized depths of consciousness itself. Mysticism approaches the divine through various mediums of experience—nature, language, religion, study, liturgy, ritual—but it is also said to be accessible in its highest states directly through our inner experience in a moment of "pure," "content-less," or "empty" consciousness.[8] Throughout its diverse historical expressions, mysticism has been associated with a personal commitment to disciplined practice that leads the individual to a process of spiritual growth and transformation.[9]

Christian mysticism, like those of other traditions, displays multiple forms and expressions ranging from the highly personal to the communal. From a primary association with the hidden meaning of scripture and the hidden presence of Christ in the Eucharist in the early church, the Christian mystical tradition also finds expression in visionary experiences and illuminative spiritual states—St. Francis's experience of the six-winged Seraph, Augustine's vision of the Divine Light, and the meditation on the humanity of Christ by Julian of Norwich. But it also refers more radically to the divine without image and name, to the "luminous darkness" of Gregory of Nyssa, Meister Eckhart's Desert of the Godhead, or Dionysius's "superessential ray of divine darkness." It was not until the end of the Middle Ages that the term "mysticism" moved toward the highly individual, subjective meaning involving a purely private, inner experience prevalent today. In these various manifestations of the mystical are certain shared elements, among them a transforming quality of being, and an experience of union, intimacy, or absorption in the divine. In addition, mystical knowledge is often termed "hidden" or "secret" because the divine is not known by mental effort but is taught through love, a knowing that is "unknowing"—knowledge through direct insight.

As one of the most enduring strands of Christian mysticism, the term "contemplation" emerges in the West from the distinction made in the Platonic schools between the "description of the soul's return to God through purification (*askesis*) followed by contemplative vision (*theoria*)."[10] In contemporary usage, contemplation often is associated with the life of prayer and mysticism with "an immediate consciousness of the presence of God,"[11] but in actual fact the two terms are used interchangeably in many Christian texts with the implication that all deeply spiritual persons are also mystic-contemplatives. Both terms refer to a quality of being associated with the mature spiritual life, and not just to the heightened, but temporary, altered states of consciousness that are sometimes associated with peak experiences in contemporary thought. Each also includes both subjective, personal encounters and those mediated by text, ritual, relationship, and community. In addition to an emphasis on a state or quality of being, mysticism and contemplation involve various spiritual disciplines, transformative processes, and meditative techniques that have been practiced by seekers throughout the long history of human spirituality.

Contemplation is most frequently associated with the practice of silent or passive (receptive) prayer. However, "the true contemplative does not strive for unity of Divine and human only at specific times of prayer, but in all circumstances and conditions of daily life: washing dishes, caring for children, family, work, sleeping."[12] Contemplation refers to an inner monastic attitude, a centering point of one's whole life and being. This centering reference may be taken in solitude or in the marketplace; but it never leaves the ground of its longing for God, turning one's whole life toward creation, hope, and love. Further, this living, daily prayer breaks through into one's mind and heart, teaching those insights, wisdoms, and realizations that uplift the soul and lead it toward what Buddhists call *prajaparamita* ("perfection of wisdom").

Far from being unfocused, ephemeral, or rare, contemplation and mysticism are said to unveil the precision of reality as it truly is and to seed a person's consciousness with the ordinary and tangible presence of mystery in every facet of existence. In a way, contemplation turns the world inside out. It illuminates the real behind appearances, concentrating one's whole being on the permanence that fuels impermanence, the love that is greater than division and fear, the inseparable goodness and holiness of self, and the crushing experience of interdependence that forever rids one of the illusion of a separated self-willed identity. Those who have discovered its living way no longer mistake the constructed for the real, and thus rightfully have rejected the imposition of any theological authority that controls or dictates one's relationship with the divine. This inseparable unity of divine and human—called by Eastern Orthodox Christians "deification"—so much a hallmark of the mystical traditions of the world's religions, subverts the notion of a distant, unfeeling deity. It often refutes sin-based theologies as well, upholding a vision of the undefiled nature of the true self.

Contemplation unleashes a distinctive mode of consciousness that is more passive than active, more illuminative than intellective, more merciful than just. This is not to say that contemplation shuns activity, the mind and reason, or justice. Rather, having opened the vault of a hidden reality, contemplation is the repository of a receptive way of seeing the world with its own set of principles and properties. This distinction between active and passive, sometimes also termed "acquired" and "infused" contemplation by Christian mystics, is important in the spiritual life because it highlights the two sides of the person's journey to freedom and love. On the one hand, we must and will struggle toward our own authenticity; on the other hand, we reach a point on the path where only the divine can lead us to our true self. Although this distinction of active and passive is applicable to all modes of spirituality, the passive dimension is most consistently reserved for the higher states of mysticism or contemplation. In Christian thought, the "active" life refers to all that we do to facilitate the journey—verbal prayer, good works, spiritual study, and practice of virtues. The "passive" reflects how the divine works in us, leading us through silence, receptivity, and openness to share in the intimacy of the divine life. It is the absence of self-willed activity, referring to the consciousness of surrender, vulnerability, and love. Teresa of Avila describes it best when she writes that active consolations in prayer "have their beginning in our own human nature and end in God," while the passive "begin in God and end in ourselves."[13] Emphasis is placed on nonaction and noneffort in contemplation as the soul is drawn to divine rest, to be bathed in the flow of God's life like water returning to its source. Agitation, restlessness, and division cease as one sinks into the center point that is love itself.

Because of the lofty language and ethereal imagery evoked in thinking about mysticism or reading the lives of saints, it is easy to romanticize a person's encounter with divinity and impose a kind of static interpretation to the prayer practices and other disciplines that are part of the spiritual life. Yet, all authentic spirituality is hard won, involving a deconstructive process that leads to fundamental changes in one's psyche, heart, and soul. Taking apart the belief in a separate, autonomous self, contemplation is profoundly dynamic, embodied, and interrelated with the whole complex that makes up the person—mind, body, soul, and spirit. As it leads to a deeper and more fundamental change of heart, the mystical encounter exposes our wounds, suffering, oppression, rejection, arrogance, doubt, and fear. It is an arduous journey, if for no other reason than contemplation requires that we get to the root of the meanings, structures, and social constructions that constitute daily life. It is radical as well because contemplation demands a certain kind

of honesty and a certain pure intention that clears away the debris of the
mind and the sloth of the heart.

The unfortunate tendency to equate the passivity of contemplation
and mysticism with nonaction, hiding from the world, and a detachment
from social change is not representative of the experience itself. True contemplation always overflows into creation—it becomes a creative act—
and some of the greatest mystics have been advocates of profound social
transformation. This emphasis on "being" over "doing" is one of degree, a
shift in perspective that allows the person to move from a deeper center
than the one normally demanded by the world. It is movement into a
certain quality of life and a certain depth of being in order to attain the
original freedom of discovering what Thomas Merton claimed was the
"one thing really necessary—the quest for *meaning* and for *love*, the quest
for [one's] own identity."[14] Concerned with discovery of our authentic
self, contemplation is a journey that takes us from inequality to equality,
from fractured, temporal love to the wholeness of divine love, and from
oppression to freedom. Those who have sought to track the wilderness
of their heart have traveled along the inner way—through those states
of knowing and feeling that are deeper than rational thought and higher
than ordinary consciousness to be directly related to the Divine Reality
itself. For these many reasons, the contemplative journey takes apart our
understandings of reality, our time-honored structures of meaning, and
our economic and social constructions to lead us to the doorway of freedom and authenticity. It is liberation—if not an ultimate or final one, then
the process of being liberated, of knowing and experiencing a liberatory
state of consciousness.

While contemplation and mysticism are associated with religions and
have developed some of their most enduring forms, they also are transreli-
gious, prior to religious formulation or institution. They exist as a fore-text
before the formation of textuality and religious discourse. As a fore-text,
contemplation informs religious consciousness but is not reduced to it.
It travels through the underlying structures, theological principles, ways
of knowing, and methods of ascent that become formalized and embodied within specific religious forms, such as Christianity, Buddhism, Islam,
and Hinduism.[15] Religion, with its views of God, cosmos, humans, and
creation, is subsumed under the domain of the mystical: silence precedes
being; *ein sof* ("the Infinite" in Jewish thought, representing the hidden
essence of God unknown to humans) flows into *ayin*; the womb of the

mother is the source of the ten thousand things. It is not only in searching for the divine embodiment of a religious tradition—be that Buddha, Jesus, Krishna and so forth—that a person finds meaning and love. Rather it is through the turn inward, toward one's own subjectivity, that the divine is discovered to be already within oneself as the ground of communion, unity, and awe. As a fore-text, contemplation cannot be contained and never succumbs to the merely religious for its own sake, but it opens out, even within religion, beyond religion to the indescribable otherness of reality. It also gives birth to the post-texts, the language that comes after every meting out of word and historical text. As the womb of new birth, as the process that leads us from known to unknown, and then beyond to a new horizon of meaning and love, contemplation is the experiential process of participation in the unendingness of what Meister Eckhart called the "eternal now."[16]

While not all of us function at the intensity of the mystical life, nonetheless there is an important association between mystical consciousness and the person's growth in wisdom and love. If, as many scholars contend, women have been systematically denied the ability to see themselves imaged as divine, then a woman's quest for her true self cannot be resolved without understanding the impact of gender on the mystical roots of her being. It is in her core, where a woman is alone with her divine source, that she works out her freedom. To have access to this language, and to understand the pathways, markers, and stages of the journey, is empowering, as we will see in reading the lives of women saints and spiritual masters. Most women who venture on the path are alone without the support of the religious traditions to which they belong. While the classical accounts of the soul's journey provide important resources for seekers along the way, there comes a point in a woman's spiritual life where she is in uncharted territory. She must forge her own path, because even her religious traditions fail her. Certainly, there always have been heroic women who stalked the wild, rocky shores of women's authentic self—and who risked the perilous journey of returning to the bunker of women's daily existence. But only a few women have left us traces of their search for a feminist God, a God who is radical and intimate enough to be on the side of women's divine humanity. Further, the writings we do have were composed under the imprint of dominant patriarchal cultures, and thus scholars ask: What is the relationship between mysticism and feminism?

Mysticism and Feminism: Academic Foundations

The Western roots of the intellectual and social movement known as *feminism* can be traced to the pioneering work of the suffragettes who, in the late nineteenth and early twentieth centuries, fought for women's right to vote and to achieve equal civil and legal status with men. Beginning with an awareness of how social structures are oppressive of women, this "First Wave" of feminism gave rise to "Second Wave" feminists in the 1960s who fought for equal pay and equal work; and to contemporary "Third Wave" feminists who emphasize the diversity of women's social, racial, ethnic, and economic locations. Some contend that we are now entering a "Fourth Wave" of feminism, which looks at the generational differences of women under thirty and relevant questions of women's rights and appropriate activism. In all of these phases, feminism is a worldwide movement that addresses "the systematic and structural character of women's oppression and a commitment not merely to obtaining redress of grievances but to the structural transformation of society."[17] In its many manifestations, there is the shared emphasis that feminism stands for the betterment and equality of men and the whole of creation, and not just the lives of women.

Feminist theologians apply the insights of feminist theory to religions, pointing out the ways in which traditional hierarchies, male God-language, and male images of God are oppressive to women. Primarily functioning as a critique of patriarchy and androcentric culture, feminist theology seeks to uncover the whole thrust of classical religious thought in which women's dignity and humanity have been systematically denied or diminished. Feminist theologians also insist that the promotion of women's full spiritual possibility is intrinsically related to our God-language. Only a God who is on the side of women's liberation is deemed to be authentic.

From its beginnings, feminism and feminist theology have emphasized women's experience as a common starting point and norm. Confronted with the historical silencing and selective social roles granted them, women use their experience to test the truthfulness of religious claims, challenge conventional assumptions and attitudes about their roles and functions, assert the right to religious authority and position, or claim the capacity of becoming divine. While a distinguishing feature of feminist theories of knowledge and interpretation, the emphasis on experience also has been critiqued on a number of fronts, especially in developing the criteria for evaluating truth claims.[18] Further, there is concern that the term "women's experience" is not a constant for every woman and that it "too often means 'white, middle-class women's experience,' in just the way that 'human' too often means 'male.'"[19] In more recent years, the diversity that constitutes women's experience is being acknowledged as voices of women from every continent, race, and social, economic, and religious background enter the conversation.

Feminism today thus endeavors to be alert to the danger of attributing a common or universal consciousness to women that silences women's voices or marginalizes their differences. The question of diversity and the critique leveled against feminism as being primarily a white women's first world and Christian movement insensitive to the power disparities and injustices of women of color and poor women must be consistently and explicitly addressed. Its visions are furthered by women scholars belonging to specific religious traditions—Jewish, Buddhist, Native American, Muslim, Christian, and others—and by women of historically oppressed or marginalized social, racial, and cultural groups such as *mujerista* (Hispanic women's theology), womanist (African American women's theology), and third world (Asian, African, Latin American, and Indigenous theology), to name a few.

Gender and Mysticism

Until recently, there has been a notable absence of voices on the role of gender in academic studies of mysticism and an uneasy tension between feminism and mysticism. While most scholars of mysticism ignored gender, feminists, for the most part, avoided mysticism. Some feminists resist mysticism as another oppressive structure of religious communities that strives toward a common definition of the universal and essential at the detriment of women's real lives. This concern has been described variously as the polarity between "difference" versus "equality" feminists or as the debate of "essentialism versus constructivism" or "nature versus nurture." In the analysis of equality-difference, for example, emphasis is placed either on women's attainment of equality with males in all areas of life, or on affirming rather than minimizing women's sexual difference and special needs.

A similar polarity is found in essentialism-constructivism, which questions whether women's self is the result of the unchanging essentials of biology or the result of social, cultural, and economic factors. "Any view of women's nature," writes Serene Jones, "that makes universal claims about women based on characteristics considered to be an inherent part of being female" is an essentialist one.[20] Many feminists reject this appeal to nature as an unhealthy form of social determinism, which bases the subordination of women to men on natural facts rather than on cultural conditions. Moreover, "attributes that have traditionally passed for the 'essentials' of women's nature, feminists point out, are often the projections of a culture that depends upon notions of sexual difference to justify its division of labor."[21] Other feminists argue that positive forms of essentialism are necessary to establish and to value women's bodily presence and to empower their ability to construct new futures. Mary Daly, in *Beyond God the Father*, emphasizes the biological foundations of women's ways of being and the importance of affirming women's unique embodiment, as has Luce Irigaray, the French feminist psychoanalyst.[22]

On the side of "nurture," feminists take the position that social and cultural factors have a tremendous role in the construction of the ideology of "woman." The myriad ways in which socialization impacts on women and girls implies that gender is formed rather than given. Feminist constructivism ranges broadly in describing this gender-formation from thinkers who contend that social factors imprint on top of a core essence, while others argue "that culture so profoundly determines human beings that no point beyond convention . . . exists from which to ascertain what is 'nature' (the clay, raw material of personhood) and what is 'nurture' (the potter, culture) with respect to sexual difference."[23]

Feminists writing in the theological and spiritual traditions are acutely aware of these difficulties. Christian feminist Sandra Schneiders asks: "Did God create one human nature in which women and men participate fully and equally, or is human nature dual with men called by nature to full participation in the Christian mystery in the image of God and the likeness of Christ and women called to a derivative identity and role in the likeness of men?"[24] Judith Plaskow reflects on a similar exclusion of women—"At the central moment of Jewish history, women are invisible"—from the Torah verse that describes God's covenant with the Jewish people on Mt. Sinai.[25] In the area of spirituality, Carol P. Christ contends that constructivism in its more extreme expressions overlooks the importance of the spiritual in shaping women's self-identity, alienating women from that mystery that can never be reduced to culture.[26] On the other hand, feminist theologians ask the question, If they wholly accept the argument that women are essentially different from men, will their spiritual lives become defined by patriarchal cultures and oppressive church politics? Within these various approaches are women from fundamental and evangelical traditions who are comfortable within their religion's patriarchal base, and women who have rejected all forms of religious discourse as gender-biased, and who define themselves as post-Christian or post-Jewish, for example, and thus outside formal denomination or tradition. Many feminist theologians take a strategic position between the two poles of the nature versus nurture debate, drawing on the wisdom of each when appropriate.

Mysticism is susceptible to these debates because of the tendencies among its early researchers to emphasize its essential or universal nature, and to interpret "the mystical" as an experience common across culture, religion, and gender. To associate the mystical with feminism raises concerns about whether women are identified with a "common core" experience that is everywhere the same.[27] For this reason, feminists have been cautious of mysticism if it is used to mask differences, make universal claims about women's spirituality, avoid social ills, or confine women to gender stereotypes. Feminists also contend that the characteristics usually associated with mysticism, such as passivity, selflessness, silence, and absence of desire, further women's oppression by assigning normative expectations to their behavior.[28] "The path of renunciation," observes Luce Irigaray, "described by certain mystics is women's daily lot."[29] These are legitimate concerns. All too often the quest for universals becomes another invasion of women's identity and another excuse used to extend gender-biased controls from the social sphere into women's spiritual lives.

Recent scholarship has exposed the notion that mysticism somehow transcends gender and social situations, and has come under scrutiny as being susceptible to power politics and clerical elites. In *Power, Gender, and Christian Mysticism*, Grace Jantzen makes an impassioned case for the social construction of mysticism, and the transference of social controls from class and church hierarchies into the deepest realms of women's consciousness. She contends that a mysticism of the intellect based on Greek philosophical notions became the standard bearer of the Christian mystical tradition, a tradition in which women were identified as "misbegotten males" belonging to the inferior world of flesh and procreation. Jantzen contends that this split between spirit and body shifted the focus of mysticism to the intellective life and away from the more embodied, emotional spirituality central to women's concerns. Mysticism in the early church was closely tied to reading scripture and celebrating the sacraments, activities performed by men. As women were barred from education and positions of clerical authority and most could not read, they were effectively prevented from participation in and attainment of spiritual mastery. By the end of the sixth century, "the subordination of women and the domination of men," she writes, "were firmly placed in Christianity, not least in Christian spirituality."[30] The summation of this historical shift is that woman is not, in herself alone, divine.

The rejection of women as substantive of the divine—and thus defining them as representatives of inferior forms of knowing, loving, and being—distorts the world's spiritual traditions. "As long as woman lacks a divine made in her image," Jantzen writes, "she cannot establish her subjectivity or achieve a goal of her own. She lacks an ideal that would be her goal or path of becoming divine. If she is to become woman, if she is to accomplish her female subjectivity, woman needs a god who is a figure for the perfection of her subjectivity."[31] This wrenching loss of self-identity, which is not merely a personal defect but emerges out of an entire cultural climate of suppression, signifies the soul suffering of woman. Luce Irigaray describes the spiritual void many women feel:

> We women, sexed according to our gender, lack a God to share, a word to share and to become. Defined as the often dark, even occult mother-substance of the word of men, we are in need of our *subject*, our *substantive*, our *word*, our *predicates*, our elementary sentence, our basic rhythm, our morphological identity, our generic incarnation, our genealogy.[32]

The establishment of privileged social roles exclusively for men was an effective device for keeping women tied to domestic affairs and away from positions of power. Yet, this unequal assignment of value did not end with external forms of control. It also permeated the religious imagination to such an extent that the mystical path—its categories of consciousness, visions of God, structure of language, and methods of prayer—was defined in such a way that few women had access to study and practice. Despite the fact that male clerics served in certain cases as champions of women's mysticism, the dominance of patriarchal ideologies designed to subordinate women was not significantly altered or changed. Greater and more dangerous than the suppression by clerical authorities of women as mystics was the way in which the male construction of mysticism transferred the debasing and wounding of the female from the social and cultural sphere to the deepest levels of woman's soul. Jantzen contends that even mysticism is imbedded within and constructed by centuries of male-dominated thought.[33]

The fact that gender does play a role indicates that the spiritual journey, as depicted in its archaic and classical forms, does not address the complexity and depth of women's mysticism. This lack of a language and literature to speak to a woman's inner life perpetuates a divide deep within the souls of women, contributing to the subjugation of their consciousness. Without a language to name their experience, and without the benefit of women spiritual teachers who have mapped out the structures of consciousness and stages of the soul's journey explicit to their gender, women struggle toward their image and likeness to God. Unable to conceive of her self as a subject of her own experience, a woman lives within what Howard Thurman, in writing about the experience of Black Americans, called "an intimate climate of poverty . . . [that] is an inner atmosphere of the spirit [that] dries up the springs of self-esteem and often renders impotent confidence in the meaning and significance of the private life."[34]

Convergences between Feminism and Mysticism

Aware of these various critiques, other feminist scholars insist that despite the domination of male voices within mysticism, its importance is not diminished as a positive force in women's lives in every culture and religious tradition from ancient times to the present. Gerda Lerner, in her book *The Creation of Feminist Consciousness*, recognizes mysticism as a liberatory factor in the lives of medieval women for it granted them access to the sacred and fostered their spiritual empowerment. Mysticism afforded medieval women "the right to define the Divine," she writes, "and with it the right to define their own humanity."[35] Rather than imposing a gender-neutral, universal common ground, or contributing to spiritual and social subjugation, Lerner contends that medieval women in monastic settings had access to education, spiritual authority, and strategies of advancement unknown to the majority of their contemporaries.

Dorothee Soelle, who was a leading European theologian and activist, concurs with Lerner and finds in mystical literature a refreshing liberation from categories of thought that belittle and denigrate women's spiritual lives. She insists that mysticism can help us step outside the site from which women are subjugated into silence, to that reality which precedes women's oppression and patriarchal violence. We learn from mysticism in our search for a new language because it "offers God-symbols without authority or power," Soelle remarks, "thus without a chauvinistic flavor. The recognition of the higher power, the adoration of domination, the denial of one's own strength, have no place in mystical piety. Religion for mystics is sensitivity, union with the whole, belonging not subjugation. People adore God because they sink into God's love, which is called ground, or depth, or ocean."[36]

Another important correlation between mysticism and feminism is the primacy placed on personal experience in understanding reality. Soelle emphasizes that mysticism is intrinsic to feminist values in that it is based on a personal experience of the Divine and not on authority; the God of the mystics is not a God of dominance, power, might, or exclusion, but the source of intimacy and communion; mysticism thus "helps us learn the Great Surrender."[37] Mystic and feminist must search for one's true self, claims Deidre Green, by an exploration of interior validation, irrespective of culturally imposed patterns. Both point toward a transformation in consciousness: the mystic searches for the true nature of reality outside of social conditioning or established religion; feminism seeks a transformation in consciousness of women's roles, expectations, and abilities. Fundamentally, mysticism and feminism are premised on a holistic worldview of the interconnectedness of reality. Also, each elevates feeling and intuition as primary tools of knowing, and denies that reason and logic alone describe the fullness of our knowledge of the world.[38]

Women's capacity to handle suffering and their ability to overcome adversity and affliction become for Ursula King the mystical foundation of women's compassion and wisdom. Faithfulness to the daily round of duties that confines most women's lives is its own spiritual journey, training women to be present, caring, and understanding of others. She also affirms that although peace, joy, love, and harmony are qualities that are not unique to women, women by the very nature of their experience have often developed and embodied these qualities to an unusual degree. "The multiple threads of their life's journeys and stories" writes King, "provide a rich tapestry of the spiritual life which above all is a proof of women's powers of radical love and self-surrender to a reality greater than themselves."[39]

From these examples we can see that the relationship between mysticism and feminism is dynamic; neither pole is fully determined by or reduced to the other. Rather, the creative interplay of mysticism and gender provides insight into the ways in which social factors impact the spiritual consciousness of women and how women's resistance pushes back the boundaries of male-dominated traditions, leading to a definable women's spirituality. As many women can attest, there is an inseparable link between what is universal about mysticism and what is particular to gender. Any attempt to suppress the dynamism between mysticism and gender only leads to the creation of an artificial set of absolutes—either mysticism is universal, applicable to all without reference to gender, racial, or religious differences, or mysticism is always susceptible to the variables of social reality and thus relative to historical circumstances. Most scholars agree that further study and research is needed to know whether women contemplatives experience radically different views of God than their male counterparts or if there exists an essential experience that is uniquely women's.

The dialogic relationship between mysticism and feminism implies that the study of mysticism cannot remain abstract but is compelled to address its cultural, social, religious, and spiritual dimensions. As lived experience, contemplation is not free of the gender bias, clerical exclusion, and theological subordination of women in patriarchal cultures. Similarly, the goal of feminism—the dignity of women—cannot be waged in isolation from the deep mystical and contemplative dimensions of women's struggle. Feminism is inseparably related to the transformation of the whole interpretive framework of unjust and sinful relations that women use to construct meaning in their lives. The categories of consciousness that surround and confine the spiritual life of women are embedded in and tainted by dominant religious norms. "There is no alternative for feminists except contemplation," insists Constance FitzGerald, "if they are to avoid the trivialization of their own religious experience."[40] It is precisely the mystery of feminism and the inability of any theory, theology, or social construction to address women's particular spiritual location that provides an ongoing challenge to women's assertion of dignity and empowerment.

However, like other words that end with the suffix "-ism", feminism is susceptible to extreme positions on both sides of the political spectrum. Labels incite resistance and resistance leads to conflict, retrenchment, and sometimes overthrow. The lived experience of women's struggle for dignity cannot be represented by a name. The extent to which the label "feminism" weakens women's positions in the world gives pause to the use of the term. I celebrate it, nonetheless, for another reason. Feminism—as representative of various social, intellectual, and spiritual movements that struggle to affirm the pluralism of women's voices and social, racial, or religious locations—applauds genuine critique, investigation, and diversity. It demands an uncovering of surfaces, veils, and deceptions, as well as an awakening in which women's ancient amnesia is brought from the dark recesses of the unconscious into full light. This quest for the real beneath appearances, the dignity that makes meaning of our suffering, is fundamentally spiritual. Further, this radical process of self-inquiry so central to feminist theology is evident in the thought of the medieval women mystics as well. Feminism and spirituality, and their associated words "contemplation" and "mysticism," are interrelated and one. There is no true feminism without the consequent awareness of the spiritual implications of freedom. As I use the terms, feminism and a redefined mysticism are indivisible. The search for woman's true self, and her dignity and empowerment, requires confrontation with one's gender, both in oppression and freedom. Further, as feminism underscores the awareness of the need for healing, mysticism reminds us that the divine leads each person to dignity and freedom. Any form of social injustice is antithetical to the truly mystical—if by that we mean union, oneness with God. Thus, feminism and mysticism are partners in drawing us closer to the divine nature, and to providing a vision of a future truly whole and healed.

Alongside the vast literature in feminist theology, the focus on issues of gender in women's mysticism and the spiritual process that takes women from oppression to freedom deserve further attention. I intend here to add to the discussion without trying to resolve the theoretical debates. In fact, these tensions cannot be resolved. The mystery of our lives, the mystery of women and feminism, subverts easy identities. Evolving over centuries of human experience, women's mystic voice is an appropriate place to start. It articulates precisely those realities that transgress the boundaries of everyday consciousness and develops a literacy that speaks to the heart of women's deepest possibility. "For we are ourselves paradox, mystery, born and being born out of Mystery Itself."[41]

chapter three

Goddesses, Mother Jesus, and the Feminine Divine

I am the mirror of radiant purity, in which God saw himself from the beginning.

I was with him when he fashioned all creation, he gazed at me constantly in his eternal desire. . . . I am the throne the Godhead never left since God slipped into me. My throng is altogether noble. I am God, she is God, he is God, this I withhold from none: I am the Father-Mother, he is truly my Mother-Father.[1]

Women in Benares offer *pujah* (worship) to her, asking the goddess Durga for blessings and grace. She is revered by Orthodox Christians as Theotokos (Mother of God)—"the one who gave birth to the one who is God"[2]—and praised by Muslims as the highest form of love. Holy churches have been erected in her name; Catholic faithful have flocked to Mary's apparition sites in Lourdes, Medjugorje, and Fatima; and mystics and saints have called her by many names—Sophia, Shekhinah, Lakshmi, Kuanyin, Woyengi, and Frau Minne. At one time the goddess rose in prominence and was the dominant deity, the most holy and mysterious divinity. Some cultures revere her still. But the time in which she was creator and ruler of the cosmos and named the way of the world is past. Whatever her power in archaic cultures, the feminine divinity has been fractured and dispersed. More primordial than religions themselves, what was the Feminine Divine before she was co-opted by dominant religious cultures and her message suppressed?

One of the difficulties in answering this question is the ambiguity and subordination of the feminine in Western religious thought. "Never in recorded history," writes Barbara Newman, "has a monotheistic religion worshipped a goddess. Where goddesses reign, gods hold sway also, and where God is One, that One is male."[3] Rarely accorded full divine status, the feminine is often imagined as an attribute of God the Father, or as one of God's manifestations, consorts, or spouses. Often invisible or discounted, there is a definite incompleteness about the feminine in religious thought. Commenting on Sophia literature, Susan Cady writes: "Her development was cut off prematurely. Both in the Hebrew scriptures and in the New Testament, she is cut off or disguised so that her image is never fully formed."[4]

Yet traces of her full potential are present as a powerful, if latent, element in the spiritual life. The Divine Feminine is exalted in the Sophia (Wisdom) literature of the Hebrew Bible, and in later Jewish mystical texts as Shekhinah (feminine "indwelling presence"); she is similarly expressed in the Hindu Shakti and in the Chinese Buddhist personification of Kuan-yin, Bodhisattva of Compassion, as pure light, eliminating darkness and extinguishing the fire of pain. As Devi, goddess, she appears in numerous manifestations in Hindu scriptures and popular piety. To Muslims she is the "womb" (*rahim*) of the All-merciful, established in a famous *hadith*: "My mercy precedes My wrath" (*rahmatî sabaqat ghadabî*). To Jews she is the "heart" (*lev*) of God. As the source of life-giving mercy, her tears overflow into creation, healing our sins and woes. She is the sacred heart of Mary and *mater dolorosa* (mother of suffering) to millions of Catholics. Source of the ten thousand things in Taoist philosophy, she holds creation in her womb. She is nondual consciousness, who encompasses emptiness and form; *yin* and *yang*; happiness and sorrow; heaven and earth; creation and destruction; birth and death. Through her, all things come to be; in her, life bears fruition. She is pristine awareness, undefiled mind, and sinless purity.

In Nigerian creation stories, Woyengi (Great Mother) molds human beings in her image and breathes life into creation.

> In the beginning Woyengi seated herself on a stool and with her feet firmly planted on the Creation Stone and a table before her, she began to mold human beings out of earth. As each person was completed, each was embraced by her and each became a living being as the Great Mother breathed into each.[5]

In the *Lakshmi-tantra*, a popular Hindu text, Creator Goddess Lakshmi pervades all creation with vitality, will, and consciousness. Undertaking "the entire stupendous creation of the universe with only a one-billionth fraction of herself, [she is] so transcendent . . . so beyond the ability of the mind to circumscribe her, that only a miniscule fraction of her is manifest in the creation of the universe."[6]

I alone send (the creation) forth and (again) destroy it. I absolve the sins
of the good. As the (mother) earth towards all beings, I pardon them
(all their sins). I mete everything out. I am the thinking process and I
am contained in everything.[7]

Thus, despite the dominant image of God as male, and the debasement
of females in patriarchal cultures, worship of the feminine divinity was
never completely suppressed. Although the female—both as deity and as
person—often was depicted as spiritually, intellectually, and physically inferior, the Feminine Divine nonetheless has maintained a vital role in the
practices and prayer lives of countless humans through the centuries. The
predominance of goddess figures in indigenous traditions, Eastern religions,
and Old Europe, and the extent to which members of the clerical elite and
popular culture worshiped a feminine divinity or employed female images
to describe the divine, highlights her significance in the religious imagination. This suppression and elevation of the Feminine Divine is so vast and
complex—intertwined as it is with the fate of civilizations, religious fac-
tions, wars, and economies—that just a small fragment of her glory in the
history of Western mysticism will be explored in this chapter.

The Feminine Divine in Jewish, Islamic, and Christian Mysticism

While feminine imagery is found in all historical periods of the world's
religious traditions, between the twelfth and fifteenth centuries female mysticism and feminine images of the divine flourished in the West. Flowing
out of Jewish, Christian, and Islamic sources and traditions, the great river
of the mystical feminine experienced a resurgence that lasted for more than
four centuries. Many writings of the period, drawing from earlier scriptural
sources, establish a feminine divine figure as an eternal presence and creator.
In the *Book Bahir,* an important twelfth-century work of Jewish mysticism, the feminine indwelling presence, Shekhinah, is eternal, not created.
In other kabbalistic texts, She is not just a personification or quality of God
but "is always God Himself."[8] Similarly, in the Book of Wisdom, Sophia
is Creator at the beginning—"When God set the heavens in place, I was
present"—and also part of the ongoing creative process who gives birth
to humans, creation, and God. "Her radiance never sleeps. In her coming
all good things came to me, and at her hands incalculable wealth. All these
delighted me, since Wisdom brings them, though I did not then realize that
she was their mother" (Wis. 7:10-12).[9] One of the clearest declarations of

the Feminine Divine comes from the Sufi master Jalal al-Din Rumi. In a passage from his *Masnavi* praising the feminine qualities of kindness and gentleness, he says: "Woman is the radiance of God, she is not your beloved. She is the Creator—you could say that she is not created."[10]

In the Jewish and Christian scriptures, the feminine divinity resides in the divine spheres just as she dwells here below. As the mother of the upper world in kabbalistic thought, Shekhinah is identical with the Written Torah, the divine eternal Word, and in her lower manifestation, she is the Oral Torah, which comes down to earth and enters the world in the form of daughter. Similarly, St. Paul proclaims Jesus, mediator of the divine and human, as Sophia, identifying the union of the divine Word and the world: "The hidden Sophia of God which we teach in our mysteries is the Sophia that God predestined to be for our glory before the ages began" (1 Cor. 2:7).[11] Ibn al-'Arabi, the renowned thirteenth-century Islamic mystic, also situates the essence of the feminine in both the heavenly and earthly worlds, and as prior to and inclusive of male and female.

> Furthermore, he made the final term [prayer] correspond to the first [women] in its femininity, placing the masculine term [perfume] between them. He begins with 'women' and ends with 'prayer,' both of which are feminine nouns, . . . since man is placed between the Essence [a feminine noun] from which he is manifested and woman who is manifested from him. Thus he is between two feminine entities, the one substantially feminine, the other feminine in reality, women being feminine in reality, while prayer is not.[12]

The feminine contains both passive and active elements. As a reflection of the divine polarity, "woman," Ibn al-'Arabi writes, "is the most complete and perfect [contemplation of Reality], because in this way he [man] contemplates the Reality in both active and passive mode, while by contemplating the Reality only in himself, he beholds Him in a passive mode particularly."[13] In the *Book Bahir*, Shekhinah is the receptive "vessel" (*shidda*) in which all the divine powers are contained and mediated to the world, and is symbolized by the ocean in which all the rivers of the world flow. She is the crown within which all creation is held and she is "understanding" (*binah*) itself. She is the innermost chamber of mystery and "to this humankind . . . has no access."[14] We cannot see our mother's place of origin.

At the same time, she is the active force who illuminates the earthly world and "it is only through her . . . that humans can find their way to

God."[15] She is prophet and redeemer who, out of compassion for the human condition, dwells within the material realm. "Only in this state," states kabbalistic scholar Peter Schäfer, "can human beings see her and speak with her; her actual place, however, the place of her origin, continues to be hidden from their view."[16] She is erased; we are her unveiling. In her dwelling among us as Shekhinah she willingly goes into exile from her divine origins and suffers "isolation" (*meyuhad*) and the tragedy of the human condition. When we sin, she mourns. When we follow truth, she rejoices. She is the embodiment of the highest form of love—mother-love—and we use the metaphors of daughter, sister, and mother to express the "exceptionality and intensification of this love."[17] Our love is the overflowing of her love; our earth, the formation of her plenitude; our body, her holy temple.

As prophet, Sophia calls aloud in the streets; she raises her voice in the public square; she delivers her message at the city gate: "You simple people, how much longer will you cling to your simple ways?" (Prov. 1:22). Like Sophia, Shekhinah plays an active part in our destiny. "She alone belongs to both worlds," writes Peter Schäfer. "It is only through her that the earthly world can be reconciled with the heavenly one and only through her that humans can find their way to God. . . . Without her the heavenly world would be incomplete, and the earthly world would neither have been created nor be able to find its way back to its creator."[18]

Speaking her own Word, the Feminine Divine is associated with the mystical theory of language. Rabbi Isaac of Acre wrote that "the holy language comes into the souls of the mystics of Israel from the radiance of the glory of Shekhinah. . . . And understand that 'language' is the secret of Shekhinah, and 'words' allude to the divine name formed of 72 [units] whose letters are 216."[19] An obscure rabbinic source also states that "*Shekhinah* spoke from the throat of Moses" in secret.[20] Once the holy language is born, a voice is heard that is audible to human ears. Similarly in the ancient Hindu text *The Rig Veda*, the "origin of sacred language" (*vak*) is a feminine noun for goddess. The hymns of the *Vedas* are sacred re-creations of feminine speech: "I am the queen, the confluence of riches, the skilful one who is first among those worthy of sacrifice. I am the one who says, by myself, what gives joy to gods and men."[21]

In the Book of Wisdom, Sophia is both teacher and what is taught. We are "not just to learn from her, [we] are to learn her."[22] She Herself is what is to be learned. Her teaching is not in the content itself, but in the way in which every content is approached. The commitment is not to a certain kind of knowledge or to a certain secret dogma. It is a commitment to the task of living from *Her* perspective. "Send her forth from your throne of glory . . . to teach me what is pleasing to you, since she knows and understands everything" (Wis. 9:10).[23] Expressed in erotic love imagery, Sophia is the one to marry, the bride to be possessed. Yet *She* cannot be possessed or owned; every attempt to claim her is aborted. "She smiles, for though they have bound her, she cannot be a prisoner. Not that she is strong, or clever, but simply that she does not understand imprisonment."[24] "By those who love her she is readily seen, and found by those who look for her. . . . In every thought of theirs, she comes to meet them" (Wis. 6:13, 16).[25] Then, it is we who are invaded by her Spirit, claims Wisdom, we who are filled with her love. We follow her truth to our nature.

> Although she is alone, she can do everything;
> Herself unchanging, she renews the world,
> And, generation after generation, passing into holy souls,
> She makes them into God's friends and prophets;
> For God loves only those who dwell with Wisdom.
> She is indeed more splendid than the sun,
> She outshines all the constellations. (Wis. 7:27-30)

Feminine Imagery in Medieval Christian Texts

This expression of the feminine divinity witnessed an unprecedented development in Christian spirituality during the High Middle Ages. The quantity and quality of women's mystical writings from the twelfth century on underscore Bernard McGinn's sense that a "new mysticism" was taking hold in Christianity.[26] The usage of vernacular writing, courtly personification plays, and the mutual dialogue between male and female voices distinguishes the later Middle Ages as one of the most remarkable periods in the history of Western mysticism. So vibrant and diverse was this outpouring of texts, images, and figures by female mystics that, Luce Irigaray claims, "this is the only place in the history of the West in which a woman speaks and acts so publicly."[27] Further, characterized by new attitudes toward the world and cloister, new forms of language, and new modes of mystical consciousness, feminine imagery found expression in ever more innovative and provocative ways by mystics of both sexes. Two important themes—the feminization of Jesus and the usage of goddess figures—reclaim this period in religious thought as one of the most fertile in establishing a context within which to address women's contemporary concerns and a feminist pathway to God. Yet, as female mysticism grew in power and authority, "many champions of orthodoxy feared it more than heresy itself. Reaction followed the Great Schism in the fifteen century. The High Middle Ages ended as they began with a great silent void where the voices of women should have resounded."[28]

Mother Jesus

Early in Christian history, Wisdom (Sophia) as a feminine persona in the Hebrew Bible was identified with the male Jesus. This tension between the grammatical gender and usage of Wisdom in the Hebrew scriptures and her co-optation by the demands of Christology contributed to the suppression of Sophia literature in the patristic period. "During the formative period of Christian theology, 'it becomes evident,' according to Jaroslav Pelikan, 'that the basis for the fullest statement of the divine in Christ as Logos was provided not by its obvious documentation in John 1:1-14 but by Proverbs 8:22-31 (LXX)'—an aretalogy [reflection on the deeds] of Sophia. The fourth-century Arian controversy seems to have broken out over the interpretation of this very passage."[29] This change in the status accorded to Sophia in Jewish scripture contributes to the demise of the singularly feminine in Christian thought, and paves the way for the identification of Sophia with Jesus in its mystical texts.

In associating the power and wisdom of Sophia with Jesus, the feminization of Jesus in male and female writers becomes a prominent feature of patristic and medieval theology. Clement of Alexandria, in his *Paedagogus*, produces one of the most compelling images of Jesus as mother in the early church. Proclaiming that "men and women are alike under the Instructor's [Jesus'] charge," Clement compares the milk of the breast to Christ's spiritual nourishment of the soul: "As nurses nourish new-born children on milk, so do I also by the Word, the milk of Christ, instill into you spiritual nutriment."[30] Other patristic authors, like Origen, Irenaeus, John Chrysostom, Ambrose, and Augustine, "all describe Christ as mother," Caroline Bynum writes. "In general the Greek fathers, particularly those influenced by gnosticism, seem to have been more at home with maternal metaphors."[31] This emphasis on sophiology and mariology remains a constant feature of the Greek Christian tradition, as it continues today to incorporate feminine figures, symbols, and metaphors in liturgical and mystical practice.

But it is in the twelfth century that we begin to see a genuine devotion to the motherhood of Jesus and a more critical reflection on the role of males and females in the divine economy. In her book *Jesus as Mother* Bynum claims that descriptions of God in feminine terms were found more prominently in male than female writers during this century, and were part of a growing tendency to emphasize the approachability and intimacy of God. "Two trends," she writes, "that differentiate twelfth-century devotional texts from the early church are the rise of affective spirituality and the feminization of religious language."[32] Bynum contends that three basic stereotypes are assigned to the female based on her bodily function of mothering. She is generative and sacrificial in her generation through giving physical birth; she loves and is tender because a mother cannot help loving her own child; and she is nurturing, feeding the child with her own bodily fluid.[33] In a medieval association of breast milk with blood, Jesus is depicted as a mother giving birth, nursing the soul at his breasts, and consoling, holding, and nourishing the person.

These maternal images frequently were applied to male religious authorities—particularly abbots, bishops, apostles, and monks—to signify their Christlike qualities of humanity, compassion, gentleness, fairness, and love. Anselm of Canterbury compares Jesus and Paul to mothers who care for the soul, and Jesus as a hen gathering chicks under his wing. At the same time, he writes in his *Monologion* that the term "mother" cannot be applied to God, "because male is superior to female and because the father contributes more to the child than the mother in the process of reproduction, but nonetheless . . . associates 'mother' as well as 'father' with engendering and stresses the mother as one who gives birth, even dying to give the child life . . . and the one who loves."[34]

Bernard of Clairveaux, the most prolific conveyer of female imagery during this period, also uses images of breasts, mothering, and nursing to express the outpouring of love and nourishment that Jesus offers the soul. He applies the term "mother" to himself and fellow monastics to emphasize the tender care with which he holds his novices as teacher and the pain felt when the student is "torn from the breast": "I nourished you with milk when, while yet a child, it was all you could take. . . . But alas! . . . You too were torn from my breast, cut from my womb. My heart cannot forget you."[35] Among women, the most celebrated and thorough theology of the motherhood of God is that of Julian of Norwich in the fourteenth century, whom we will turn to in part 2. But other women mystics—Gertrude of Helfta, Mechthild of Magdeburg, Hildegard of Bingen—also describe Jesus in feminine terms as mother, lover, spouse, and healer who nourishes the soul, leading them to intimacy and divine union.

The increasing use of images taken from uniquely female experiences of childbirth, nursing, and feeding is found in both male and female authors. Medieval thinkers tended to use masculine and feminine imagery fluidly, mixing and fusing the genders. The soul, for example, was predominately pictured as female, while female erotic and sexual experience was used "steadily from the twelfth century on . . . to describe the soul's union with Christ."[36] Monks, nuns, and lay practitioners of both sexes referred to themselves as "weak women"; male hagiographers extolled the virtues of saintly women as "virile." Women used self-deprecating terms in either a serious or an ironic sense, calling themselves "wretched" and "weak" to highlight their special status before God, to deflect an inquisitional temperament, or to lament their weakness as a sign of humility. Adopting images from courtly love poetry, women mystics described themselves as manly "knights" in their spiritual lives.

Goddess Figures

Not only was the divine nature pictured in feminine images and language, but goddess figures also were prevalent in the writings of male and female mystics. The dominant object of worship in Old European cultures, goddesses appear with amazing regularity in mystical writing and in popular piety of the High Middle Ages.[37] "The manifestation of goddesses in transcendent landscapes," Paul Piehler contends, "constitutes the central psychic experience in medieval allegory."[38] Male usage of goddess figures is evident in a number of medieval texts, among them St. Francis's celebrated devotion to Lady Poverty; Beatrice, the feminine muse, representing faith and grace, who guides Dante out of purgatory and into the celestial realm; the personification of Charity as a feminine force independent of God in Hugh of St. Victor; and Cornelius Agrippa's bold association of the feminine persona of Divine Wisdom, Sophia, with women.[39]

However, one of the most expansive usages of a goddess figure appears in the *Horologium Sapientia* (*Wisdom's Watch upon the Hours*), composed by Henry Suso. Scarcely consulted today, but one of the most widely read devotional texts in Medieval Europe, the *Horologium* was completed in 1334. The text "oscillates between two versions of the divine love affair: sometimes the writer speaks as the female Soul pining for her divine Bridegroom, but more often as the male Disciple ravished by love of his heavenly Bride."[40] A gifted disciple of Meister Eckhart, Suso interweaves in the text meditations on the cross with "fervent professions of love to . . . 'the goddess of all beauty'"— "none other," writes Barbara Newman, "than Eternal Wisdom (Sophia or

Sapientia), acknowledged in her female form as the friar's courtly mistress and spiritual bride."[41] In a reversal of the standard erotic imagery of the female mystic as a bride of the male Christ, Suso takes as his celestial bride Eternal Wisdom, the "only beloved daughter [of the] Supreme King . . . and somehow made me [Suso] his son-in-law."[42]

While many of the women mystics paid scant attention to goddess figures, or focused instead on Jesus as divine spouse or mother, others like Hildegard of Bingen, Mechthild of Magdeburg, Marguerite Porete, and Christine de Pinzan place goddess figures at the center of their writings. Hildegard, the celebrated mystic–healer, draws from the books of Proverbs, Wisdom, and Ecclesiasticus to develop a cosmological view of creation, redemption, and transformation in the figure of Sapientia (Wisdom) or Caritas (Love). Applying this sapiential theology to Jesus, the cosmos, and Mary, Hildegard situates the feminine divinity at the center of the wheel of life, as the source and power of healing, and as the mothering figure of the church (*Ecclesia*). Sapientia or Caritas exemplifies the ultimate mystery of the cosmos, and the inseparable bond between creator and creation. "Hildegard," writes Barbara Newman, "saw this as the dimension in which mediation or union between Creator and creature can be achieved. Where the feminine presides, God stoops to humanity and humanity aspires to God."[43]

At the center of Hildegard's cosmological wheel of divinity is Sapientia. Her immanence is supreme; she is everywhere, generating, circulating, and greening all of life. In Hildegard's *Book of Life's Merits*, Caritas is both the elemental force that invigorates nature and the spiritual force that instills new life in the soul. "I am the air, I who nourish all green and growing life, I who bring ripe fruit from the flower. For I am skilled in every breath of the Spirit of God, so I pour out the most limpid streams. From good sighing I bring weeping, from tears a sweet fragrance through holy actions."[44] She is creatrix and *anima mundi* (soul of the world), who gives life to the cosmos by existing within it and not by molding it or ordering it from on high. "Hildegard's keen sense of divine immanence led her to envision the creative power not as a force propelling the world from without but as an ambience enfolding it and quickening it from within."[45] Further, as the source of creative and healing forces, the Feminine Divine is not associated with any fixed or precise dogma in Hildegard's thought. "She is, rather," contends Newman, "a unique perspective on them—a whole realm of associations, images, and spiritual perceptions that may bear on aspects of Christ, or Mary, or the Trinity, but cannot finally be reduced to them."[46] In a way reminiscent of Ibn al-'Arabi's understanding of the feminine and the Jewish depiction of Shekhinah, Hildegard depicts Mary as the celestial foreshadowing of Wisdom and the embodied fertility of Eve. She thus unites the celestial with the earthly, the divine with the flesh.

Mechthild of Magdeburg and Marguerite Porete, two beguine mystics born in thirteenth-century Germany and France, respectively, continue this weaving of goddess figures into Christian spirituality. Mechthild's *The Flowing Light of the Godhead* and Marguerite's *The Mirror of Simple Souls* both begin with a dialogue between the soul and the figure of Lady Love. In Mechthild's text, Lady Love (Frau Minne) instructs the Soul or "Lady Queen" on how to empty herself and achieve annihilation in God. In the dialogue that ensues, the soul laments that Love has consumed her, taking everything away from her, including youth, wealth, honor, and health; while Love counters with the spiritual benefits the soul has received in return—freedom, virtues, knowledge and purity. The passion that flows between the two describes the soul's abandon to Love, in a total surrender beyond the bounds of social convention or theological decree.

The heights of erotic love are contrasted with the "sinking humility" and "constant estrangement from God" that exposes another dimension of divine love.[47] The mature soul must experience all aspects of Frau Minne's love, even as she is drawn into the humility of the "love-rich soul." This "sinking humility . . . chases her up into heaven and drags her down again into the abyss."[48] An imposing presence, Lady Love "demands absolute dispossession" of the soul's attachments in order that the soul will come to possess her and thus God and all the world.[49] She is depicted as the "Love who wounds and binds her devotees, who sickens them and slays them and asks everything of them in order that she may bring them to an undivided will and a mutual interchange of desire, to make love manifest."[50] Seeking to free the soul from its attachments to anything less than intimacy and total love, Lady Love leads the soul through its temptations, wounds, resistance, fear, and sorrow in order to center her whole being on Love herself, on the goddess figure "who coexists with and even overpowers the Trinity."[51] Demanding everything of them, Frau Minne brings her lovers to an undivided communion and an interpenetrating binding of intimacy to make the divine manifest.

Marguerite Porete also situates feminine divine figures as central actors in *The Mirror of Simple Souls*. Burned at the stake in 1310 for refusing to stop circulating her manuscript after the church had condemned it, Porete's personal tragedy strangely parallels the dialectic that takes place within the text between Reason and Love. Creating a distinction between desirous love and divine love, Porete follows what Michael Sells calls an "apophasis of desire" in which utter selflessness is the medium through which the soul gives up its will and is annihilated and ravished by its divine lover.[52] The main dialogue in Porete's drama takes place between the goddess figure Lady Love (Dame Amour) and the Enfranchised Soul, also called the Annihilated Soul. Another dialogue occurs between Dame Amour and Reason, who is associated with the theological schools and masters and is thus unable to understand the finer points and paradoxes of this courtly divine love. The only male character, FarNear (Loingpres), is identified with the Trinity and is depicted by Porete as the divine lover of the annihilated soul who never speaks. In this mystical love play, the characters debate with one another about the proper relationship of the human and the divine and how this relation fosters the soul's spiritual ascent to God. Of special interest is how the two main dialogues take place between three female allegorical figures—Love, Reason, and Soul.

In guiding others on the mystical path, *The Mirror* enacts an itinerary that progresses through seven stages of spiritual growth and three deaths—to sin, nature, and spirit—which move the soul toward mystical perfection. The transition from desirous love to divine love cannot take place until the soul dies to its own will and, finally overcome by the "abyss of humility into which she has fallen," is annihilated in the divine will.[53] It is the transition or death from the three beginning stages to the final four stages that marks the soul's ascent in which both self and other are made empty in an ecstasy of love. The soul is now so completely possessed by Lady Love that it is powerless to accomplish anything on its own, for it wills and knows nothing. "The central event of the drama is the death of Reason who, after continued questioning of Dame Amour over the paradoxes of love, finally dies (chap. 87), 'mortally wounded by love.' This theatrically constructed event marks a major transformation in the annihilated soul, who is now freed from reason and able to 'reclaim her heritage.'"[54]

An even more radical but parallel usage of goddess figures is found in Christine de Pizan's *The Book of the City of Ladies*. Completed in 1405, *City of Ladies* explores the suffering and oppression of women. A widowed mother of three at the age of twenty-five and with no inheritance, Christine supported herself through writing in a time when women were kept out of the public economy through illiteracy and social restrictions. She is remembered as an accomplished poet and the official biographer of Charles V; her most memorable writings are those that address and defend the status of women. In a direct confrontation with the "utter falseness of 'masculine myths'" concerning women, Christine wanted to provoke a more perfect realization of women's potential by insisting that females must be educated and that the betterment of women's lives is a social and religious responsibility.[55] Although Christine was aware of medieval class structure and its detriment to women, she did not advocate its overthrow. Instead, she wanted to assist women from all social classes and levels of accomplishment to achieve their true nobility of soul and to affirm their "kingdom of femininity."

Her text is premised on the redemption of womankind by the workings of God's celestial daughters. Claiming that God can choose to manifest a feminine Trinity, Christine posits a Virgin Queen who invokes both a male and female Trinity whose divine wills coincide in splendor at her coronation. This feminine Trinity is composed of Reason, Rectitude, and Justice, who join forces with pagan and Christian goddesses and female saints to valorize the female as a genuine representative of God and to deconstruct gender identities harmful to women. "It was not her authorship as such," writes Barbara Newman, "but her mission of deconstructing and reconstructing the history of women, that she needed to authorize with this convention of visionary literature."[56] Modeled on Augustine's *City of God*, de Pizan's *City of Ladies* is widely inclusive, bringing into its vision the outcasts of society—"biblical women, amazons, Christian martyrs, transvestites, pagan goddesses, contemporary queens, and classical heroines, including a few notorious criminals, all under the queenship of Mary."[57] In order to affirm that women as well as men could be representatives of the divine, Christine emphasizes both her female authorship and female representation of the divine. Drawing on this *"universal history of women*, which encompasses pagan and Christian women up to Christine's present," *City of Ladies* stands out as one of the first vernacular feminist literary genres.[58]

This attraction to the feminine divinity did not result, however, in changes in attitudes toward females. It is without question that medieval attitudes toward women as compared to men were strongly negative. Women were depicted as physiologically weaker, spiritually inferior, and defective in body and moral fortitude. The ancient polarity in which females are but a miserable imitation of the more valorous and superior male is evident in the following statement by John Gerson (1363–1429), chancellor of the University of Paris:

> The female sex is forbidden on apostolic authority (1 Tim. 2:12) to teach in public, that is either by word or by writing. . . . All women's

teaching, particularly formal teaching by word and by writing, is to be held suspect unless it has been diligently examined, and much more fully than man's. The reason is clear: common law—and not any kind of common law, but that which comes from on high—forbids them. And why? Because they are easily seduced, and determined seducers; and because it is not proved that they are witnesses to divine grace.[59]

Despite its significance, beauty, and vitalizing strength, this renaissance of women's mysticism and feminine divine figures was not to be a permanent fixture of Christian culture, but was pushed underground again during the Reformation, remaining a hidden tributary until the modern era. As Barbara Newman explains:

> In sum, we may posit that the high medieval centuries constituted a golden age of goddesses without in any way implying that the era was a golden age for women, feminist theology, or the genial toleration of dissent. But during the great religious upheavals of the sixteenth century this tolerance for goddesses came to an end. Torn apart by religious warfare, heresy, and schism as never before, a beleaguered Church could no longer sustain the freewheeling religious culture and began to enforce a new mandate for uniformity, not only in doctrine but also in devotional literature, spirituality and art. . . . With the Reformation . . . the goddesses dwindled until they faded from common sight; and with them, a remarkable era in the history of Christianity came to an end.[60]

Women, Feminism, and Intimal Mysticism

Feminist scholars claim that the "imaginary" of patriarchal consciousness has so penetrated the symbolic order—language, text, scripture, imagination—in which we think, live, and breathe that it cannot be dismantled or transcended simply by virtue of retrieval or reconstruction.[61] In the High Middle Ages, we have touched briefly on how female and male mystics used women's experience as a hermeneutic (an interpretative framework) within which to re-imagine self, deity, and world. From the bodily experience of women—mothering, breast-feeding, nursing, birthing, pregnancy—writers drew new metaphors and symbols of the divine life. From female spiritual experience—visions, locutions, and soul sufferings—they discovered a contemplative process that cultivated a new or alternative symbolic order. The particularity of women's experience in body and spirit was used to frame women as "other" and to contain their experience under the auspices of

male control and prerogative. But it also served to open up new interpretations of God, temper the austerity or distance of divinity, and re-imagine
ultimate reality in female figures and symbols as nurturing, compassionate,
and intimate.

Although women were officially prohibited from preaching or adminis-
tering sacraments, many women mystics had disciples and followers whom
they counseled and instructed. Their reputation as spiritual authorities and
leaders was based on their mystical experiences. Female mysticism, especially the more extraordinary visionary, ecstatic, and erotic, served to legitimate female spirituality, allowing women to develop an authoritative body
of wisdom, and to plumb a depth of meaning unhampered by the university theologians. As Bynum, Newman, and others have shown, the focus of
female mystics on the humanity of Christ, suffering of the soul, importance
of the Eucharist, goddess figures, and mothering symbols constitute the first
documented cases "that a particular kind of religious experience is more
common among women than men" during the medieval period.[62] While
we clearly are unable to get inside their experience or to declare a certain
universally applicable female consciousness, it is possible to detect in their
writings an embodied or "intimal" mysticism.

Medieval women's intimal mysticism functions for us today as a guide-
line to a distinct type of consciousness and to the inmost *processes* whereby
new interpretation, symbol, and understanding of reality emerge. From the
Latin *intimus* or *intumus*, the word "intimal" refers in medical usage to the
innermost membrane of some organ or part of a body. Where female imagery and women's mysticism are dominant, intimal mysticism appears as a
perspective on reality most clearly distinguished by its "within-ness"—its
ability to dwell within what it perceives, touches, or knows. Whether males
employ feminine images or females explore male and female metaphors and
symbols, traces of an intimal consciousness are apparent in the turning of
the text to perceive reality from the perspective of a divine-human intimacy.
Based on a prior willingness to offer over the rational distinction between
self and other central to all expressions of mystical union, intimal mysticism
does not function solely in highly rarified spiritual realms but also becomes
embodied, leading to a new type of perception and a new way of approaching the divine.

Defined as a caring, closeness, or affection between two subjects that is
inmost to them, intimacy is a central feature of women's mystical texts. As
Dame Amour, Mother Jesus, Frau Minne, or Sapientia the soul is drawn to a

communion so total that the distance and exclusion that mark and demarcate self and other, deity and world, male and female are overturned. At the highest states of mystical consciousness, intimacy—as the collapsing, fusing, or annihilating of boundaries between self and Other—*is* interpretation. Reforming our conditioned view of reality, this vantage point leads to an awareness of the suffering world and a desire to lift it up to its highest spiritual potential by turning the face of intimacy to suffering itself. By dwelling within pain, pain is experienced and perceived in a new way; it is also transformed, for even suffering cannot withstand the healing and curative properties of Intimacy. When the subject comes down or comes out of nondual mystical consciousness, she often looses sight of the Intimate, clothing her pure nakedness in gowns of beauty and fragrance, or sometimes in cloaks of armor and defense. Nevertheless, the experience cannot be wiped away, cannot be merely dismissed or forgiven. It takes root or dwells in the core of the person, healing and reforming the causes and conditions that generate soul pain.

It is precisely these deeper expressions of divine intimacy that subject the women mystics to scrutiny, accusations of heresy, and, in some cases, death. Because their understanding of intimacy was not divorced from embodiment or the daily human condition but was inmost within them, women mystics often turned attention to the suffering and healing of their brethren, and to the reformation of political and church affairs. Each had to struggle to find within herself that point of intersection that liberates whatever prevents or aborts her living out of her highest potential—the place where she breathes and sees from God's (read Intimacy's) perspective. The loving, caring closeness that she finds in this inmost union is transposed into a way of understanding what liberation and divinity mean in this world.

While our medieval foremothers may differ from us in their sexual, racial, cultural, religious, or economic orientations, their process of naming and claiming their own voice is something women today can relate to and understand. The intimacy of the mystical encounter is central to the writings and the lives of medieval women. Jesus, Frau Minne, Dame Amour, Sapientia, Sophia, and Caritas take a personal interest in their hopes, sufferings, and joys. Their experience as women is not discounted or dismissed, requiring subservience to neither God nor men. Evidenced by the variety and scope of their literary and spiritual contribution, women's embodied mysticism honors and cherishes each woman's search for God and for her true self. This profound commitment to becoming divine is the doorway to their empowerment, and not to the adherence of a stereotypical or universal view of God or women.

The women mystics clearly held their divine lover in the highest esteem. Yet, this bond of lover and beloved is the antithesis of anything harsh or without mercy. Their appropriation of the feminine Jesus as a hermeneutic for life was the healing of dogmatism, exclusion, or violence. He is transposed through the bond of love into a fount of intimacy, becoming for Teresa of Avila—as well as for Julian, Hildegard, and others—a guiding light in her earthly sojourn. Teresa takes his intimacy on the road; she takes his longing for her freedom into her heart; she takes his advice over that of her male confessors; she privileges the message: love me unto the cross, see the suffering I see, and embrace the whole world in love. This understanding is very far from the injunction to convert the whole world to a superior or final dogmatic claim. Mystical experience becomes, then, both a savoring and an honoring of the power and beauty of our differences *and* a devotion to the one whom each calls Beloved. Teresa does not try to hide her adoration of Jesus; she does not try to deny that she longs to lead all souls to loving "His Majesty." But, she does this from a primary injunction to do no harm—to honor intimacy's hold on her interpretation of reality.

If this intimal mysticism represents an entire perspective on reality—a hermeneutic of a feminine divine way—and not just an aspect, dimension, fragment, or association that modifies or revises a prior male deity, or patriarchal construction of gender, then the articulation of what constitutes, interprets, and names the feminine is a subversion of a dominant worldview. In medieval women's texts, I believe we see traces of this breaking through of a true contemplative feminism that by virtue of its expression necessarily becomes a critique of dominant religious and cultural norms. As a vision of women and the feminine seen through God's eye, contemplative feminism can be defined as the study of the relationship between women's spiritual freedom and engaged social concern.

While the women mystics themselves may not have intended this radical stance, the very fact of their speaking—of their naming reality from an intimal vantage point—was a threat to the established order. To the extent that this is so, the women mystics bring to theology a new language and a new *presence* that revise our understanding and interpretation of the world. This intimal quality of evaluation, perception, and speech that underlies female mysticism maps a territory of hope in which we discover an integral manner of approaching life's problems, perceiving God-consciousness, and restoring our planet.

chapter four

Contemplative Feminism

Transforming
the Spiritual Journey

History has shown us women whose mystic experience in what I call the "mystic circle" moved from contemplative prayer as learning love into intense social involvement. . . . Valid mystical feminism reaches out, then, to our neighbor; it is social, rooted in love and ablaze with concern.

Reading this quotation one can immediately ask whether there is something like "mystical feminism" and "feminist spirituality" and what are its main characteristics. The emphasis lies undoubtedly on a new self-concept and new relationships, on a breakthrough in consciousness and on a spirituality which is embodied and undivided, that is to say integral and holistic.[1]

After centuries of suppression, the spirituality of the feminine is revealing itself once again both within and outside the bounds of formal religious traditions. Like our medieval predecessors, we are at a distinctive juncture in the history of consciousness marked by the ascension of feminine wisdom from its ancient dwelling place to assume a leadership role in human cultures. Similar to prior historical shifts in our understanding of God and the world, we stand today between old paradigms of religious consciousness facing challenges and new ones struggling to be born. Central to its time is an urgency voiced by students of history: that the sacredness of the Feminine Divine must not succumb to the pressures of materialism or be driven underground. Scholars and practitioners realize, as well, that the explosion of interest in female deities and goddess figures is tied to feminism as a whole, and that an inseparable relationship exists between the heights of mystical consciousness and contemporary women's concerns. In all this, many feminists acknowledge that the activism that drives them is sustained and nourished by a deep, contemplative attitude.

This conscious joining together of the spiritual processes that lead women to self-liberation with women's prophetic activism for social change has been variously referred to as *contemplative* or *mystical feminism*. A postmodern version of the classical ideal—in which contemplation and action are inseparable and one—contemplative feminism studies and maps the spiritual practices and structures of consciousness of the mystical traditions as a resource in women's liberation and in the transformation of our world. It is a method of inquiry and interpretation that probes the contemplative processes, prayer forms, and mystical techniques women employ to heal inner oppression, liberate soul wounds, and empower personal dignity and self-worth. Charting the journey that compels women to achieve their highest spiritual potential, the contemplative side of feminism concentrates on states of consciousness and deep mystical processes at work in women's struggle for equality. A woman's inner life and freedom to pursue the mystical center of her being are integral to her self-worth, dignity, and empowerment.

Contemplative feminism also investigates how oppressive social and religious institutions affect a woman's ability to reclaim her original nature. Alert to the ways in which the holy has been denied and desecrated in its manifestation as mother, sister, daughter, wife, lover, and friend, the feminist side of contemplation reminds women that their full spiritual potential is dependent on reclaiming and upholding in daily life their integrity and worth. The social activism that fuels feminist discourse insists that women's liberation cannot remain a purely interior act. It must spill over into the world, empowering women's prophetic voice to transform human conditions that breed violence and hatred. This commitment to women's embodied holiness involves an arduous spiritual process that initially is bounded on all sides by darkness, doubt, and aloneness. Born out of the intensely female experience to heal the ancient fracture in consciousness that distorts the feminine, women must push through the anguish that "there is no way out of, no way around, [and] no rational escape from, what imprisons one."[2] Yet, it is also a journey that is "more lovely than dawn," for it is the process by which a woman claims her undivided self and champions her *full presence* in the world. Combining resources from the wisdom of the contemplative and feminist traditions, women's soul strength and moral commitment are revolutionary forces of social good.

Transforming the Spiritual Journey

In seeking an authentic spiritual life today, the context and content of women's experience as *women* refine and transform the spiritual journey—its interpretations, techniques of enlightenment, and understanding of divinity. Women's discovery of their divine core challenges the classical understanding of mysticism, altering the dynamics of the inner life, the process of spiritual development, and the various maps of the journey. The mystical process of negation by which a woman discovers her self as a *subject* in the divine is vital to mapping a feminine way to God. An inseparable relationship exists between women's recognition of their need to transform deep spiritual wounds and the birth of mystical feminist consciousness. Understanding this dialectic offers us a unique way of approaching God-questions. We ask: What spiritual paths, soul strengths, and dark nights do women discover in their journey toward divine intimacy? How does women's mystical awareness contribute to a new understanding of our world, and to healing the soul oppression of others? How does cultural pragmatism mask deep spiritual injuries and trivialize ancient vocabularies that speak of wisdom and inspire the human search for meaning? In what way can women bring their spiritual gifts to bear on global issues?

As a spiritual journey, mystical feminism provides a starting point for an interpretation of reality that turns in two directions, inward toward the divine center of the self, and outward toward the world. Turning inward, it refers to the path women follow toward union and intimacy with God. It maps the geography of women's soul, concentrating on the rare and subtle movements of women's quest for wholeness, a subject of infrequent comment in the history of human spirituality. It tracks the development and growth of women's mystical consciousness from despair, doubt, and loss of hope to freedom and empowerment. It recognizes that abusive speech and misogynist views of women penetrate into deep structures of consciousness, violating women's self-esteem, dignity, and right to seek union with God. Further, it draws on women's soul force, tapping into an ancient storehouse of wisdom, strength, and nonviolence built upon centuries of women's heroism and prayers.

Turning toward the world, contemplative feminism sees women from the perspective of a divine concern and looks at the world through women's eyes. It deals with the spiritual values, ethical visions, and moral implications of seeing the world through the vantage point of the female body and fem-

inine consciousness. It recognizes that God suffers the violation of women
and the feminine in our world. Women's suffering is divine suffering; divine
suffering is women's suffering. What injures a woman, harms her soul, or
violates the feminine in creation touches God. This bonding between
divinity and womanity, a bonding measured by an intensity of vulnerability and intimacy, indicates the depth at which violence reverberates in a
woman's soul, harming what is most receptive and sensitive in her nature.
To cite an example, the worldwide economic and social marginalization of
women, and their historical status as a permanent underclass are violent acts
that rob a woman of self-worth, creating hidden scars in her being. Further,
the global dimensions of women's suffering—rape, trafficking in women,
wife-beating, bride burning, infanticide of girl babies, as well as more subtle
forms of social, religious, and economic violence—are indicators of the vast
and tragic failure of the world community to honor and protect the intrinsic rights of more than half the human race. These are the most political of
acts; they are thinly veiled attempts to mute the prophetic voice, blind the
eyes that look upon our concerns, and deny the compassion for human
frailty that comes through and by women. In combating these injustices,
contemplative feminism explicitly uses resources drawn from women's spiritual traditions for insight into positive forms of social change.

The interaction of mysticism and feminism rises from the transformation
of the deepest source of a person and not just the mind. As a spiritual journey, it embraces the struggle of not knowing, the uncertainty of darkness
and void, and the sting of betrayal and rejection. Likewise, it rewards with
moments of profound illumination, wholeness, and awe. The pioneering
efforts of women's spirituality most likely arise from the ancient challenge
to experience and bring to speech what has been deeply heard and fiercely
felt. This journey of return and rebirth digs at the core of a woman's emotional fabric and spiritual being, and is a catalytic force in the mending of the
human heart. Expressing a divine concern with the suffering of women, the
human family, and all creation, contemplative feminism uses the resources
of the Wisdom traditions to improve conditions that breed violence, subjugation, and hatred. At the same time, it calls on the power of women's
prophetic voice and the strength of women's soul to make the world a better, more compassionate and loving place. Women's ability to embody the
highest spiritual values—determination, resiliency, strength, intimacy, compassion, and love—inspires a radical, living faith in their moral authority
and prophetic commitment to societal transformation. Every effort made

toward raising women's inherent dignity and worth is a self-loving that mirrors the divine-loving in our souls.

Joining Resources

When we apply feminist theory to contemplation, we are asking the following questions: Who benefits from descriptions of the interior life? In what way did men's experience influence and dominate the language and categories of the spiritual journey, and to what extent has that language become normative and universal for all persons? What spiritual strengths, resiliencies, weaknesses, abuses, or wounds arise in the soul of a woman, and what is spiritually necessary for women to attain their full potential? In analyzing the effects of patriarchy on women's spiritual health, feminism makes a distinction between the naming of reality by dominant cultures and the use of that naming as an oppressive tool to control the rights of women and other marginalized groups. With respect to religion, the feminist critique in its broadest sense deals with both. It denies, even with the best intentions, that spirituality and an understanding of divinity that has been primarily described by one sex can and do speak for all humanity and creation. Further, it critically investigates the motives and outcomes of this male-defined spirituality to see in what way it has been used as a tool of domination over women and other subjugated groups.[3]

Conversely, the usage of "contemplative" as a modifier of the term "feminism" highlights that women's freedom is at the center of the divine-human relationship. A woman's quest for liberation is related to the inseparable bond of love between the divine and human in her soul; it thus always involves a mystical dimension. According to medieval women mystics, their experience of the divine nature is never dominating, oppressive, or diminishing of them. Rather, as Teresa of Avila, Julian of Norwich, Hildegard of Bingen, Gertrude of Helfta, and others illustrate, it is in their God-experience that they derive an inner assurance and certainty that liberates them from social constraints and brings awareness of their equality, wisdom, freedom, and authority. Through disturbing the ideology that surrounds these two words—contemplation and feminism—we wrest from them a more authentic representation of women's lived experience, peering beneath the veneer of women's subordination into the hidden chambers of the sacred feminine.

In joining together the resources of the contemplative traditions and feminism, three spheres of influence, in addition to the mystical, are apparent—

personal, social, and theological. On a personal level, a woman's actualization of her full potential involves growth and development of her mystic consciousness. Without this inner confrontation, a woman remains imprisoned in an unconscious assimilation of patriarchal cultures, unable to claim subjectivity in her own right. Further, in the social and political arenas, the justice that feminists seek is inseparably tied to women's spiritual well-being. A working concept of social justice that is defined solely in terms of cultural, political, or economic gain is not only inadequate, but also potentially dangerous. Inadvertently it may endorse social abuses that objectify women as a class, potentially legitimizing structural forms of violence at the risk of women's spiritual health and moral agency. In theological terms, images of God that exclude, marginalize, or diminish women contribute to the tragic failure of religious communities to affirm women as representative of the holy. "Women's exclusion from full participation in their communities is not caused merely by social arrangements," claims Mary Bednarowski. "It is embedded in traditions' theological understandings of how the universe operates."[4]

Contemplation is always revolutionary, for it takes apart what is comfortable and convenient, asking us to see the world from God's perspective. Applied to feminist concerns, it protests the fragmentation and distraction of women's lives and repudiates the selfless renunciation that is women's daily lot in much of the world. Further, it challenges the rampant materialism that makes women's bodies and the body of creation objects to be bought and sold. The fact that the spiritual journey itself is dominated by patriarchal thinking, unjust relations, or oppression of women and feminine states of consciousness indicates that there is a dimension of the soul that is not free, a place where we have not yet found total redemption, salvation, liberation, or enlightenment. The injustices that taint the religious imagination of Western culture are found in the spiritual as well—its techniques of enlightenment, roles assigned to women, areas of practice taught, kinds of spiritual experiences given credibility, and images of the divine sought.

Naming and Eliminating Spiritual Oppression

[After they become nuns], they do not realize the great favor that God has done to them by choosing them for Himself, and by rescuing them from being subject to a man in the outside world; a man who often kills their bodies, and God forbid, could also kill their souls.[5]

Teresa of Avila's astute awareness of the peril lurking on the margins of every woman's imagination still rings true in the lives of women today. The many dimensions of social, religious, and economic violence against women have played an important part in feminist activism over the last one hundred years. One of the key convictions of feminism is that a person's spiritual and emotional problems cannot be divorced from current social, historical, and economic contexts. Secular feminists have been vigilant in investigating these various faces of cultural and political oppression. Iris Young, for example, describes "five faces of oppression" in North American culture—exploitation, marginalization, powerlessness, cultural imperialism, and violence—and how these have affected women's health and moral agency. In this and other accounts of women's oppression, the focus is on the individual and collective violation of women's cultural and material rights and the impact it has on women's well-being, health, and security.[6]

Feminist *theology* builds on the contributions of secular feminism by exposing the religious roots of violence against women. It tracks the suffering of women left out of religious community, pushed to the margins of ecclesial structure, or abandoned by the theological tradition that is supposed to uplift and heal. Responsible for perpetuating a socially oppressive relationship with women, classical theology has been used to justify and condone burning of witches and mystics, torture and rape of heretics, and murder in the name of its absolute truth.[7] Feminist scholars from minority traditions continue to educate about the crippling effects poverty, racism, sexism, and domestic violence exert on future generations of women and children.[8]

Feminist *spirituality* addresses issues of sexism in women's religious experiences, the relationship of gender to mysticism, and women's ability to value and affirm themselves as an authentic reflection of divinity. Rooted in various religious traditions, feminists who write about spirituality assert its intrinsically social nature, investigating how patriarchal religions create and maintain a culture of domination, which restricts women's mature spiritual development and curtails relationships of mutuality and collaboration.[9] It studies how religious traditions, primarily revealed and embodied by men, employ languages and structures of consciousness that are not representative of women's experience. Even when a woman finds meaning and value in the wisdom of her religion, something of her nature is left out.

Aware of the emphasis feminists have placed on issues of injustice and inequity in civil society and religious community, contemplative feminism analyzes the deeper spiritual causes and consequences of a subtle but equally powerful form of oppression—the oppression of women's soul. I refer to this as *spiritual oppression* and contend its recognition and healing are fundamental to women's liberation. The core of this theological stance is that *women's spiritual oppression is the foundation of all her other oppressions*. What harms a woman's soul reverberates in her physical, emotional, and mental spheres, generating suffering in every area of her life. Similarly, violations of a woman in the social realm have a direct impact on the health and integrity of her spirit.

But what is spiritual oppression? The word "oppression" signifies an unjust exercise of authority or power by one person, group, or institution over another. Serene Jones describes six dimensions of feminist theories of oppression. She first suggests that multiple factors of cultural and material oppression interact and contribute to the diminishment of women. Material factors that keep women in underpaid labor forces, for example, must be understood as profoundly tied to "how a particular culture perceives and devalues women's voices." She then argues that material and cultural oppression is often the result of relations of domination in which women occupy a place subordinate to men in the power dynamic. Third, relations of domination not only are embedded in individuals but are frequently institutional as well. In addition, individual oppressors need to be held personally responsible for the harm they inflict, as women need to be challenged to resist and contest their oppression. As insiders to their own suffering, women must be attentive to the power of their emotional authority as well as to the ways in which harm diminishes a woman's capacity to carry out an analysis of her oppression. A fifth dimension of what Jones calls the "eschatological character" of theories of oppression relies on a vision of the flourishing of women. Finally, she cites the practical character of feminist theories "to work for the good of women's lives. Theories do this when they illuminate what women already know quite intimately but have not yet theorized."[10]

Because the oppression I am referring to here is spiritual in nature, these varied interactions of personal, societal, and institutional control over women exert their influence beyond external events to invade a woman's psyche and soul. Further, these abuses cannot be fully understood without recognizing how profoundly connected they are to cultural and religious devaluations of women as spiritually inferior to men. This fundamental belief in women's spiritual inferiority inevitably permeates the cultural imagination, and contributes to and fosters violent acts against women, as it most often remains unacknowledged and unnamed. A stark example of how spiritual oppression becomes embedded in social discourse and functions to dominate, humiliate, and possess women is evident in the following quote from Francisco de Osuna, a contemporary of Teresa of Avila and a noted theologian.

> Since you see your wife going about visiting many churches, practicing many devotions, and pretending to be a saint, lock the door; and if that isn't sufficient, break her leg if she is young, for she can go to heaven lame from her own house without going around in search of these suspect forms of holiness. It is enough for a woman to hear a sermon and then put it into practice. If she desires more, let a book be read to her while she spins, seated at her husband's side.[11]

Osuna's candor about attitudes toward women in sixteenth-century Spain were played out in Teresa's life as she, too, was subjected to powerful forms of clerical and church censorship. The presumption of male domination over the most private and solitary aspects of Teresa's life—her right to be holy—can be seen as a manifestation of a deeper and more insidious spiritual oppression. Overt forms of violence against women repeat on a physical level a prior spiritual privilege that is asserted by men over women's interior lives. Codified in scripture and institutionalized by religious and secular law, rights granted men to invade Teresa's inviolable solitude led to serious psychological, political, and spiritual consequences for her. Spiritual domination, which undergirded the economic and social marginalization of women and their historical status as a permanent underclass in sixteenth-century Spain, created hidden scars in Teresa's soul.

The attempt to control or conquer Teresa's inner life and the naming of her experience by dominant religious norms were a tragic imposition on the development of her maturity, dignity, and positive self-identity. Since medieval theology gave privilege to male experience and male power, its spiritual traditions also reflected gendered discourses that were not free of the theological and political advancement of the guardians of (male) orthodoxy. For it is in spiritual experience—its categories of growth, pathways to God, and techniques of prayer and contemplation—that the Church aimed its most potent weapon against women's full equality. Through a sustained and often concealed undermining of women's spiritual rights, men granted to themselves (under the guise of divine truth and ecclesiastical decree) the authority to name, own, and dictate Teresa's relationship with God. At the same time, however, her eventual realization of these various forms of women's oppression empowered Teresa to resist and may have contributed to what scholars call her "rhetoric of femininity," a linguistic devise she used to subvert authority and to champion her own mystical path.[12]

From this brief example of Teresa's life, which will be studied further in subsequent chapters, we can include within the category of spiritual oppression anything that marginalizes, dominates, violates, humiliates, shames, diminishes, or silences a women's spirit. Acts of spiritual violence also may involve possession, transgression, or exploitation, and more serious efforts to injure, harm, or forcefully control a woman's inner life, or destroy women's spiritual dignity and humanity. When I say that all forms of women's oppression are fundamentally spiritual oppression, I mean that acts of violence against women—overt or subtle—are directed first and foremost at the core of a woman's nature. Often fueled by unconscious motivations, spiritual oppression is the wrongful violation of the sanctity of a woman's self. Violence against women—personal and structural—can be seen as nothing less than a desire to harm or destroy women's unique and particular embodiment of the divine.

Women's spiritual oppression, because it injures the site of a person's greatest holiness, sensitivity, and mutuality—their relationship with God—is frequently an unnamed, forbidden territory. The possession of women's ability to be relational, receptive, and vulnerable—to reflect an outpouring of Divine Intimacy—is a form of spiritual violence maintained through complex relationships of shame and blame. Women's openness and vulnerability are possessed through the same dynamics of domination and subordination that mark unequal sexual relations. Once their soul is invaded and the injury consummated, women are ashamed of their receptivity and blamed for their inability to resist. Yet, this invasion of a woman's being may not involve any overt sexual act. Instead, it is the process by which one person or group claims spiritual privilege over another's integrity and dignity, right to solitude, and ways of being and knowing.

Corporate forms of spiritual violence are present when a religious community institutionalizes women's inferiority or denies them rights granted to men, such as ordination to the priesthood or other recognized religious titles held by males. Institutions that promote unequal spiritual relations, prevent women's full participation in divine life, deny women access to spiritual authority, or commodify women as objects to be owned and sold contribute to worldwide suffering. The social structures that allow the unequal distribution of spiritual goods and that exploit or dictate women's spiritual abilities effectively possess a woman's soul, for they control in what way and in what measure women are representative of divinity. Despite rhetoric to the contrary, institutional structures that prohibit women's full representation in positions of authority granted to men reinforce the sin of omission: women are not capable of representing divinity. Because structural violence invades the foundation of women's consciousness, it touches deep archetypal roots of women's understanding of God, religion, and gender roles. It is frequently pre-theological and pre-verbal. It is often the last place women look for healing.

Contemplative feminism investigates how this suppression of women and girls in personal and institutional settings afflicts us in heart and mind, harming the growth of our full humanity and betraying the vulnerable and fragile in us all. As spiritual practice, contemplative feminism is alert to naming, healing, and eliminating spiritual oppression in its many forms. Damaging on various levels, spiritual oppression:

- injures a woman's soul, creating a barrier, a divide, between her deepest wisdom and her true self;
- fractures a woman's languages and ways of knowing, inserting a dominant linguistic structure that is often foreign to what she knows and is;
- exploits the spiritual goods women produce in religious, social, and family settings because women are structurally prevented from sharing fully in the benefits of their labor;
- marginalizes women as a category of people expelled from useful participation in spiritual life and thus potentially subjects them to spiritual deprivation and possibly death;
- distorts a woman's reflection on and experience of God and imposes a spiritual method that conflicts with her inner life;
- denies women the spiritual authority to be prophets, masters, and founders of new wisdom traditions that may be outside or beyond current determinate religions; and
- possesses or co-opts women's soul force, creating a sense of false powerlessness and dependency that cripples women's full participation in the building of a divine community on earth.

The presence of spiritual oppression in a woman's life is the most significant indicator of her inability to quiet the restlessness that divides her soul, and awareness of its causes and conditions is primary in her healing and empowerment. Yet, the mystical dimensions of women's suffering lack adequate recognition and appropriate language. The majority of women have no words to name the grief, rage, and violation they feel. All too often, classical accounts of the soul's journey do not express the depth and anguish of women's wounds. Frequently, the spiritual remedies tradition-ally applied—prayer, spiritual guidance, humility, and surrendering to God's will—offend women and distract them from a problem with roots deeper and more primordial than the religious interpretation used to "cure" their woes. This difficulty can be traced to the lack of references to women's spiritual development and to the fragmentary documentation of women's mystical lives and struggles.

As a spiritual director, I have learned that spiritual oppression injures women in particular and unique ways. It frequently damages the most receptive aspect of a woman's nature and divides a woman against herself. Elusive and difficult to grasp, spiritual violence invades the integrity of a woman's psyche and soul at such a primary level that most women cannot recognize or name what has harmed them. Unable to identify the source of their pain, women often blame themselves and develop strategies to protect their oppressors. This quality of soul suffering, which survives at the cost of women's spiritual diminishment, inflicts on women an unequal burden of sin and blame. Thus, without understanding the subtle ways in which her soul is violated and the fierceness that marks the site of her affliction, a woman cannot resolve her inner conflict. Often unspoken, denied, and ridi-culed, or dismissed as unimportant and emotional, women's soul wounds must be brought to consciousness to avoid the trivialization of their experi-ence and for healing to occur. It is in their anguish and despair, sorrow and betrayal, rage and tears that women discover the freedom that comes from the feminine heart of divinity. This process of bringing to consciousness the violation of women's spiritual rights moves women beyond fragmentation and false passivity to wholeness and empowerment.

In attempting to eliminate these diverse forms of oppression, mystical feminism directs attention to theologies and ideas that dominate, judge, or shame females as violations of women's moral dignity and spiritual rights. Without addressing the fundamental violation of women's spirit, women cannot achieve the liberation they seek. It is not just in theological lan-guages and metaphors that women are betrayed. Even when women do achieve a form of enlightenment, there frequently remains a deeper layer of misogyny embedded in the cultural or religious imagination that resists extraction. In the conquering of her inner life and the naming of her experience by unjust and injurious religious norms, a woman's access to her original, non-separated self is always an accommodation made against the background of a prior deflection—of her image reflected back through a broken mirror. In this aggressive fracturing of women's divine image, true sins have been committed. The ancient and ongoing wounds that women sustain, and the language structures and mind-set that have formed over thousands of years of male theological privilege, can block a woman's ability to know the truth of who she is at the deepest level of her being and to bring this truth into word.

Women's afflictions are soul afflictions; their souls suffer the experience of being females in this world. The fullness of what women know and are, as well as their spiritual salvation or freedom, cannot be actualized until they reconnect to the great mother river flowing within them, where symbols and words are not broken and women's language and ways of knowing and being are still holy. Women always will be divided against themselves unless they come to this. Yet, this way of the feminine runs parallel to the spiritual paths articulated by the great wisdom lineages but flows through the soul more deeply and silently; thus, while it is related to classical spirituality, it is not identical to it. As women piece together the mirror of their divine reflection, shattered in some ancient time by men's colonization of a woman ancestor they cannot name, they discover that the world's spiritual traditions can be used as a partner in women's quest for freedom. As long as women do not deny the current of their own strength and wisdom, those enduring truths and conceptual categories of women's religious practices can help women connect to and name the road they have taken. But since the pain of being female is foremost a violation of her spiritual being, she can only begin the process of integration by crossing the borders of other dark nights and soul sufferings that every woman experiences and knows. It is not the dark night of the soul, but the further dark night, the dark night of the feminine that women have to discover and surrender to now.

Feminist Koan: Healing Women's Oppression

One of the greatest concerns that many women I know as friends, colleagues, and students raise is their fear that there is no way out of women's oppression and no way to heal their soul wounds. These beliefs keep many women trapped in unequal relations, curtailing development of a mature spirituality and subverting their resiliency and strength. Yet, women who have turned to the deeper and more mature forms of contemplation and mystical practice recognize that ancient technologies and processes do exist that can assist women in their revolutionary desire to heal and eliminate the underlying causes and conditions that breed oppression. I call this contemplative process of naming and healing spiritual oppression the *dark night of the feminine*, holding that it transforms the soul suffering imprinted in the core of a woman's self-identity and masked, in men, as an interior battle against the feminine.[13] Understood as a deeper phase of the soul's purgative contemplation, and discussed in greater detail in the life of St. Teresa of Avila in chapter 7, the night of the feminine marks the mystical passage in which women's abused consciousness is experienced, named, and healed. Women who enter the unmarked passage of the night of the feminine confront an ancient and historic rent in consciousness that continues to fragment, injure, and divide. They suffer the roots of violence against women and the taking apart or erasure that results from women's depiction as weak or defective males—inferior and miserable imitations of the supposedly greater, more valorous patriarchal self.

Constituted by a particular apophatic spiritual process of emptying and letting go, the dark night of the feminine is simultaneously embodied and transcendent. Premised on an understanding that in women's spirituality there is the discovery of a deeper core of consciousness, the night of the feminine reaches down into women's soul wounds and lifts them up to the silence that heals. Women cannot simply reject, trivialize, or suspend internalized feelings of worthlessness or pain; nor can they easily transcend or spiritualize them. Rather, the women mystics illustrate that they must live out these wounds—confronting, feeling, naming, and transforming them through the divine spark within the sanctuary of the self. The process is marked by intense states of suffering, pain, and impasse, alternating with glimpses of bliss, exaltation, and freedom. Yet as a mystical process of healing, women do not endure these wounds alone; rather, it is the divine within that becomes an active participant in tenderly embracing and healing all forms of soul suffering. There is no pain or injury beyond the force of divine love, dwelling in the depth of the soul, which restores the person from the inside out.

In a widely read article, "Impasse and Dark Night," Constance FitzGerald makes a correlation between the depth of women's alienation from Christian belief systems and the dark night of the soul depicted by St. John of the Cross. She contends that women spiritually function in impasse—at a profound level they feel trapped between patriarchal religions and views of women that are no longer acceptable to them and an unknown future they have yet to become. "By impasse," FitzGerald writes, "I mean that there is no way out of, no way around, no rational escape from, what imprisons one. . . . In true impasse, every normal manner of acting is brought to a standstill, and ironically, impasse is experienced not only in the problem itself but also in any solution rationally attempted."[14] While the felt experience is one of abandonment, fear, frustration, and anguish, the actual process that is taking place is one of healing and restoration. The soul of a woman is undergoing the throes of a profound spiritual transformation when the wounds made by all that diminishes, marginalizes, rejects, and abhors her are mended. This healing process, because it takes place in the hidden depths of a woman's life, frequently does not fit into the framework of psychological or social analysis, and seldom is completely understood even by religious professionals. A woman works out her freedom often unaware of the great potential within her and often alone and isolated from others. Because the roots of a woman's oppression reach into the core of her self, there comes a time when she is no longer able to makes sense of her suffering through the force of her own will, psychological awareness, religious belief, or intellectual insight. At this point, the movement into contemplation is necessary and essential. Finally only God, Spirit, Goddess, or *bodhichitta* (awakened mind) within us can break us of illusions and free us from centuries of self-inflicted and other-inflicted violence. Only that which is outside a woman's alienation and pain—the divine at the center of her being—can lift up and empty out the content of all that injures, rejects, and diminishes her.

When women turn inward to their most authentic center, they cannot avoid the pain, despair, and anguish of exploitation and domination. Tearing apart the very fibers of her soul, a woman's dark night of impasse is "revolutionary and seditious," writes FitzGerald. It leads a woman to experience in her being and bear in her body "all the marks of crucifixion"—when everything that has defined her as inferior and insubstantial is taken away in order to restore her to an embodied and integrative equality. FitzGerald's treatment of this phase of spiritual growth is worth quoting at length:

> Contemplation, and ultimately liberation, demands the handing over of
> one's powerlessness and "outsider-ness" to the inspiration and power of
> God's Spirit. Although the God of the dark night seems silent, this god
> is not a mute God who silences human desire, pain, and feeling, and

women need to realize that the experience of anger, rage, depression, and abandonment is a constitutive part of the transformation and purification of the dark night. This very rage and anger purify the "abused consciousness" of women in the sexism they have internalized.[15]

This deep spiritual impasse is a challenge to women "to be mystics," FitzGerald contends, "who, when human concepts disillusion, symbols break, and meanings fail," are guided by a deeper faith to a new horizon.[16] Only a deep personal encounter with one's God can heal the roots of a woman's suffering and reveal her original holiness. It is not merely a spiritual way of living or code of conduct, it is God living in us and uniting us to God's own life and unity. The fundamental liberation women seek, and the emergence of a realized feminist spirituality, comes through the integration of contemplation and action.

"Imprisoned in a night of broken symbols," the feminine impasse that marks the experience of many women today replicates this journey through pain into empowerment.[17] Unable to find meaning in dominating, exclusive, or triumphal images of God, many women have reached the limit of their respective religious tradition, realizing that they cannot go forward without a radical accommodation of their truth. Further, women are no longer content to live a lie or continue to deny that no religion in recorded history has been truly and completely open to and inclusive of women. Exhausted by making accommodations for the failings of their religion, women look for new ways to interpret, understand, and reconstruct. It is here that the intensity of impasse often grips a woman's spirit. Trapped between patriarchal images of God that offend and unknown futures not yet born, women struggle through a lived and embodied paradox—an inscrutable feminist koan—in order to be finally free and whole. Through recognizing and experiencing these failures, lies, and denials that constitute spiritual sexism (when women no longer avert their face from what is painful and abhorrent—when they *feel* the violation of their own holiness), women find the courage to live out of their deepest ground.

In this feminine impasse a woman "bears all things." Although usage of the word "bearing" may conjure up unhealthy images of women's sacrifice, in a positive sense it can refer to a gestational state of consciousness in which the complexity that exists among mind, body, spiritual energies, and divine wisdom is acknowledged as essential to women's spiritual health. As we will discover in the women mystics, their journeys were not ones of just knowing or feeling but were far more complex, involving an integrated, bodily dimension. One of the distinctive features of medieval women's mystical accounts is the degree to which they acknowledge how one's whole self participates in and transforms consciousness. In the process they transmute what is unconscious, instinctual, and intuitive in them into a realized awareness. For them, wisdom is not only known but also borne; it has to be planted in heart, mind, body, and soul, and allowed to gestate and grow.

In writing this, I have thought often of Maura O'Halloran, the Irish-American woman who found enlightenment in a Japanese zendo, and who died soon after at the young age of twenty-seven.[18] She is revered today in Japan as a saint, but I wonder how she handled the harshness, even abuse, of Zen masters, all men. Would she always have been able to transcend her ego, break through her resistance, and overlook their words if she had lived? Would her first enlightenment have led to deeper enlightenments, and to further death experiences in which she too would have had to surrender to the dark night of the feminine? Had she already crossed its borders? Or is it all ego anyway? No matter which way we go, do we all have to let go, and is the night of the feminine just another way of shouting: *mu! mu!* (Nothing! Nothing!)?

I cannot answer my own question. Spiritual life is so personal. But I do know that the women I've seen over these last thirty years sustain specific types of soul suffering because of their womanhood. And whether or not the dark night of the feminine is an ultimate religious category, women must spiritually experience the suffering of the self and the violation of the spirit that prevent them from being whole. If God reveals God-self to all of us, and not just to the powerful, the mighty, the priests and the men, women's exclusion from the full range of spiritual wisdom and authority is a desecration of God. Whatever denies women full participation in spiritual life, violates women's spiritual integrity, or objectifies women's wisdom and knowing is contrary to Her intention. As a spiritual practice, contemplative feminism provides a starting point for healing oppression in its many forms.

Mapping the geography of the soul, identifying and healing soul wounds, and reclaiming women's divine image will be more fully explored through the lives and thought of two medieval Christian mystics—Julian of Norwich and Teresa of Avila—to whom we now turn.

Part Two

Women Mystics
of Medieval Europe

chapter five

Women Mystics and a Feminism of the Inner Way

Hail, my Salvation and Light of my soul!. . . May thanks be given you by all things that are under the cope of heaven, within the circumference of the earth . . . and the depths of the sea, for the exceptional grace by which you have led me to know and consider the interior of my heart which until then I had heeded as little, if I may put it thus, as the interior of my feet. . . . With this loving courtesy you drew my soul toward you, to the touch of a more intimate union, a more discerning contemplation, a freer enjoyment of your gifts.[1]

The women mystics of medieval Europe developed a distinctive spirituality and literary style based on an integration of theology and profound mystical concerns. Theirs was a theology rooted not just in salvation or redemption, but in the highest reaches of mystical intimacy and freedom. Metaphysics was always in service of personal liberation, truth, and perfection. Theology was always indebted to and subsumed by the basic need for communion, wholeness, healing, and love. A person was measured not against an abstract horizon of doctrinal decrees and linguistic sophistication, but by one's depth of concern for the suffering of others, and one's ability to diagnose the state of the soul.

More than any other legacy, it is their ability to integrate the highest states of mystic contemplation with the pastoral needs of their sisters, neighbors, and friends that sets apart women's mystical legacy. Today we often interpret their thought to be representative of an embodied, integrated spirituality, one in which the concerns of the body, feeling, and mutuality are paramount. This is part of their genius. But to stop there is to truncate and domesticate the great contributions of women mystics, by coercing the complexity of their thought into modern sensibilities. More aptly, we should see them as spiritual masters without formal position or structural authority. We should re-imagine them as women who crossed the boundaries between the sensible and the majestic, and returned with new visions of the world and God. In doing so they learned how to read souls, turning their transcendent vision to the subtle movements by which the person grows in love of the divine. Confronted with their personal transcendent experiences, they "conquered this territory, and charted and interpreted it, using feminine eyes, outlook, speech, and writing."[2]

An intense yearning for union with God propels their lives and their texts. From this vantage point, they turn their attention to the spiritual life, often co-opted by ecclesiastical authorities and submerged in academic theology, and to the daily trials by which a soul ascends in grace. In them, we find a body of wisdom through which we can map the souls of women, their journeys toward the highest states of enlightened consciousness, and their pains and illuminations along the way. They were not, by the standards of our times, defenders of women's rights or feminists in any contemporary sense. Yet, were they alive today I have no doubt they would be ardent champions of the rights of women as intrinsic to the soul's freedom, an act of bravery commanded by the very God they loved. This piercing sight, by which they gained themselves and the world, would have seen that women's liberation is of the highest mystical concern; it is essential to any authentic spiritual life, reaching into the deepest core of women's relationship with self, others, and the divine. Theology that fails to address oppression, or worse, is itself guilty of oppression, cannot serve the purpose of the women mystics who knew that mysticism is more than a onetime *experience* of divine presence, or even a sustained and infused *feeling* of divinity; it is, in fact, a far more powerful, seditious, and existential condition of *deconstruction* and *disruption* of everything and anything that stands in the way of the original freedom between God and the person. So all encompassing was their mystic insight that upon one's first encounter, a mysterious and hidden process begins to take place. The divine now becomes the true center of the soul, touching, strengthening, and consoling, often without its knowledge or consent. Jesus becomes for them lover, healer, and *magnus medicus* (great physician) who works in the depth of consciousness to heal the wounded, free the imprisoned, raise the downtrodden, restore the sight, and open the heart of stone.

Part of their genius was the realization that to be "woman" was more than to serve socially defined roles, including the needs of family, husband, children, society, and friends. These holy women recognized that every endeavor and all meaning were founded on a primary motivation and intention—devoting one's whole heart to God. If this total commitment were present, they crossed the threshold into a new freedom, one that brought them to dignity and empowerment. If we define feminism not in terms of contemporary social criteria, but in terms of the attainment of this inner freedom, then we can see women mystics as forging in their own lives and times a kind of inner feminism that recognizes and subverts women's traditional gender roles.

Julian and Teresa: Sisters in Spirit

Among the many accounts by the medieval women mystics of the interior life, Julian of Norwich and Teresa of Avila stand out for their wise and mature guidance. Although separated historically by almost two centuries, their spiritual lives and theologies are remarkably resonant with each other and with women's contemporary concerns. Julian and Teresa were astute spiritual thinkers who explored the contemplative process that took them from fragmentation, self-denial, and inequality to the formation of spiritual principles based on wholeness, intimacy, and mutuality. As marginalized females in predominately male-dominated cultures, it was through their contemplative experiences and prayerful dialogues with God that they worked out their personal wounding and social concerns. In their struggles toward spiritual equality they mapped out an inner feminism—the territory of the soul by which mysticism becomes the site of women's empowerment and dignity.

Julian was a fourteenth-century English mystic who lived as an anchoress—a female who chose a life of solitary enclosure usually connected to a church—during a time of social and political unrest, and under the scourge of the Black Death. Little is known of her life and scholars speculate that she was not a member of a religious order, but a lay woman (perhaps even widowed) who was one of the great mystics and theologians of her time. As an anchoress, Julian's life was hidden from the prying eyes of the world, but her spiritual wisdom and theological acumen were "the very antithesis of a privatized spirituality that turns away from the world to some safe and unengaged cocoon."[3]

Her story is well known: she prayed for a vision of Christ's passion, a bodily illness, and three spiritual wounds, of contrition, compassion, and longing with the will of God.[4] In May of 1373, when she was thirty and a half years old, Julian's prayers were answered as she became severely ill and received sixteen visions, or revelations, that form the basis of her whole life's study. Her intention in these prayers was not for personal gain, but to experience Christ's love as her own and to suffer what he suffered for the world. Surrounded by her mother and a priest brought in to prepare her for death, Julian's mystical experience is graphic and raw, for she contemplates the thirsting face and crucified body of Jesus on the cross. Yet, while the vision is of Jesus' bloodied head, the theology that emerges from it is one of flourishing, healing, and loving the world. Julian emphasizes that God wraps all of creation in love, caring for even our humblest bodily needs so that "we, soul and body, [are] clad and enclosed in his goodness."[5]

Soon after her vision, she composes the first commentary, or Short Text, of her *Showings*, which she revises some twenty years later, after further thought and reflection, in her Long Text. During the interim period, Julian reflects on questions of sin and suffering, human goodness and God's mercy, and the motherhood of God and women's dignity. She develops a distinctive theology of the feminine in which the meaning of sin and suffering is transformed and her worth as a woman is affirmed. Conceptualizing this journey through the image of the motherhood of God, Julian works out her equality and dignity of personhood, and the sinlessness of her fellow Christians. For example, the harsh language Julian initially uses to describe herself—"disregard the wretched worm, the sinful creature to whom it [revelation] was shown"—is reduced in the Long Text, and in its place is a clear insight into her role and authority as a woman mystic.[6] Although she uses the rhetoric of frailty, weakness, and ignorance to describe herself, she also asserts "because I am a woman, ought I therefore to believe that I should not tell you of the goodness of God?"[7]

One of only three women doctors of the Catholic Church, St. Teresa of Jesus was born in Avila, Spain, on March 28, 1515. A descendent of *conversos* (Jews converted to Christianity), she maintained an awareness of social injustices all her life. This sensitivity was no doubt related to her family history and to the public confession her paternal grandfather was forced to make in 1485 over his secret practice of Judaism.[8] As a young girl, Teresa de Ahumada was lively and extraverted, determined and disruptive, yet she was drawn to the religious life, entering the Monastery of the Incarnation at the age of twenty against her father's wishes. An ardent lover of all things divine, Teresa assumes her new role with enthusiasm and commitment, eventually becoming prioress of the Incarnation and founding seventeen reformed

Carmelite monasteries. The first twenty years of her profession are marked by periods of illness and defeat, as well as states of illumination and authority, as Teresa passes back and forth between the intensity of mystical experiences and her inability to quell her active and highly social personal life.

In her thirty-ninth year, Teresa, like Julian before her, has a profound experience of the suffering face of Jesus in which she discovers the mystical link between her personal shortcomings and the conditions of the world. In 1554, during the season of Lent, Teresa is transported by a statue of the "wounded Christ" to identify with his pathos for humanity. While Teresa is struggling with her attraction to gossip, honor, position, money, and trivial concerns, the vision of the wounded Christ incites profound compunction in her. She experiences how her sins increase God's wounds, and "how poorly," she writes, "I thanked Him for those wounds that, it seems to me, my heart broke."[9] This felt pain for what God suffers on our behalf shatters Teresa's understanding of her self, impacting on her sense of responsibility to her sisters and spiritual friends. Pivotal to Teresa's future ethical stance, this conversion ignites the moral fiber necessary to awaken her deepest feelings and turn her life around. Taking Christ's wounds into her heart, Teresa is no longer free to act of her own self-will, but must evaluate her subsequent behavior, response to moral issues, and responsibility for her growth in virtue and perfection against the horizon of all she has witnessed.

An astute spiritual director and mystic theologian, and in obedience to her confessors, Teresa writes extensively about her life, methods of prayer, and spiritual trials, becoming a chronicler of her soul and of the contemplative processes that assist her growth in perfection. Writing during a time of Spain's heightened political power and an Inquisitional church acutely suspicious of heresy, Teresa came under scrutiny from many different fronts, yet never failed to guide others on the road to God and inner freedom. What Julian accomplished in a reasoned theological reflection from her anchor hold, Teresa experienced in a much more public and fiery fashion, through an anguishing twenty years of rejection, ridicule, and self-doubt. In a period spanning the middle of her adult life, Teresa struggles with issues involving her status as a woman and her achievement of her own style of contemplative prayer, with the ridicule and suspicions she aroused in those who felt her experiences were suspect and "from the devil."

Mystically, however, Julian and Teresa each arrive at a theology of integration and affirmation based on conversion experiences of personal and divine suffering, and develop distinct contemplative vocabularies to describe the process by which a person achieves and fully accepts oneself as beloved of God. This personal realization of divine self-acceptance is foundational to Julian's and Teresa's ethical and social concerns and to the battle that Teresa eventually wages to dignify the rights of women, girls, *conversos*, and others.[10] Julian, cloistered anchoress, and Teresa, founder of monastic orders, both find in their mystical lives a mirror of their world. Through it Julian and Teresa map the geography of the soul, developing a comprehensive understanding of its typology, the operation on the inner life of suffering and sin, and the contemplative processes that take them from oppression to freedom and from human love to divine love. This chapter begins the journey by looking into five qualities of Julian's and Teresa's mysticism—longing to love, great determination, inner monastic heart, spiritual detachment, and the annihilated self.

Longing to Love

Clearly, the women mystics were mapping new and distinctive ways to God. Despite protestations of worthlessness, wretchedness, and frailty, they also were insistent on the value of their visions and practices in leading their fellow Christians and others in their charge to deeper love and communion with God. In the midst of condemnations of heresy, Inquisitional suspicion, and the often-misogynist climate of medieval societies, women mystics championed the rights of others and stood their ground. Hildegard of Bingen's community was silenced for refusing to exhume the body of a nobleman buried on convent grounds in opposition to the local prelates; Marguerite Porete went unrepentantly to the stake for refusing to stop circulating her book, *The Mirror of Simple Souls*; and Teresa of Avila was in constant danger from the Inquisition for her bold writings and far-reaching reforms. Yet the intensity of their inner compass compelled these mystics to assert—often after years of struggle, self-doubt, and suffering—the significance of a woman's journey to God and the determination with which it must be practiced, followed, and protected. Aware of the particular limitations women faced, these master teachers of the inner way sought to dispel fears and inspire in their sisters and communities an intense desire to know and long for God. "Do not be frightened, daughters," Teresa consoles in *The Way of Perfection*, "by the many things you need to consider in order to begin this divine journey which is the royal road to heaven. A great treasure is gained by traveling this road; no wonder we have to pay what seems to us a very high price. The time will come when you will understand how trifling everything is next to so precious a reward."[11]

Central to this inner way was a longing and passion for God. These spiritual women did not want God as humans want materials things; rather they wanted to know God as God knew them—they wanted to experience the intensity of love between soul and divinity. Julian of Norwich, for one, places this passion at the core of her mystical life, establishing a relationship between Christ on the cross and her request for a "longing with the will of God."[12] Her most ardent prayer is an extended passion—the desire to be given divine desire—to share in the longing that God has for us. This very equality of possibility raises Julian up to an advanced state of mystical awareness where she sees and understands the reciprocity that exists between Jesus' "unquenchable desire for human salvation and bliss" and our unending restlessness until we rest in God.[13] As the "foundation of your beseeching," God's desire for us is never one-sided, according to Julian, but is held equally by lover and beloved, causing us much mourning and weeping until we, too, respond to divine love.[14]

> For even though our Lord God dwells now in us, and is here with us, and embraces us and encloses us for his tender love, so that he can never leave us, and is nearer to us than tongue can tell or heart can think, still we can never cease from mourning and weeping, seeking and longing, until we see him clearly, face to his blessed face, for in that precious sight no woe can remain, no well-being can be lacking.[15]

This reciprocity of desire fuels the soul's growth in love and grace. As it taps into a deeper level of passion—this longing that longs to die to all that is partial, fragmented, and withheld—the soul understands the essential link between true life and death. Teresa's poem sings, "To this life worldly love adheres; Love divine for the other sighs. Eternal God, without You, Who can live? *Longing to see You, Death I desire.*"[16]

The passion of giving of oneself totally and of seeking to know the true nature of reality is the primary impetus for the whole journey inward. Julian and Teresa felt that the soul is so close to the divine nature, so attuned to the rivers of longing that flow between the divine and human heart, that a woman only knows herself when she knows God. By seeing the divine reflected in the mirror of her own longing, Teresa realizes the limitations of human interpretations of women and recognizes that God alone can assist her in true self-knowledge. "In my opinion," Teresa instructs, "we shall never completely know ourselves if we don't strive to know God."[17] Our longing for God is the expression of God's longing in us. The divine love was increased in Teresa to such a degree that she was dying with desire to see God—"*Muero porque no muero*"—"I die because I do not die," Teresa laments.[18]

As the central metaphor and spiritual matrix of their lives, the mutuality of passion flowing between God and the human person not only inspires the journey but also is the very process that heals and restores. Longing for God reciprocates God's longing for the soul. In this mutuality of love rests a microcosm of the whole macrocosmic universe. For this reason, Julian also claims "we cannot come to knowledge of it [the soul] until we first have knowledge of God."[19] In their discovery of the mourning and moaning that leads to divine longing, Julian and Teresa break through the limitations of conventional life. Here, they find their own feminine divinity and extend the great desire and mutuality of love to the whole world. Theirs was not an ascetic, life-denying mysticism, but one in which the fullness of being is celebrated and affirmed in a continuous flow of love toward God and creation. Further, Julian and Teresa taught that the soul was not to be ashamed, humiliated, or embarrassed by its intense longing and love of the spirit. Offering one's heart totally and completely was the goal of the mystic life, for longing *is* the intention that breaks through ordinary consciousness to an inner realm of wisdom with its own interpretation, understanding, and view of reality.

A Great Determination

In Teresa's life many factors conspire to weaken or divert her from her goals. Subjected to the turmoil rampant in sixteenth-century Spanish religious circles, she aroused the Church's suspicion because of her insistence on the value of mental or contemplative prayer in the spiritual life. In her *Way of Perfection*, Teresa writes at length about her struggle and commitment to prayer as the *camino* (road, path, or way) leading to perfection or as the fount of living water that quenches the soul's thirst. In order to overcome the fears of starting out on this road, Teresa recommends three attitudes that assist seekers to achieve self-knowledge and communion with God—determination, surrender, and courage. The manner or attitude with which one begins is all important, if a traveler on this road of prayer wants to overcome obstacles along the way and continue until she reaches the end. Most important "to those who want to journey on this road" is having what Teresa calls *muy determinada determinación*—"a great and very determined determination to persevere until reaching the end, come what may, happen what may, whatever work is involved, whatever criticism arises, whether they arrive or whether they die on the road."[20]

Because so many fears arise on the path to God—both within the self and from the world—determination expresses a personal commitment to give of one's time wholly, without taking back what is given. It also suggests, according to Teresa, the manner in which we reciprocate the care given to us by God, warding away "the devil" that is repelled by determined souls. Like a soldier in battle who knows if he is conquered, he will be killed, the determined person fights to live the inner or true life with God. The soul's courage to preserve will be rewarded, as God will not allow us to die of thirst, Teresa consoles.[21] Yet determination and persistence without surrender and humility are like wild horses, undisciplined and unfocused. True desire involves the persistent pursuit of one's longing through the practice of giving over one's whole self to God. "Surrender and determination go together," Teresa states. "One must be determined to follow . . . [Christ] in this way even though the dryness may last one's whole life. His majesty wants this determination, and He is a friend of courageous souls."[22] Surrender of self-will is necessary for one to travel along the divine road as it winds through valleys of nourishing waters and deserts of dry and sparse vegetation, to reach the rarified air of mountain summits and mystical ecstasy.

The idea or practice of surrender does not function in Teresa's thought to repeat the passivity or dainty submissiveness of women. Instead, it is an empowering recognition of what it means to commit to inner fidelity—to a truth that takes away women's subordination and restores their equality. Seldom in life do we give ourselves so totally and fully to the one necessary thing—to find the true self and to know God. Yet Julian and Teresa remind, and even caution, that without this giving of one's whole self—this dying to everything constricted, withheld, and partial—we will never reach the heights and depths of women's possibility. Pouring the self out for God takes place not only in praise and thanksgiving, but also and sometimes more profoundly in lament and pain when everything that falsely defines a person is let go. Astute to the ways in which we humans fool ourselves, they were quick to point out how our own limited commitment is transferred to the divine nature and used to justify defeat. Teresa's treatment of this area is direct and earnest:

> We don't give ourselves completely to this path [to be a servant of love through the path of prayer], and therefore we do not attain the blessings we desire in a short amount of time. Because: it seems to us that we are giving all to God, whereas the truth of the matter is that we are paying God the rent or giving Him the fruits and keeping for ourselves the ownership and the root. We resolve to be poor . . . but then we often turn back to being anxious and diligent about possessing not only the necessities but superfluities as well and about winning friends who might provide these things for us. . . . Since we do not succeed in giving up everything at once, this treasure as a result is not given to us all at once.[23]

For Teresa surrender is an expression of humility, which is truth. "Once I was pondering why our Lord was so fond of this virtue of humility," she writes, "and this thought came to me: It is because God is supreme Truth; and to be humble is to walk in truth."[24] The most intense form of courageous humility is surrender of will, for it operates on a determined faith that there *is* something greater than the individual self. Courage to follow God's will in all things, even when the path is fraught with confusion and doubt, is instrumental in strengthening the soul. Reminded of how determination, courage, and surrender are interrelated, Teresa notes that on some days she has great intentions and "wouldn't turn from anything of service to God," and on others when put to the test, "I won't find the courage in me to kill even an ant for God if in doing so I'd meet with any opposition."[25] Courage is the gift of God fortifying the soul to withstand the onslaughts of persons who "frequently make objections," Teresa tells her sisters, to their way of prayer: "'There are dangers'; 'so-and-so went astray by such means'; 'this other one was deceived'; 'it's not for women, for they will be susceptible to illusions'; 'it's better they stick to their sewing.'"[26]

Julian's fifteen-year reflection on her revelations, and her persistent questioning of God and meditating on theological points that were unclear to her, also mirrors the power of determination in achieving life goals. Not submissiveness, but an expression of self-knowledge and self-worth, the soul surrenders itself "with true confidence," Julian says, "whether it be seeking or contemplating . . . [and] taught me to understand that the soul's constant search pleases God greatly. For it cannot do more than seek, suffer, and trust."[27]

Inner Monastery

Perhaps the most essential and revolutionary element of Julian's and Teresa's teachings is the transposition of the physical monastery from a material reality to a state of consciousness. Julian and Teresa were teaching fellow Christians, especially women in their care, a method of achieving perfection in this life. Despite the biblical prohibition against women as teachers, their writings are replete with instructions, practices, and cautions about how to achieve the cloister that is uncloistered—a monastic heart. In direct subversion of church politics, both Julian and Teresa democratize the spiritual life, taking authority away from clerics and institutions and placing it in the hands of the individual person. In *The Way of Perfection*, written expressly to help her sisters in the spiritual life, Teresa explains how the soul can maintain an inner paradise and close the door to the whole world, in "this holy fellowship" with God, without hindering its solitude. Further, this ability to achieve inner paradise is neither dependent on the intervention of priests and lords nor supernatural, but it is "something we can desire and achieve ourselves with the help of God."[28] "For the love of God, daughters," Teresa instructs, "don't bother about being favored by lords or prelates. Let each nun strive to do what she ought."[29]

> So in this temple of God, in this His dwelling place, He alone and the soul rejoice together in the deepest silence. . . . Here an abundance of water is given to this deer that was wounded. Here one delights in God's tabernacle. Here the dove Noah sent out to see if the storm was over finds the olive branch as a sign of firm ground discovered amid the floods and tempests of this world.[30]

Essential to their travel along the divine road was the formation of a monastic heart. While physically cloistered to a greater (Julian) or lesser (Teresa) extent, they nonetheless realized that the true monastery was not dependent on the enclosure of walls. It was, rather, a quality of consciousness or a state of heart that involved a daily commitment to maintain an inner aloneness—that place where God and soul dwell alone, in intimacy. Fostered by the practice of prayer, silence, and solitude, this monastic quality of heart was applied to all relations and every question, evaluating reality from a unitary perspective. This indivisible intimacy between God and the soul is maintained through a commitment to self-discipline and self-awareness.

Sustaining the sanctuary of one's own heart requires a "gradual increase of self-control and an end to vain wandering from the right path," Teresa instructs. "It means conquering, which is a making use of one's sense for the sake of the inner life."[31]

Far from denying love for others, inner focus generates an intense loving toward all relations. When distracted by daily events and obligations, Teresa reminds her sisters how often women are not aware of the great potential that awaits them. As contemplatives, one's whole being and soul serve as God's own dwelling place and the center of all outward works. Without a conscious stabilization and return to this well of meaning and love, women in their active lives would be continually torn by worldly events to give up their interior spiritual focus and be pulled away from the center of love. To assist others in maintaining this monastic heart, Teresa provides a daily practice.

> If you speak, strive to remember that the One with whom you are speaking is present within. If you listen, remember that you are going to hear One who is very close to you when He speaks. In sum, bear in mind that you can, if you want, avoid ever withdrawing from such good company; . . . if you can, practice this recollection often during the day; if not, do so a few times.[32]

What constitutes this monastic heart? Not allowing anything or anyone to trample or block the road that leads to the temple where God and the soul are one. "However softly we speak," Teresa reminds, "he is near enough to hear us. Neither is there any need for wings to go to find him. All one need do is go into solitude and look at him within oneself."[33]

Teresa provides the vibrant language of an inner, or metaphorical, monastery that Julian lives out as a cloistered anchoress. But, we should not assume that Julian becomes estranged from social concerns within her anchor hold. In fact, she clearly demonstrates how the monastic heart is fired with a love for all suffering and for the reconciliation of humanity. Silence and solitude are necessary to the formation of a mature spiritual life. Time to ponder, reflect, and hear the voice of God within one's soul brings Julian to profound theological conclusions. Physical solitude, in which outside distractions are not allowed to invade the tabernacle of her being, becomes the sign of a greater and deeper spiritual courage that leads her to assert a theology of the feminine and mercy some interpreted as contrary to established church teachings. Centering one's attention on the inner monastery performs a spiritual repetition in our world of the intimacy between soul and divine. Just as the soul in its center is united with divinity, so a woman who focuses her attention on her inner monastery maintains that centering in all she does. The depth of this inner monastic focus generates a loving concern with life in every one of its aspects. "The true lover loves everywhere," Teresa encourages, "and is always thinking of the Beloved!"[34] "Come now, my daughters, don't be sad when obedience draws you to involvement in exterior matters. Know that if it is in the kitchen, the Lord walks among the pots and pans helping you both interiorly and exteriorly."[35]

Three Spiritual Remedies

These outward signs and choices reflect an even deeper spiritual commitment that survives, and even thrives, in the activity of the daily round of chores and responsibilities of life. In order to maintain an inner monastic focus in the midst of life's events, Teresa recommends three spiritual practices in *The Way of Perfection*: spiritual love, detachment, and humility. Spiritual love is a divine virtue that grows out of prayer. Teresa understands God's love primarily as a spiritual love that takes place in the depth of the soul. Those who experience perfect love love differently than those without it. According to Teresa, love fails from excessive attachment to persons, things, vanities, honors, and wealth. Since spiritual love gives more than it receives, it has experiential knowledge of two worlds—the one eternal, the other a dream; two loves—one for the Creator, the other for the creature; of what is gained by the one love, and lost by the other love.[36]

Spiritual love is not self-centered or otherworldly. As Julian prayed to understand Christ's suffering in order to share in his suffering for the world, spiritual love is an act of love that bears the essential work of compassion for others. Teresa is called to achieve this equality of spiritual love in order to assist others working toward love of the world. It is a love with "no self-interest at all," Teresa writes, because it imitates the love "which the good lover Jesus had for us."[37] Further, spiritual love is not dispassionate and unconcerned with another's progress in love; no, according to Teresa, it is the most impassioned love that costs the soul who loves dearly. Prayers, tears, and penances are part of the longing the lover has for those who desire it, that they will find God and make progress in the growth of true love. The person pierced by the fiery arrow of love "does everything he can for the other's benefit; he would lose a thousand lives that a little good might come to the other soul. O precious love," Teresa praises, "that imitates the Commander-in-chief of love, Jesus, our Good!"[38]

Spiritual love is the natural overflow of the integration of the active and contemplative lives. They are inseparable: the root of interior contemplation flowering in external acts of goodness and for great benefit to others. Mary, as biblical symbol of the interior life, and Martha, her active sister, illustrate the efficacy of love in Teresa's thought.

> Mary and Martha never fail to work almost together when the soul is in this state [mystical marriage]. For in the active—and seemingly exterior—work the soul is working interiorly. And when the active works rise from this interior root, they become lovely and very fragrant flowers. For they proceed from this tree of God's love and are done for Him alone, without any self-interest. The fragrance from these flowers spreads to the benefit of many. It is a fragrance that lasts, not passing quickly, but having great effect.[39]

If spiritual love is the fruit, detachment is the root that sustains the freedom necessary to surrender one's whole self to God. Not understood by Julian or Teresa as either life denying or ascetic, detachment is the spiritual practice that preserves the inner monastery, establishing this centering vision in everything one does and one loves. Given the demands on her person both as a woman and a leader of spiritual reform, Teresa recognizes that effort must be applied for her monastic sisters to be able to carve out this necessary solitude of heart. In a monastic climate that encouraged visits from family and friends, along with the maintenance of economic and social privilege, Teresa encourages detachment from relatives, vain concerns, and excessive friendships. Further, a lack of attachment to self, including pains of the body, life, and honor, and the esteem of others, was prescribed. Detachment becomes a practice of being attentive to the spiritual movement in a person's life, in which trials and happiness are measured against one's compassion for others who suffer. It is an interpretative stance in which life's problems are evaluated against the great horizon of love.

What detachment practices, humility accepts. In her longing to be perfectly united with God, Teresa learns to accept the false accusations made against her or her way of prayer. In regard to contemplation, she writes that the person cannot make prayer happen, but receives what is given by God; nor can she demand God's favors, but rejoices in what is offered. As the bride of detachment, humility burns away the dross of Teresa's soul. For our mystics, humility is the way to truth; it is the premier virtue that invites in God's compassion and love. Reversing the hierarchy of patriarchal values, they repeat in their writings the biblical injunction that in the lowest is the highest. "Taking literally the biblical promise that God chooses 'the foolish things of the world to confound the wise' and 'the weak things of the world to confound the things which are mighty' and 'things which are not, to bring to naught things that are' (1 Cor. 1:27-28), the mystic writes herself as loved and desired by God in her specifically feminine form—as 'foolish' 'weak', and . . . as one of those mysterious 'things which are not.'"[40]

The Feminine Subject and Mystical Annihilation

The various manifestations of the mystical life discussed—longing for God, great determination, detachment, humility, and spiritual love—revolve around what is variously described as the loss or annihilation of the self. A familiar and much discussed topic in the world's mystical traditions, especially those of the Asian religions, emptiness of self is the premier path to enlightenment, realization, or perfection. Described by many mystics as an ultimate stage of consciousness—even beyond mystical union—annihilation is an experience of complete intimacy and openness, which leads the person to powerful experiences of interdependence and unity with all of life.[41] In a state of absorption or interpenetration with the divine, the mystic describes the true self as empty, nothing, nondual, or indistinct—the self of intimacy, receptivity, and surrender. The ninth-century Sufi master Junayd expresses this idea in the Arabic word *fana* (passing away) of self, as the source of wisdom and compassion: "He annihilated me in generating me as he had originally generated me in the state of my annihilation. I cannot designate him because he leaves no sign, and I cannot tell of him because he is the master of all telling."[42]

"One of the recurrent themes in feminist spirituality," writes Ursula King, "is women's need to find their true self."[43] Considered to be an area in critical need of awareness and reform, scholars question whether there is a feminine form of subjectivity outside the limitations of gender roles and patriarchal exclusion. It is thus of interest how Julian, Teresa, and other female mystics of medieval Christianity, who lived in times of constrained social and religious freedom, were able to "exemplify to an extraordinary degree women's struggle for autonomy and self-affirmation, crowned by the liberating experience of self-transcendence."[44] No doubt many of them shared sentiments similar to St. Teresa's feeling of "worthlessness" that made her proclaim that just being "a woman was enough to make my wings fall off."[45] Yet despite this damaged self-image, women mystics discovered, as did many of their male counterparts, that healing the wound of inferiority comes about not from the assimilation or imitation of the independent, autonomous, individualistic self—what some call the "patriarchal self"—but rather by marching further into a particular kind of *spiritual* nothingness. I emphasize the modifier "spiritual" in order to distinguish this experience of nothingness from forms of abuse that lead women to a punishing sense of self-effacement and self-denial. The rhetoric of annihilation, emptiness, and nothingness represents that moment of absorption, melting, and absence of boundaries in which the person becomes truly aware of the great river of unity that flows through life. In becoming "nothing" one also becomes whole.

What does annihilation mean in the context of medieval women's subordination? Was it another form of female debasement and internalized self-loathing, or a new way of achieving dignity and power? For our women mystics, nothingness represents two distinct characteristics or attributes. It is first a repudiation of women's inferiority and false identity in order to relinquish whatever imprisons one. While there are traces of self-abasement in the writings of both Julian and Teresa, they appear to be rhetorical devices rather than central to their mystical development. Instead, due to women's socially reinforced lack of self-awareness and attachment to excessive selflessness and other-centeredness, nothingness functions as a kind of reverse purgative process than the one depicted in the majority of male mystics. It is not primarily about letting go of power, ego, and will, as it is passing through women's gendered "nothingness" to finally gain perspective and wisdom over their own lives. "According to Martin Gaite," writes Pérez-Romero, "St. Teresa is the perfect example of a woman who, starting from zero (by rejecting men's vantage point) interpreted her own experiences and the world around her. It did not matter that her starting point was obedience to male authority for St. Teresa 'started obeying in order to disobey,' to do things her own way, and this is her greatest glory, not only as a woman, but as a renewer of the language."[46] Confronted with spiritual directors who dismissed her religious experiences and visions of God, Teresa struggles with profound self-doubts and self-loathing. Only when she turns inward to Jesus' affirmation of her way is she able to withstand the onslaught of patriarchal attitudes toward her as a woman. This confrontation gives her the courage to transcend her prior fears and to integrate and accept her right to spiritual authority.

Annihilation also refers to the true self. The French mystic Marguerite Porete even more clearly depicts the "ecstatic freedom" mystical annihilation brings in her book *The Mirror of Simple Souls*.[47] A challenge to the doctrinal guardians of the Church, Marguerite claims for herself a new kind of being through "becoming nothing." The annihilated soul cannot be subjected to the authority of either clerical institutions or men, radically redefining one's relationship with God and with the world. Marguerite understands that the soul annihilated in love is finally secure, for it is finally open to everything: "They [annihilated souls] have no shame, no honor, no fear for what is to come. They are secure. Their doors are open. No one can harm them."[48] The freed soul is "without why," and is unburdened of all claims and attachments. Disrobing her of will, the soul gives up her honor and her shame. What remains when the self has been lost is God: "And therefore she loses her name in the One in whom she is melted and dissolved," writes Marguerite.[49] Emptiness of self—nothingness—is the highest stage of awareness for everything floods back to its source, like a river which flows back into the sea, losing "its course and its name with which it flowed in many countries."[50]

As Teresa, Julian, and Marguerite labored with heroic intensity to uncover the undivided self, they realized that the only adequate path was the journey into nothingness and unknowing. This mystical self—open, intimate, and empty—is not a miserable imitation of the supposedly greater and more valorous male self; rather it is a glimpse of the mystic's *true self* inflamed in love, perhaps realized unconsciously, or not sufficiently understood and articulated. But nonetheless, this realized woman-self that is open to life and has become secure in its own powerful dynamism of emptiness and fullness, death and birth, is the seed, the precursor, of all acts of holiness. "If it could," writes Teresa, "love would want to discover ways of consuming the soul within itself. And if it were necessary to be always annihilated for the greater honor of God, love would do so very eagerly."[51] The soul that is annihilated in love is finally whole, finally open to everything, and thus is the true source of women's freedom, strength, dignity, and empowerment. When a woman as mystic plunges into what Gertrude of Helfta calls the "abyss of tenderness" she is freed of all that oppresses and divides her. She gives up her name, property, and person; she is unable to be identified. "In effect, she is emptying out the content of the term 'woman', in the same way that the mystic empties the content of the term 'God.'"[52] A woman must bring herself to zero and thus transform all that has constructed her as the negative "other" of patriarchal cultures. Our women mystics remind us that feminine subjectivity is discovered not in separation or individuation but in intimacy and interpenetration, not in naming but in emptying out, not in claiming or possessing but in opening and freeing.

The term "annihilation" functions in their texts to repeat the primary mystical event of divine-human receptivity. Receptivity and annihilation go together, for fear of intimacy prevents women from becoming "nothing," as fear of being "nothing" blocks a person's ability to freely let go. The key to this escape is in women's rewriting of mysticism. Here, even nothingness is not the same. Rather than being a barrier to the unknowable God, it transposes into a permeable membrane passing back and forth intimacies—sweet tender kisses and loving praises. God is never closer, more intimate, more personal, more forgiving, or more freeing. Women mystics do not just know about or unite with divinity; they incarnate and embody Her, bearing in their bodies the marks of a realized intimacy. This is the foundation of a transformed being and a transformed world. No longer austere or remote, nothingness—annihilation—is the tender womb of new life. Gestating within its warm and certain fold, women are divine.

chapter six

Julian and Teresa as Cartographers of the Soul

For in reflecting upon it carefully, Sisters, we realize that the soul of the just person is nothing else but a paradise where the Lord says He finds His delight. So then, what do you think that abode will be like where a King so powerful, so wise, so pure, so full of all good things takes His delight? I don't find anything comparable to the magnificent beauty of a soul and its marvelous capacity. Indeed, our intellects, however keen, can hardly comprehend it, just as they cannot comprehend God.[1]

For medieval theologians and philosophers, the soul was a subject of intense inquiry and speculation. Seat of the unseen world, most precious jewel in God's creation, and fountain of divine wisdom and love, study of the soul occupied the thoughts of the mystics and formed the basis for all higher knowledge and meaning. To understand the inner dynamics of the soul and to chart its growth was a requirement on the path of perfection, and the fruit of natural reason, establishing the subject of many of the great medieval works of theological speculation. Yet, to be able to read souls, to pierce the veil that separates ordinary from nonordinary reality, was a higher gift of infused or supernatural contemplation. Usually associated with mystical masters, soul reading was an experiential process of discernment and guidance whereby a person was assisted in understanding and naming the subtle movements of his or her journey to God.

We have to understand from our vantage point the intense focus the women mystics placed on achieving the highest spiritual potential and on developing a sophisticated mystical vocabulary to explain the structures of consciousness, contemplative processes, and spiritual techniques in the journey of faith. Concerned, first of all, with love of God, and then with healing the whole person, women mystics probed their inner lives in order to bring themselves and others to lives of virtue, love, and beauty. Personal religious experience was never for its own sake, but was a window into a complex world of learning in which theology—study of God—and mysticism—how to become one with God—were intertwined. The fact that the wisdom of women mystics came primarily, although not exclusively, from personal experience rather than book learning situates their contributions alongside the world's spiritual lineages, among them the yoga aphorisms of Patanjali, Dogen's style of *zazen* (sitting meditation), or the prayers of John Cassian. We should not be deceived into thinking that women mystics' writings were merely conceptual accounts of privatized experiences; rather they were expansive treatises on the whole range of technologies—reading souls, spiritual medicine, contemplative prayer, spiritual discernment—that constitute the mystical world.

The primary book of learning was mystical experience itself. It alone carried the full alphabet that formed the vocabulary of the spirit, and the deepest longing and wounding of the soul. Mystical experience was not personalized—the product of the modern individual self—but was the site in which the universal broke the limits of self-identity to become apparent in the depths of subjectivity. The highest value of this self was not to become self-less, but rather surrendered—an open plain of being in which God and soul were truly free to come and go, to share an intimate friendship without restraint or fear. The fruit of this relationship was what John of the Cross called "secret knowledge," teaching that came through intimacy and love; this loving knowledge was the most elevated and intense form of approaching reality.[2] Mystical knowing was infused, meaning it came through no effort on the part of the receiver, but instead was a gift of divinity—a direct imprint of truth. Higher than rational thought or reason, infused knowing activated the contemplative, passive mind, revealing truths unseen and unstudied by ordinary, everyday consciousness. What a woman was able to bear, what she embodied, loved, and suffered became the text of a new book of wisdom.

One of the most significant by-products of this mystical learning was an understanding of the process or method whereby a person achieves oneness with God and freedom of self. Women's mystical literature was a cipher that conjoined expansive poetic language with the precision of a spiritual map showing the typology of the soul and the method of soul advancement. Underneath the protestations of frailty, ignorance, and worthlessness that mark many women's texts, and their sometime dismissive critique of what

Teresa of Avila called "womanish" needs and desires, exists a contemplative process as detailed and rigorous as any in religious history.

Rooted as we are in Western rational thought, it is easy to miss women mystics' code-talk—how they use language as a method of ascent, alternating between persuading and reprimanding the seeker; how prayer, which is available to all and acceptable to the church, is seized and adapted as a method of perfection that democratizes the spiritual life, taking spiritual authority away from religious professionals and placing it in the hands of women and common people; how visionary experience provides access to forming theological principles and mapping states of the soul; how suffering is used to explain the dynamics of spiritual growth and development; how divine-human intimacy is a learning laboratory in the interconnection of life, and thus the best teaching on how to treat others with compassion, mercy, and humility; and how God's benevolence and unconditional love form a new view of the human person as founded in goodness and blessing, limiting the effects of sin.

Julian and Teresa and other women mystics had an inner, spiritual compass that attuned them to the subtle way in which a soul progresses in love of the divine. They were able to see into the depth of another's heart, tracking the person's journey from oppression to freedom. They knew that earthly sufferings are felt on one level of consciousness, but another, greater suffering also exists that is "not in the body," writes Teresa, but is "in the very deep and intimate part of the soul."[3] To truly understand soul suffering demanded another view of life, theology, and God. Although inner truth and outer reality are interrelated, the interior level is where the great work of love takes place, leading the person to experience and understand the preciousness, vitality, and simplicity that motivate life. Because the inner core of a person is always in touch with divinity, even while she may be unaware, Julian and Teresa held that soul consciousness operates at a much more refined level of feeling, knowing, and understanding. This inner self is attuned to life's seamless oneness, suffers violation of the intrinsic bond of love between God and creation, and experiences the radical intimacy evident in those who see through eyes of gratitude and awe. Thus, the theology of women mystics has been called more embodied than abstract, more immanent than transcendent. The God, or Beloved, they saw and knew was a warm and embracing lover and a gentle and healing physician. He—and sometimes She—was the fount of mercy and goodness, forgiving of all our sins.

Mapping the Soul: Inner and Outer

> It should be kept in mind here that the fount, the shining sun that is
> in the center of the soul, does not lose its beauty and splendor; it is
> always present in the soul, and nothing can take away its loveliness. But
> if a black cloth is placed over a crystal that is in the sun, obviously the
> sun's brilliance will have no effect on the crystal even though the sun
> is shining on it.[4]

Teresa's words convey the uplifting hope at the heart of mysticism—that
the true self is always one with God. The true self can never be separated
from its divine lover, even though its brilliance may be tarnished or covered
over with the black cloth of sin and error. In Teresa and Julian, the excessive
concentration on sin that has marred the Christian religious imagination is
redeemed by their lives and visionary experiences, which spell out a different, more benevolent, view of God and person. While sin is not overlooked
or ignored, it is overshadowed by the bond of intimacy and love between
God and the soul that is always present. The paradox of human sin and original blessing becomes transposed in Julian's and Teresa's thought through
conceptualizing the soul as having an inner and outer aspect, bound with
an essential core.

  Products of a medieval worldview, Julian and Teresa inherited a view of
the soul—worked out over the centuries—as the ultimate internal principle
by which we think, feel, and will, and by which our bodies are animated. An
immaterial substance, the soul is itself absolutely simple, that is, of a spiritual
nature. While naturally related to the body, the soul is not wholly immersed
in matter; its higher operations are intrinsically independent of and interdependent with the organism.[5] Medieval Christian theologians depicted the
soul as an indivisible whole conceptually divided into two parts or activities, the sensory and the spiritual, each with its own powers and faculties.
The sensory (lower or outer) soul is related to the body and possesses the
five exterior faculties of sight, hearing, taste, smell, and touch. The sensory
soul was also sometimes associated with two interior sensory faculties that
John of the Cross termed "the imaginative power and phantasy."[6] The spiritual (higher or inner) part of the soul is directed toward spiritual objects
and has the three faculties of memory, understanding, and will. Operating
both in the sensory and spiritual parts of the soul, the faculties turn outward toward the world through their natural powers and inward toward the
divine through their spiritual or supernatural powers. Through the sensory

and spiritual faculties, the world is mediated through language and symbol, the principles and properties of consciousness perceived, and the feelings of love and mercy felt.

It was Augustine who associated these spiritual faculties with gifts of the Trinity (Father–Son–Holy Spirit) imprinted into the soul. In seeking to understand how he was able to apprehend the Divine Light, Augustine writes in his *Confessions* that humans are able to experience and know the divine because we already contain within us organs of spiritual understanding. Through centuries of Christian thought about the soul's composition and its relationship to the three theological virtues (faith, hope, and love), the Father comes to correspond to the soul's memory and hope, the Son to understanding (intellect) and faith, and the Spirit to the will and love. Because God remembers, knows, and loves us, we have the capacity to participate in and experience the divine fully, says the anonymous author of *The Cloud of Unknowing*, through love. These organs of spiritual perception function as the "eyes" and "ears" of the interior world.

In practical terms, the inner structure of the soul is directly related to a person's understanding and growth. Since the lower soul is connected to the sense faculties and thus the body, everything that affects a person in daily life—both positively and negatively—has a corresponding impact on the lower soul. As a realm of spiritual consciousness and not a material thing, all forms of energy reverberate in the highly sensitive soul. Because of the unity of the sensual faculties with the physical organism, medieval theologians held that human vices and sin caused effects in soul consciousness, dividing the lower soul from the higher and turning it away from the divine good. Similarly, whatever contributes to the disintegration of the lower from the higher soul will cause physical effects of pain and illness.

In various ways, our women mystics conceptualize the inner (or higher) and outer (or lower) soul, and how the true self is always one with God. Using images of fortified dwellings (Julian, a citadel; Teresa, a crystalline castle), each mystic distinguishes between the inner and outer soul. The inner soul remains pure and holy, turned toward communion with God, while the outer soul, turned toward the world, is susceptible to human desires, attachments, and sins. The lower soul speaks of what is achievable through human efforts and the ordinary help of grace, and is thus considered to be "active." The higher soul functions through the operation of supernatural grace; it is receptive, operating in non-dualistic, unitive states of consciousness, and deals with the "passive," or mystical, elements of the spiritual life.

Julian names this distinction between inner and outer soul by using the terms "substance" and "sensuality."[7] Substance is our essence, our pure nature made for God's love; sensuality is the soul's response to impulses and attractions that lead the person astray; this distinction between inner and outer is not representative of a dualism between body and soul. Julian clarifies that God is present in both the inner and outer soul:

> And therefore if we want to have knowledge of our soul, . . . we must
> seek in our Lord God in whom it is enclosed. And of this enclosing I
> saw and understood, . . . as I shall say, and as regards our substance, it can
> rightly be called our soul, and as regards our sensuality, it can rightly be
> called our soul, and that is by the union which it has in God.[8]

The whole "honourable city" of the soul, lower and higher, is one; for God "is the foundation on which our soul stands, and he is the mean which keeps the substance and sensuality together, so that they will never separate." Bonded together as one, "our soul is so deeply grounded in God and so endlessly treasured," writes Julian, "that we cannot come to knowledge of it until we first have knowledge of God, who is the Creator to whom it is united."[9] Conversely, Julian states that "we can never come to the full knowledge of God until we first clearly know our own soul."[10]

However, while the human person is inseparably connected to divinity, sin can cause a fracture within the soul, dividing substance from sensuality. Because there is a unity of the sensuality with the physical organism, when sin splits the outer from the inner soul it reverberates in the body as well, creating physical effects of pain and illness. "This fracture," writes Grace Jantzen, "has the immediate effect of self-alienation and thus of the mental and spiritual anguish of the inevitably restless heart; it is the woundedness at the center of the personality."[11] Similarly, the reintegration of sensuality and substance can only be performed by God, who alone heals, from the deepest center of the soul outward all those fractures in the consciousness of the person torn between pain and freedom.

Although sin, according to Julian, is responsible for the split between the inner and outer soul, it can never penetrate or fundamentally harm the soul's perfection, which always remains pure and untouched in its center. A departure from traditional Christian doctrine, the dissonance between Julian's experience of the fundamental goodness of the soul and the Church's teaching on original sin generates a conflict within her, which she spends more than fifteen years pondering. In an especially important vision of a servant and his lord, Julian works out the urgent paradox that occupied her thoughts: How was she to reconcile the ordinary teaching of "Holy Church [in which] blame for our sins continually hangs upon us" with her spiritual understanding that "our Lord God show[s] no more blame to us than if we were as pure and as holy as the angels in heaven"?[12] In the vision, a lord sits in rest and peace, while his servant stands before him ready to do his will. The lord sends the servant to a certain place, but the servant not only goes, but "dashes off and runs at great speed" and soon "falls into a dell and is greatly injured."[13] The fall causes the servant great distress because in his pain he is unable to turn his face or seek consolation from his lord who is very near him.

Julian conceives the vision in trinitarian terms; the servant is Jesus and Adam ("that is to say all men"), the lord is "God the Father," and "the Holy Spirit is the equal love which is in them both."[14] She thus interprets this teaching to signify how God looks upon his servants with such mothering mercy and tenderness. The lord does not blame his servant but realizes his fall is blameless, the result of excessive love and zeal. This excessive love told Julian how God looks upon our sins: "and then I saw that only pain blames and punishes, and our courteous Lord comforts and succours, and always he is kindly disposed to the soul, loving and longing to bring us to bliss."[15] Having pondered this vision for many years, Julian sees it as the essential manifestation of the incarnation—how through love, sin and evil are transformed.

In this sense, Julian's vision is an extended meditation on the question of integration, of joining the fragmented human self into wholeness, a wholeness that in turns teaches us about the interconnectedness of the world. The intimacy shared between lord and servant establishes guidelines for a human response to the problem of evil and sin. This intimacy of mutual sharing and feeling is exemplified in the feminine, in the bond of love between Jesus and his mother, Mary.[16] Liz McAvoy interprets the whole of the vision through the closeness of the mother-child relationship:

> Julian presents the mother figure as the one who feels in her own body every hurt her child receives, both physical and psychological, and so this lord feels the suffering of his servant and is united with him in his anguish. The pain of the fall unites them both, just as the pain of childbirth and the suffering involved in the child's acquisition of experience unites mother and child in a continuous cycle of reciprocity.[17]

Like Julian, Teresa also conceptualizes the soul as having an outer aspect that turns toward the world and is tempted by its sins, and an inner pure and undefiled core that is turned toward God. In *The Interior Castle*, Teresa describes a vision of the soul as a crystalline castle with many rooms or dwelling places that lead to Christ at its center (see diagram on p. 107). Teresa names seven of these rooms, distinguishing three outer *moradas* (dwellings) where a person confronts worldly limitation, suffering, and desire from four interior rooms infused with supernatural love. The outer three levels of soul consciousness turn toward the world and are susceptible to its pains, doubts, limits, desires, sins, and sufferings. The four interior rooms, or aspects of consciousness, are mystical and are always connected with the divine, thus remaining pure and untouched. In writing of these seven dwelling places, Teresa points out that we must be aware that "in each of these are many others [*moradas*], below and above and to the sides, with lovely gardens and fountains and labyrinths, such delightful things that you would want to be dissolved in praises of the great God who created the soul in His own image and likeness."[18]

The Interior Castle is a record of Teresa's journey of self-knowledge and self-discovery, with each room of the castle signifying a state of awareness and a quality of prayer that eventually lead to centering one's whole life in God. Teresa understands that because of human ignorance and sin, each person must undergo a journey from the outer *moradas* to the inner, from exile to home, in order to focus one's attention on "another heaven, where His Majesty dwells alone" in the soul.[19] Entrance into the castle is through prayer, writes Teresa, and her discussion of the first dwelling place chronicles how the soul "is so involved in worldly things and so absorbed with its possessions, honor, or business affairs," that it is prevented from taking time for prayer and searching for the true light.[20] The second dwelling place is for those who have taken the first steps in the practice of prayer, and who are receptive to external means of communion with God especially through books, sermons, good friendships, and trials. In Teresa's explanation of moving from distraction to formal prayer practice, the third dwelling place exists for those who long not to offend "His Majesty," and who guard against sin and are fond of "ascetical practices and periods of recollection."[21] However, because a person is still attached to worldly affairs, "any threat to wealth or honor will quickly uncover" the extent of his or her true desire for perfection and for achieving the "delectable peace and quiet of contemplation."[22]

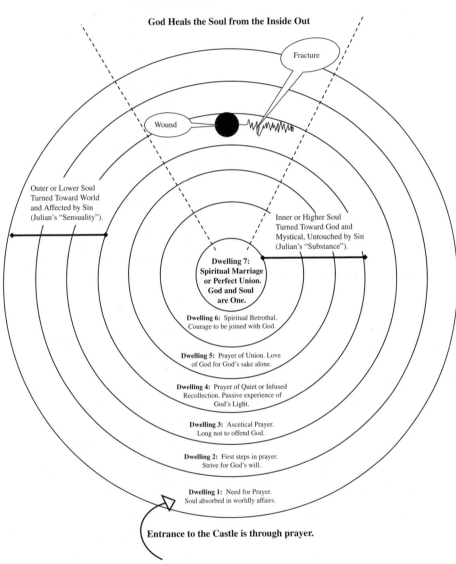

Seven Dwellings (Moradas) in the Interior Castle

God Heals the Soul from the Inside Out

Fracture

Wound

Outer or Lower Soul
Turned Toward World
and Affected by Sin
(Julian's "Sensuality").

Inner or Higher Soul
Turned Toward God and
Mystical, Untouched by Sin
(Julian's "Substance").

Dwelling 7:
Spiritual Marriage
or Perfect Union.
God and Soul
are One.

Dwelling 6: Spiritual Betrothal.
Courage to be joined with God.

Dwelling 5: Prayer of Union. Love
of God for God's sake alone.

Dwelling 4: Prayer of Quiet or Infused
Recollection. Passive experience of
God's Light.

Dwelling 3: Ascetical Prayer.
Long not to offend God.

Dwelling 2: First steps in prayer.
Strive for God's will.

Dwelling 1: Need for Prayer.
Soul absorbed in worldly affairs.

Entrance to the Castle is through prayer.

The problem of how to explain infused prayer marks Teresa's discussion of the fourth dwelling place and the beginning of supernatural or mystical states of consciousness. Central to her vision that the soul is one with God in its center, Teresa distinguishes the three outer *moradas* as active efforts a person makes to embark on this journey, which begins in human nature and ends in God. The four inner or mystical dwelling places, however, have their beginnings in God and overflow into human nature, and represent the passive or receptive experience of divine presence. Contemplative prayer begins in the fourth dwelling place. Teresa calls this prayer the "prayer of quiet," and it represents the joining together of the active or natural and passive or supernatural states of consciousness. The soul's progression from the "prayer of quiet" to the "prayer of union" occupies Teresa's description of the fifth dwelling place. This progression involves the complete stilling or silencing of the faculties, which leaves a certitude that the soul "was in God and God was in it."[23] The sixth and seventh dwelling places involve mystical or passive prayer, and how the soul is drawn into a deeper experience of intimacy through further purifications and raptures. Spiritual betrothal and then later spiritual marriage join God and soul in an inseparable oneness, inflaming the person with the courage necessary to be co-equal in love with her divine spouse.

This pilgrimage of the spirit involves an intense mystical process designed to move the person from denial and doubt into direct awareness of truth—the inseparable relationship between divinity and humanity. As the soul advances toward the center of its castle, consciousness moves from oppression to freedom, from human love to divine love, and from doubt to certainty. The most difficult aspect of this spiritual process, according to Teresa, is not the trials one endures, but the immensity of divine benevolence: God wants the soul's freedom; God draws the soul toward healing and integration, toward its true nature and source. Despite the noise, disruption, and wasted time that occur "on the outskirts of the castle," the soul is completely joined with God in the dwelling places very close to the center. "Terrible trials are suffered," Teresa laments, "because we don't understand ourselves, and that which isn't bad at all but good we think is a serious fault. This lack of knowledge causes afflictions of many people . . . [who] don't reflect that there is an interior world here within us."[24]

For Teresa, the love and goodness in which the soul is enclosed subvert our notions of sin, and take away punishment and pain. Negative views of the self cannot be sustained and no sin is outside forgiveness, for there is nothing that divine mercy cannot heal. Progression from outer to inner soul, and from "wretchedness" to self-dignity, is depicted in bridal imagery as the person is first betrothed, and then wedded, to God. The spousal encounter conveys a mysticism of intimacy in which the person moves from occasional touches of divine union to a more sustained union found in spiritual betrothal in the sixth *morada*. However, even in betrothal, "union with the Lord passes quickly" Teresa instructs, [and] "in the end the two can be separated and each remains in itself."[25] It is only at the center of the castle that the soul and God are joined in an inseparable unity "that is like what we have when rain falls from the sky into a river or fount; all is water, for the rain that fell from heaven cannot be divided or separated from the water of the river. . . . The soul always remains with its God in that center."[26] The intimacy achieved in mystic contemplation impresses on Julian and Teresa how the soul in its essence is always one with God, despite errors, omissions, and sins. So powerful was our mystics' understanding of the undefiled love between God and the soul that this equality of intimacy became the founding impetus of their lives and theologies.

In practical terms, Julian and Teresa conceive of the spiritual life as one in which the person must learn to detach from the temporary attractions of the world through determination and practice in order to experience a higher order of freedom and happiness. Beginners in the spiritual life are aware of two things: the struggle to mend an inherent division within oneself and the ability to achieve moments of illumination, truth, and love. Those more advanced in the spiritual life feel the pain of longing to be reunited with their beloved, of no longer living a divided life. Those who long for spiritual unity with God recognize that the more arduous and fruitful path is one by which conflicting attractions give way to centering one's whole life in God. For our two women mystics, a person's capacity to grow spirituality and to be harmonious and joyful is dependent upon healing the division between inner and outer soul. Whatever afflicts our hope, faith, and love in this world has a corresponding impact on the deepest core of the self, affecting the soul's ability to be in touch with and experience the great goodness in which it is held.

Subversion and Liberation in Prayer

Let all the learned men in the world rise up against me, let the world of creation persecute me, let the evil spirits torment me; but you do not fail me, my Lord, for I already have experience of the great deliverance you offer to the soul who places its trust only in You. . . . While I was going through this distress, only the following words were good enough to give me liberation and peace: "Do not fear, my daughter; it is I; I will not forsake you, do not be afraid." . . . Only those few words were necessary to give me peace, strength, courage, and security . . . and in such an amazing way that it seemed to me that I would have disputed with the entire world that my way of prayer was God's way.[27]

In the above passage Teresa struggles with a dilemma: she has found a contemplative way of prayer that is better, quicker, and more authentic to the spiritual life of her sisters than the salvation that occurs through sacraments, penances, confessions, and the mediation of the academic theologians. Teresa's way of prayer is attacked, ridiculed, and dismissed by clerical authorities; she is accused of arrogance, chicanery, consorting with the devil, and lack of humility unbecoming to a woman. Yet despite these attacks, Teresa is clear that her form of contemplative prayer is from God and not created by her own will. "Up to this point The Life was my own. The Life that I have lived," she writes, "since I started to declare the way of prayer is The Life that God lived in me."[28] Her life and writings are testament to her determination to achieve self-worth and to her courage in affirming herself as a teacher of contemplation who found a deeper, quicker, and more effective way of reaching perfection. '

To comprehend the radical stance Teresa takes, it is valuable to recognize that in sixteenth-century Spain, prayer was practiced primarily in a vocal, communal setting. Silent, contemplative prayer was suspect, considered to be a "waste of time" and effectively suppressed by the church with the Inquisition's banning of books on contemplation, an act that had a profound effect on Teresa. In the midst of this hostile environment to the individual seeker of truth, Teresa nevertheless accepts the great benefit and strength that comes from freely seeking divine wisdom on her own. In her monasteries, Teresa sets about teaching the sisters in her charge of the great good attainable through silence and practicing contemplative prayer.

Foundational to the whole mystical life is prayer and reflection, which Teresa calls "the gate of entry to this castle [of the soul]."[29] Prayer is the surest method by which the soul moves from oppression and fragmentation to freedom and wholeness. As the primary mode of communion between God and the soul, a specific type of nondual, infused prayer—Teresa's prayer of quiet, union, betrothal, and marriage; and Julian's prayer of mothering and unity or "one-ing"—is central. This is not the prayer of subject and object, of lord and damsel, but the fiery passion of lovers who share in the fullness of each other's joys and sorrows. For both Julian and Teresa, prayer is the vessel or enclosure within which God's longing for human redemption takes root and grows. Like human relations of intimacy, prayer grows in the eyes of the beholder, changing from one that involves effort and practice to one of complete ease and rest, a coming home to the beloved. Teresa uses various descriptions and images to describe this growing intimacy of communion between God and the soul. She makes a distinction between different modes of prayer: vocal and mental prayer, meditation, and pure contemplation. However, all types of prayer are essentially contemplative, rooted in Teresa's understanding of mental prayer as an "intimate sharing between friends: it means taking time frequently to be alone with him who we know loves us."[30]

Highly imaginative and creative, Teresa describes in graphic detail her famous four degrees of prayer, from early to advanced stages, in various writings. Beginners on the path she likens to persons trying to cultivate a garden in very barren soil, full of weeds. God assists beginners by pulling up the weeds and planting good seeds, but these seeds now have to be watered. The way in which the garden is watered becomes a creative metaphor for the progress the soul makes in giving over its will and resting in God. Using the image of filling two troughs from two different water sources, Teresa distinguishes between meditation, the prayer of beginners, and contemplation, the prayer of proficients. Meditation is compared to drawing water from far away through the construction of numerous aqueducts and the use of human skill. It is obtained "through thoughts, assisting ourselves, using creatures to help our meditation, and tiring the intellect." In contemplation, the "source of water is right there, and the trough fills without any noise."[31] The spring of contemplation comes from its own source, which is God. It is thus always abundant, overflowing in a continuous stream without human effort or skill, and produces "the greatest peace and quiet and sweetness in the very interior part of ourselves."[32] Meditative prayer offers *contentos* (tender consolations) that begin in human nature and end in God. Contemplative or supernatural prayer "begins in God and ends in ourselves," favoring the soul with *gustos* (spiritual delights).[33]

Beginners in prayer are unaware of how God is always within them, calling them to union and love. Thus, they labor to recollect their senses and tire themselves in the effort, a fact Teresa relates to drawing water from a well. She writes, "the tedious work of often letting down the pail down into the well and pulling it back up without any water [makes them want to] abandon everything."[34] Fetching water from the well corresponds to the rational work of the intellect, which desires to understand and thus struggles with watering the soul. The movement from effort and self-will to rest and receptivity constitutes the maturing of the practice of prayer, and the soul's journey from natural to supernatural states of consciousness. Teresa names the second degree of prayer the "prayer of quiet." Here watering the garden of the soul takes place by means of turning the crank of a water wheel and by aqueducts. More water is obtained with less labor. God is so close that the soul can speak with "Him itself and not by shouting since He is so near that when it merely moves its lips, He understands it."[35] Communion with God takes place in the depths of the soul, when the intellect is stilled and the spark of divinity at its center is enkindled by love and desire. The ease with which water now flows brings all the flowers to bud, and the soul sees very clearly.

Drawing closer to its divine source, the garden of the soul is now irrigated with water flowing from a river or spring. This third degree of prayer requires very little effort, as God so desires to "help the gardener here that He Himself becomes practically the gardener and the one who does everything."[36] The soul desires an intense freedom, and its virtues and good deeds are stronger than in the prayer of quiet. The flowers of the garden are in full bloom, offering life-giving fragrance. Yet, this third degree of prayer does not culminate in further stillness or inactivity "rejoicing in the holy idleness of Mary," but joins "both the active and contemplative life together" as did Martha.[37] Teresa claims that the person is able to conduct works of charity and business affairs even while the best part of the soul is elsewhere.

The "prayer of union," or fourth degree of prayer, is compared to water falling from heaven. Nothing can be done to bring the life-giving waters of rain; its blessing is simply received. The gardener is now joined with heavenly love and experiences intimate communion with God and the greatest tenderness in the soul. The gift of the prayer of union softens the soul "by living in great detachment from self-interest [and] ... begins to be of benefit to its neighbors almost without knowing it or doing anything of itself."[38] Inseparable from its divine source, the heart of the soul is one with God and the eyes of the soul are opened to the vanity of the world.

In her most mature synthesis of the spiritual life, *The Interior Castle*, we have already seen how Teresa creates a bridge between these degrees of prayer and the seven *moradas* or dwellings. Yet, amid Teresa's illuminating insight into the depths of mystic contemplation and her efforts to convey these truths to others are found poignant and painful stories of the criticism and persecution leveled against her. The prayers of quiet and union and her transformed self arouse suspicion and jealousy. Teresa is accused of trying to make herself out to be a saint, and of being unfit for the consolations of grace she receives. The wrenching self-doubt she confronts and the subsequent empowerment she achieves transpire as she passes through a "painful prayer" in which she suffers a mystical crucifixion of the soul, which will be discussed in the next chapter.

Teresa's annihilating prayer that is a "one-ing" (to use Julian's term) of God and the soul finds resonance in Julian as well. "Prayer unites [*onyth*] the soul to God," Julian says, "for though the soul may be always like God in nature and in substance restored by grace, it is often unlike him in condition, through sin on man's part. Then prayer is a witness that the soul wills as God wills, and it eases the conscience and fits man for grace. And so he teaches us to pray and to have firm trust that we shall have it; for he beholds us in love, and wants to make us partners in his good will and work."[39] Contemplative prayer is prayer without praying "because when man is at ease with God he does not need to pray, but to contemplate reverently what God says. For in all the time when this was revealed to me," Julian writes, "I was not moved to pray, but always to keep this good in my mind for my strength, that when we see God we have what we desire, and then we do not need to pray. But when we do not see God, then we need to pray, because we are failing, and for the strengthening of ourselves, to Jesus."[40]

Whether prayer is vocalized alone or in community, or silently progresses into deeper and deeper forms of communion, it is centered on this desire to remain attentive to God, one's "intimate friend." In these deep wells of pure contemplation, normal mental activities are suspended and the person is not even aware of how these great gifts occur. "The will is fully occupied in loving," Teresa insists, "but it doesn't understand how it loves. The intellect, if it understands, doesn't understand how it understands; at least it can't comprehend anything of what it understands."[41]

Suffering and Exaltation

The greatest oppositions which exist are the highest bliss and the deepest pain. The highest bliss there is, is to possess God in the clarity of

endless light, truly seeing him, sweetly feeling him, peacefully possessing him in the fullness of joy. [Yet] our spiritual eye is so blind . . .
that we cannot see clearly the blessed face of our Lord God. No, and
because of this darkness, we can scarcely believe or have faith in his
great love and his faithfulness, with which he protects us. And so it is
that I say that we can never cease mourning and weeping.[42]

If prayer is the essential form of communion that allows entrance into
the soul, the experience of suffering and exaltation, or pain and bliss, is the
contemplative method or process that guides the soul toward integration
and the eventual centering of one's life in God. For both Julian and Teresa,
this spiritual process is the direct result of their contemplation on the suffering face of Jesus, which involves identification with God's longing and
concern for humanity, and bearing of the two-fold wounds of Christ's passion—one human and the other divine. Their encounter with the suffering
face of Christ results in an increased awareness of the great joy and bliss with
which God enfolds us, and an increased sensitivity to the suffering of others. At least three distinct causes of suffering can be detected in Julian's and
Teresa's writings: suffering from identification with God's own suffering;
suffering due to the pain felt when sin fractures the soul; and suffering from
longing to be reunited with God.

Participating in God's own suffering, the contemplative's method of
alternating states of pain and bliss emerges from human and divine roots.
The soul experiences the afflictions of its most receptive nature, both in
terms of the painful wounding sustained from bearing the sin and violence
of the world, and the joyful touching of Divine Wisdom that opens it to
deeper reserves of communion and oneness. Thus, the intense suffering over
the world's afflictions is connected to the immense exaltation of love God
offers to the soul. Inner soul wounding and outer worldly offense exist in
reciprocal relationship to the overflowing love between God and the soul.
The depth of the soul's ability to invite in God's love for the world exists in
proportion to the intensity of love's wounding of the soul. The communion
that takes place between God and the soul in its center teaches how close
God is to all things and the manner in which we share in and bear with God
the pain and happiness of our world. The movement between suffering and
exaltation follows the logic of lover-beloved, which for Julian and Teresa is
exemplified in the passion of Christ as "the standard by which love itself
must be measured."[43]

Teresa contends these sufferings are felt "in the very deep and intimate
part of the soul" and mystically repeat the wounds borne by Jesus.[44] Yet, she

makes a radical departure from traditional theology when she states that Jesus' sufferings while alive were much greater than what he experienced in his passion, because "all things were present to Him and He was always witnessing the serious offenses committed against His Father."[45] For those who are intimate with God's presence in the world, human sin strikes into the very core where God and the soul are one. Teresa reflects on her own awareness of the suffering of the soul that is intimate with God and how difficult it is "to see the many offenses committed so continually against His Majesty . . . that I believe that only one day of that pain would have been sufficient to end many lives."[46]

Further, as women mystics in male-dominated cultures, the paradox of suffering and bliss was deeply personal for them. Throughout their lives, Julian and Teresa experienced moments of heightened love and rapture alongside the most intense of physical and spiritual pains. Drawn to the center of their souls by a process almost too elusive for them to name, our women mystics attempt to put into language an inner realm of consciousness, a place in which the soul is torn between bliss and pain. Aware of the difference between physical and spiritual pain, they remind us that, of the two, soul suffering is the most intense and all consuming. Yet, they also are quick to say that one glimpse of the divine face is enough to erase every suffering endured. "All other fears," Julian contends, "she [the soul] counts among the sufferings and bodily sicknesses and fantasies which she must endure; and therefore, though we be in so much pain, woe and unrest that it seems to us that we can think of nothing at all but the state we are in or what we are feeling, let us, as soon as we may, pass it over lightly and count it as nothing."[47]

In spiritual suffering, Julian and Teresa see into the heart of reality itself. Through the image of Christ's wounds they recognize how we damage and harm the most tender, receptive, and gentle part of creation, and how God continues to love and alleviate suffering. The whole of Julian's first revelation, which occupies nine chapters of her Long Text, can be expressed in the juxtaposition she creates between the bleeding and suffering Jesus and the vision of a tiny object, "no bigger than a hazelnut," that she ponders lying in the palm of her hand. She asks about the meaning of this tiny hazelnut and is shown how God loves it into existence. Love is at the center of being; it is love for which we are made; our essential core is pure, verdant, growing love—never stagnant or tainted. The sweetness and tenderness with which God loves creation overflows the hearts of those who are God's lovers into a concern for all others: "In all this," writes Julian, "I was greatly moved in love towards my fellow Christians, that they might all see and know the same as I saw, for I wished it to be a comfort to them, for all this vision was shown for all men."[48]

In a mystical commentary on "his precious crowning of thorns,"[49] Julian expresses the union between God and the soul, the joy of the Trinity as "our maker . . . our protector, and our everlasting lover," and the familiar love in which God enfolds and embraces creation.[50] Julian emphasizes that God wraps all of creation in love, caring for even our humblest bodily needs, so that "we, soul and body, [are] clad and enclosed in the goodness of God."[51] In the paradoxical association of images of suffering and bliss, Julian emphasizes the great pathos God has for our sins, and the immeasurable joy that comes through realizing and transforming all that fractures this great love. Spiritual suffering opens our hearts; it moves us from individual needs toward concern for the flourishing of others. Her understanding that everything "lasts and always will, because God loves it" forms the basis from which Julian's thought and action are generated.[52]

Julian writes one of the clearest and most precise descriptions of this movement between bliss and suffering in religious literature, and thus I quote her at length:

> And after this our Lord revealed to me a supreme spiritual delight in my soul. In this delight I was filled full of everlasting surety, and I was powerfully secured without any fear. . . .
>
> This lasted only for a time, and then I was changed, and left to myself, oppressed and weary of myself, ruing my life so that I scarcely had the patience to go on living. I felt that there was no ease or comfort for me except hope, faith and love, and truly I felt very little of this. And then presently God gave me again comfort and rest for my soul. . . . And then again I felt the pain, . . . now the one and now the other, again and again, I suppose about twenty times. And in the time of joy I could have said with Paul: Nothing shall separate me from the love of Christ; and in the pain, I could have said with Peter: Lord, save me, I am perishing.[53]

This vision was shown to Julian to teach her that God is with us and loves us as much in sorrow as in joy. The alternating experiences of bliss and suffering are a divine method that strengthens our souls and prepares us for greater heights and depths of love. From these experiences of pain and happiness we learn to preserve our consolation and bliss, which lasts forever, and to discover that even the greatest pain is reduced to nothing by God's love.

In *The Book of Her Life* and her many other writings, Teresa of Avila also contributes an enormous body of literature to understanding the contemplative process a person follows in her longing to love God and to be healed. Nowhere else is this more evident than in Teresa's emphasis on the relationship between pain and joy, suffering and bliss. "Two experiences, it seems to me, which lie on this spiritual path," she writes, "put a person in danger of death: the one is this pain, for it is truly a danger, and no small one; the other is overwhelming joy and delight, which reaches so extraordinary a peak that indeed the soul, I think, swoons to the point that it is hardly kept from leaving the body—indeed, its happiness could not be considered small."[54]

Every suffering has a purpose; every pain is measured against the horizon of Divine Love; every sorrow healed by the Beloved's own touch. The soul is so close to its God, so intimate to the shimmering, sensitive, rapturous divinity at its center, that all life is witnessed through the lens of a different quality of consciousness. Pain and joy are not opposed, Teresa teaches, but are two aspects of one process of drawing closer to God. We are wounded by events in our world, pained by our own and others' folly, and felled by the magnificence of gifts we cannot ever repay. All of this—every breath of air we take, every heart we touch—represents the joy and sorrow of life's unending majesty.

Teresa reminds us that we should not abandon passion or substitute the banal in its place, but grasp its full strength, holding onto it until every shame and every fear of truth are taken away. There is danger on the path, but it is the danger of the one who dares to risk everything for the sake of a greater love. Contemplatives are drawn to a deeper sharing in the life of the divine and, thus, Teresa instructs, "do not bear a lighter cross" of pain and suffering. To strengthen them to endure greater trials, God gives contemplatives many spiritual delights because "the more He loves them, the greater the tribulations."[55]

This inner participation in God's suffering compels in our mystics a desire to share in the world's sufferings in an outpouring of solidarity with those who are marginalized, ridiculed, and rejected: "I desire to suffer, Lord, since You suffered," Teresa writes. "Let your will be done in me in every way, and may it not please your majesty that something as precious as your love be given to anyone who serves you only for the sake of consolations."[56] Through this intimacy of divine-human suffering—"for I wished that his pains might be my pains"—Julian also recognizes that "identification with Christ must include identification with those for whom he suffered," writes

Grace Jantzen, "and hence with their suffering."[57] In Julian's and Teresa's confrontation with the vulnerability of Jesus' face, body, and wounds, their hearts are torn and whatever traces of self-centeredness remain are consumed by the fiery flame of sorrow for human arrogance and sin. Yet, this mystical emptiness of self initiates an unreserved responsibility in which our mystics reclaim their dignity as women and articulate a new feminine way of liberation for themselves and for others.

chapter seven

The Soul of Woman and
the Dark Night of the Feminine

It seems to me that the soul is crucified since no consolation comes to
it from heaven, nor is it in heaven; neither does it desire any from earth,
nor is it on earth. The experience resembles the death agony with the
difference that the suffering bears along with it such great happiness
that I don't know what to compare it to. . . . In this pain the soul is
purified and fashioned or purged like gold in the crucible.[1]

Teresa's account of her soul's simultaneous suffering and joy was written almost twenty-seven years after she entered the Monastery of the
Incarnation. Because she was no longer a novice in matters either of spirit
or world, it is tempting to think that she would have left behind the more
agonizing aspects of the journey long ago. Instead, one discovers that the
longer Teresa progresses on the path, and the more she is attuned to the
relationship between her inner freedom and outward oppression, the more
arduous is her path. This period of Teresa's life, from the age of forty-five
to her death at sixty-seven, is marked by three significant themes: greater
awareness of herself as a woman, greater acceptance of her divine gifts, and
greater empowerment of her spiritual teaching. Teresa even clarifies for her
readers, in order to encourage them in their own spiritual quest, that it
"must not be forgotten that this experience of pain comes after all those
favors that are written of in this book."[2] How are we to understand Teresa's
continued movement between deeper resources of suffering and greater
heights of mystic comprehension?

In this chapter, I return to the "un-saying of woman" raised in chapter
1—the contemplative process by which a woman leaves behind societal and
often anti-female views to gain dignity, power, and self-worth. Through the
lens of Teresa of Avila, I map an additional stage of the mystical life—the
night of the feminine—to highlight her specific soul suffering and liberation

119

as a woman. As defined here, the dark night of the feminine shares many characteristics with the depiction of *la noche oscura* (the dark night) of St. John of the Cross. A friend and spiritual companion of Teresa of Avila, who was his elder by twenty-seven years, John is one of the greatest explicators of the soul's apophatic experience. An astute spiritual physician, John found in Teresa a fountain of wisdom, insight, and strength, as she praised him for his gifts of spiritual direction and mystical sanctity. In this chapter, I use John and Teresa's experiential knowledge of the dark night as a conceptual framework to explore when the soul of a woman turns inward to heal her deep divide and to claim her equality. Together, John and Teresa offer to us, as they did for each other, guidance on the struggles we undertake in the journey toward the undivided self.

St. John and the Dark Night of the Soul

En una Noche oscura	One dark night,
Con ansias en amores inflamada	Fired with love's urgent longings
—Oh dichosa ventura!—	—Ah, the sheer grace!—
Sali sin ser notada,	I went out unseen,
Estando ya mis casa sosegada.	My house being now all stilled.

This first stanza from the mystical poem of St. John of the Cross begins a commentary on the soul's passage from bondage to liberation. One of the most profound in religious literature, the poem traces the soul's growth from separation and darkness to intimacy and oneness with God. Refining the classical journey of purgation, illumination, and union, John names this period of spiritual darkness and suffering *"una noche oscura"* (one dark night). Inserting the dark night as an additional stage of transition between purgation and illumination, and between illumination and union, he provides three reasons why he calls the soul's passage a dark night. First, it is a releasing of all our attachments and desires, the road of faith a person travels toward union with God, and God's secret, loving communion with the soul. "The first has to do with the point of departure," John writes, and the deprivation of our desire for worldly possessions, whether physical, mental, emotional, or spiritual. The second reason refers to "the road along which a person travels toward this union. Now this road is faith, and for the intellect faith is also like a dark night." The third reason "pertains to the point of arrival, namely God," and how

God's intense communion with the soul, expressed through such terms as "inflow," "infusion," "nursing," and "illumination," appears as a dark night to a person in this life.[3]

In John's mystical theology, the dark night holds a special and unique place. Unlike the beginner's stages of the spiritual life, which purify the outer aspects of one's feelings and perceptions, the dark night is the necessarily desolate space of transformation of the soul's deepest attachment and identity as a separate being. St. John's usage of the term "dark night" implies a confrontation with *nada* (nothing) and signifies the critical transition each person makes across the frozen pond of human ego to the liquid waters of liberation and intimacy. Exceeding in quality and intensity all previous spiritual growth, John's dark night is both the anguishing confrontation with the roots of the soul's inordinate passions, and the glad and lovely night in which lover and beloved are united.

As we have seen in the cases of Julian and Teresa, John is also an inheritor of medieval theological thought who understands the soul to be divided into two parts—the sensory or lower soul turned toward the body, and the spiritual or higher soul directed toward spiritual objects. Using this typology, John perceives the dark night through the lens of a four-fold classification of consciousness—the night of the senses (corresponding to the lower soul) and the night of the spirit (corresponding to the higher soul). Each of these has two degrees of interiority: the active and the passive. John explains that there is an active and passive night of the senses when the person is cleansed of sensory and material attachments, as well as an active and passive night of the spirit in which God's purifying light draws the person into relinquishing all manner of spiritual things. Although the two nights are actually aspects of one deepening process of interiorization and receptivity, John distinguishes the active nights as those efforts a person makes to control the senses, from the passive nights, where the soul can do nothing in its own power and is taught by God's secret, perfect love.

The distinction John makes between active and passive is crucial to understanding the importance he places on the sublimity and power of the dark night in a person's growth. Activity refers to one's response to the desire to attain wholeness and includes all those intentions, both positive and negative, which lie in one's spiritual power to enter this night. It is what *we do* to find God: join in community with like-minded seekers, consult with masters and other pilgrims on the path, devote ourselves to prayer and meditative practices, and learn through errors and realizations. Despite moments of darkness and confusion, the soul is still supported by collective structures of religious life: language, prayer, ritual, and community.

In the active night of the senses, the soul begins the process of integrating the physical and the spiritual. Since the lower part of the soul is turned toward the world and is susceptible to human failings, the active night purifies "the sensory and spiritual faculties of everything contrary to a life of perfect faith and love."[4] In the passive sensory night, God grants the person relief from her attachments, and begins to "wean the soul [from worldly desires] and place it in a state of contemplation."[5]

As in the night of senses, John divides the night of the spirit into active and passive states. The active night of the spirit is distinguished from its counterpart in the sensory night by its interiority and intensity, specific focus on purification of the spiritual faculties, and presence of the feminine in the figure of Wisdom (Sophia). Important to these efforts, John says "the intellect must be perfected in the darkness of faith, the memory in the emptiness of hope, and the will in the nakedness and absence of every affection."[6] In the active spiritual night, the soul is still nourished by the collective structures of the spiritual life: prayer, ritual, and community. Because in activity we are able to cling to something known, and we rely on the ego-self, John emphasizes that the active nights are not as foreign or intense as the passive. In the passive spiritual night, God draws the soul into the most intense, hidden, and wrenching experiences of the spiritual life, healing the soul of its suffering in a special infusion of Divine Love. In this realm of forsakenness and emptiness, the soul is lifted above the three faculties of memory, understanding, and will to pass over to a dark and incomprehensible union with God.

John depicts the soul's suffering as a transformative stage prior to self-integration and divine union. Torn by a wrenching inability to assuage the desolation of this dark passage, a person feels worthless and abandoned in the eyes of God. Yet the soul is being raised up to an illumination so bright it appears dark to the disordered and suffering spirit. The soul cannot see what it is or name what it knows. This dark night is the secret teaching of love in which God releases the soul from oppression and draws it into a special realization of Divine Intimacy. The soul is being absorbed into an experience imprinted in its original nature, to something wondrous and profound. Thus John says the dark night is also "that glad night," "guiding night," and "night more lovely than dawn" in which lover and beloved are reunited.[7]

Wisdom (Sophia) in St. John

In John's four major works, which are centered on Wisdom as the crucified one, the feminine divinity becomes the compelling force of the soul's trans-figuration and eventual experience of completion in love.[8] While John does not explicitly address women or employ the word "feminine" in his writings, he makes numerous references to the books of Proverbs and Wisdom, two biblical texts with strong feminine imagery, and frequently depicts the soul's spousal relationship as a union with Jesus Sophia.[9] Wisdom appears in the beginning stages of the soul's journey "like a loving mother," writes John, "who warms her child with the heat of her bosom, nurses it with good milk and tender food, and carries and caresses it in her arms."[10] As it matures in intimacy with God, the soul is weaned by Wisdom-Sophia from her loving presence and is led to the source of its woundedness and to a more painful and revolutionary healing. Just when the soul's consolations are most high and "divine favor is shining most brightly on [it]," he cautions, "God darkens all this light . . . and weans [it] from the sweet breast so [it] might be strengthened."[11]

John's explicit association of emptiness and annihilation with Wisdom is an acknowledgement of the integral role of the feminine in the dark night. It is interesting to reflect on the fact that John and Teresa were close friends—she encouraging him to join her order, while he served as her confessor and spiritual companion. While John's writings clearly contain a feminine aspect and are systematic and eloquent, Teresa's thought is often digressive and repetitive, centered more explicitly on Jesus and less frequently on Feminine Divine imagery. Nevertheless, upon a close reading of her texts, it becomes apparent that she is confronting another dimension of transformation not contained within John's writings. It is unmistakable that Teresa is grappling in large measure with being a woman and a mystic in a society that brutally marginalized and subordinated women to the dictates of men. Teresa took her battles with the world into her interior, and wrestled them out with God. Her confrontation with her own unworthiness, despair, and grief, magnified by the pronouncement by male spiritual directors of her lack of worth, becomes the medium of her liberation. It is, in fact, this quest for union with God that leads her from subordination and oppression to subversion and empowerment.

In her journey toward freedom and wholeness, Teresa experiences the root pain and "terrible anguish" of stripping away human and super-natural knowing. Having known God primarily through the authority of a male-dominated church, Teresa struggles to reconcile Jesus' loving affirmation of her whole person with the harsh and punishing views directed against her. She recognizes that even Church-sanctioned spiritual directors and prayers mediated by her male confessors do not capture the fullness of her spiritual life or the pain of the purgative contemplation gripping her soul. She confides in her books and letters over and again that a critical element of her and her sisters' spiritual struggles *as women* is left out. There comes a point on a woman's journey when even classical accounts of the soul can be a hindrance because women assume that male depictions of the spiritual life are charting the same territory they need to cross. In *The Book of Her Life*, Teresa recounts how she is continually made to let go of her attachment to the advice, demands, and criticism of male clerics, Inquisitional authorities, and even her community in order to claim Jesus'—and her own—loving and sometimes radical advice.

Perhaps the problem is that classical descriptions of the soul's journey touch the latent, unconscious feminine, which Teresa experiences in an active, conscious manner. Or it could be the theological assumption that the soul's suffering is self-inflicted (a result of its intemperance, inordinate desires, and corrupted will) that Teresa eventually reacts against. Further, medieval spiritual writers did not associate the attainment of soul perfection with the healing of any particular social, religious, or gender oppression. Since Teresa knew silently and intuitively that women's self-doubt and self-loathing not only were the result of personal failings but were formed also from deep social and religious roots, this omission becomes another source of her conflict and pain. For contemporary women, John's category of dark night can be a detriment because women may further internalize the sin-based theology associated with medieval culture. The self-blaming aspects of these classical depictions of soul suffering reinforce gender differences and often turn women away from the wisdom contained in John's thought.

Night of the Feminine in St. Teresa of Avila

In keeping with the feminine gender signified in the Spanish noun *noche* (night), I call this most interior and additional passage the "night of the feminine." Using St. John's four-fold typology as a conceptual guide, I insert the dark night of the feminine as a contemplative process that includes and yet goes beyond, or is more interior than, John's passive night. The night of the feminine shares many characteristics with John's description, but it has an added dimension: it specifically locates a woman's struggle to achieve fullness of being within her soul's internalization of the misogyny particular to her world and God's suffering of the violation of her womanhood. In Teresa's case, the night of the feminine is a continuum of consciousness that brings her to another level of alienation and fragmentation. This intensification of suffering precludes a breakthrough into a new life of integration in which Teresa experiences her mutuality with men and God, and a new-found certainty and strength.

The addition of the night of the feminine to our religious vocabulary emphasizes its distinctiveness in a woman's spiritual life and refines our understanding of the soul's journey. When I say it is a feminine night, I mean the soul suffers the afflictions of its most receptive and intimate nature, in terms of both the negative wounding sustained from the violence of the world and the positive touching of Divine Wisdom that opens it to deeper reserves of communion and oneness. It is a dark night of the feminine not only because it occurs in women, but also because the experience itself is the healing of the injury women sustain in the most receptive part of the soul. In *The Interior Castle*, the soul progresses from the outer dwellings (depicted through the masculine imagery of her day: soldiers defending the castle) to the inner dwellings that are represented by qualities she associates with the feminine: vulnerability, surrender, and annihilation. This is the gestational ground in which Teresa's soul offers its separate identity into the fiery flame of divinity to be transformed into a life of intimacy, relatedness, and communion that is not a negative sacrifice of autonomy, but a new and exalted quality of being.

Although she does not name it explicitly, Teresa uses many different images to describe this feminine night, placing it sometimes within the purgative contemplation prior to union, and in other texts as an additional stage after union. As a more radical "unsaying of woman," the night of the feminine turns Teresa away from the purely spiritual realm and back to material reality to experience the suffering of embodiment—the wounds of being female, and the denial of her dignity as it relates to her gender. As the most vulnerable and embodied of the mystical life, the night of the feminine does not withdraw her soul from the world in an ascetic detachment nor does it shield her from the world's cruelty and disgrace. Teresa must confront the desecration of the holy and the violence directed against her as a woman in every aspect of life. Strengthened by her previous trials and consolations, God reaches out in tender loving care to remove the scars that have formed over her soul's hidden anguish, exposing the rawness of her wounds. No longer able to stave off the profound dismissal, cruelty, and gossip wielded against her, Teresa is torn by doubt, confusion, and grief.

Teresa's Unsaying of "Woman"

While her status as a woman colors her whole spiritual life (in a sense, we could say that Teresa's entire dark night experience *is* feminine), Teresa experiences an extended phase of her suffering that is an intensification of the feminine night. Here she is now more clearly aware of how mysticism relates specifically to her gender, and she recognizes the seeds of equality that will bear fruit in her life and those of her sisters.

If we study the progression of Teresa's self-affirmation and growth in divinity, we find that she moves through three major phases or dimensions of the dark night of the feminine.[12] In the first, she confronts her alienation from her self, her friendships and interests, her "womanish" weaknesses, and her lack of confidence in her own way.[13] In the second phase, she suffers alienation from God due to her extreme lack of self-worth and belief that, as a woman, she is unworthy of receiving God's love and intimacy. Yet, through these trials she becomes more certain of her path, even rejecting the advice and criticism of male confessors. This initial certainty is not complete, however, and she succumbs to a deeper confrontation with the roots of her fragmentation as a woman. It is during this third movement that Teresa, now older and more aware of God's presence in her life, suffers the offense of clerics who brand her divine graces as visitations "from the devil" and attempt to curtail her thought. She experiences the most profound desolation of her life: complete abandonment and estrangement as she struggles to reconcile the world's debasement of her with Jesus' unqualified love and encouragement. It is from these experiences that Teresa eventually becomes boldly empowered, speaking out for the rights of women and girls, *conversos*, and her Carmelite sisters.

First Phase of Un-saying

Teresa spends almost twenty years in an interior battle between her need for friendships and worldly ambitions and Jesus' offering of intimacy and love. During this first phase of her unsaying, Teresa chides herself for being unable to make a choice, abandoning the conversation of intimate prayer for human conversation and superficial pastimes. As we have noted previously, a statue of the "wounded Christ" finally calls her to conversion, healing her tired, broken, and weary soul. "I was utterly distressed in seeing Him that way," she writes, "for it well represented what He suffered for us. . . . Beseeching Him to strengthen me once and for all that I might not offend Him, I threw myself down before Him with the greatest outpouring of tears."[14] Teresa places herself in the aloneness that Jesus must have felt and realizes that Jesus had to accept her, as she became a companion to him in her own faith struggles. She also recognizes how her love for Jesus and his love for her is related to her acceptance of positive self-love. From this point, Teresa strives to feel the experience of God's presence in her life, and begins to sense the kind of equality God's love calls her toward.

Second Phase of Un-saying

From these initial experiences, Teresa enters a second phase of mystical transformation during which her inner freedom, autonomy, and strength grow. She is called by God to give up her attachment to the counsel of her confessors who critique her visions and make her fear her own truth, abandon her dependence on human words of encouragement, and free herself from being a victim to the criticism leveled at her by those who do not understand her spiritual path. Encouraged to validate her inner wisdom, Teresa labors to be the founder of the Carmelite reform and a woman teacher of prayer. She writes with great passion in *The Book of Her Life* of her yearning to put her desires into action. "The trouble is that for persons as useless as myself there are few opportunities to do something. . . . Others were women, and they have done heroic things for love of You. . . . Fortify my soul and dispose it first, and then ordain ways in which I might do something for You."[15]

However, Teresa could not really accept the love and favors God shows her. Because she is overcome with her fear of ignorance and lack of education, the consolations Teresa receives from God only increase her sense of unworthiness as a person. The most crushing difficulty centers on her confessors' inability to understand that God was calling her to be the architect of a distinct contemplative path. She writes, "During the twenty years . . . I did not find a . . . confessor, who understood me, even though I looked for one. This hurt me so much that I often turned back and was even completely lost, for a master would have helped me flee from the occasions of offending God."[16] These very favors God gave her increased Teresa's sense of inferiority to God and to men, and while she is under obedience to write an account of her gifts she says, "As for everything else, just being a woman is enough to have my wings fall off—how much more being a woman and wretched as well."[17]

Third Phase of Un-saying

Teresa now enters the most crucial and agonizing aspect of her search for subjectivity. As Teresa's visions, favors, and experience of God's presence increase, her confessors and community subject her to further scrutiny and ridicule. She enters a third period beyond her "prayer of union," and even beyond the next stage that she calls "raptures" to a "painful prayer, a painful experience, a deep pain."[18] I would distinguish this period as Teresa's clearest or formal night of the feminine because of her awareness that her pain is even beyond descriptions of the soul: "Thus it seems that the soul is not in itself, but on the roof or housetop of itself and of all created things because it seems to me to be even above the very superior part of the soul."[19] Teresa depicts her suffering and exaltation as a crucifixion in which there is no consolation from heaven or on earth.

> Receiving no help from either side, it is as though [the soul is] cruci-
> fied between heaven and earth. . . . The desert and solitude seem to
> the soul better than all the companionship of the world. . . . The body
> shares only in the pain, and it is the soul alone that both suffers and
> rejoices on account of the joy and satisfaction the suffering gives. . . . It
> must not be forgotten that this experience of pain comes after all those
> favors that are written of in this book.[20]

The intensity of Teresa's pain is magnified by her feelings of being alone and without human support. She discusses how her confessor thought the devil or bad spirit might be involved with her since he told Teresa that her imperfections were "incompatible with the [spiritual] favors [she received] and that these gifts were bestowed on persons who were already advanced and mortified."[21] Teresa's fear of the world's opinion of her made her forget all she had gained in self-worth, plunging her into a deeper desolation and despair. "I was like a person in the middle of a river trying to get out," she wrote. "Wherever she goes she fears greater peril there; and she is almost drowning. It is a very severe trial, this one; and I have suffered many of these. . . . And certainly it is a great one, the trial that is suffered, especially with women, because our weakness is great, and a lot of harm could be done by telling us outright the cause is the devil."[22]

Yet Jesus does not abandon Teresa, nor does Teresa abandon herself. In the subsequent period of anguish over the world's perception that she lacked humility and that her prayer life and visions were temptations, Teresa cries out: "All fails me, my Lord; but if You do not abandon me, I will not fail You." Her calm and courage is restored when Jesus appears to her, saying, "Do not fear, daughter, for I am, and I will not abandon you; do not fear."[23] This dialogue signals another fundamental turning point in Teresa's life because she understood that God was infusing her whole self with Wisdom—it came from inside and could not be controlled or co-opted by the world. By these words she was empowered to claim her own truth and was lifted out of inferiority, self-deprecation, fear, and abandonment. As Teresa writes, she saw her self as another person and "would have disputed the entire world that these words came from God."[24] Writing to her nuns a few years later in *The Way of Perfection*, Teresa remembers her suffering and says, "Since the world's judges are sons of Adam and all of them men, there is no virtue in women they do not suspect."[25] She and Jesus had become partners in affirming and accepting her worth.

During this period of Teresa's heightened acceptance of her equality in God's love, she continued to be counseled to give up her path and was torn by her inner conflict:

> There were enough things to drive me insane . . . for the opposition
> of good men to a little woman, wretched, weak and fearful like myself,
> seems to be nothing when described in so few words. . . . If the Lord
> hadn't favored me so much, I don't know what would have happened
> to me.[26]

Teresa had won the battle over her own inferiority, lack of worth, and divided soul. She claimed her right as a woman to be a person of wisdom and strength, and she was no longer intimidated by oppressive words and "decisions of fearful men" into denying her call to deep contemplative prayer. Teresa turned to her inner wisdom and began to see women from God's perspective, as equal and free. What her age could not give—equality of personhood, an understanding of her own subjectivity—she received from the depths of her prayer life, from God. Having healed the fracture in her own soul, Teresa becomes a forceful advocate for women's wisdom. Some years later, although she continued to suffer society's misunderstandings about the interior life and mystical experiences, especially in women, Teresa boldly defended mental prayer:

You will hear some persons frequently making objections: "there are dangers"; . . . "it's not for women, for they will be susceptible to illusion"; "it's better to stick to sewing." . . . What is this, Christians, that you say mental prayer isn't necessary? Do you understand yourselves? Indeed, I don't think you do, and so you desire that we all be misled. You don't know what mental prayer is, or how vocal prayer should be recited, or what contemplation is, for if you did you wouldn't on the one hand condemn what on the other hand you praise.[27]

The night of the feminine carries Teresa through trials and exaltations to an affirmation of her self-worth. In addition, it reveals the mystical process that "unsays" and heals her false identity as a "little woman" and frees her from gender stereotypes. Through this powerful experience of struggle toward dignity and authority, Teresa passes on to her sisters a distinct women's contemplative path, spreading the seeds of monastic reform. The goal of the spiritual journey—to know God directly and to know oneself—is undertaken in the context of Teresa's fully human experience. For her, there is an inseparable relationship between the heights of mystic contemplation and the healing of the soul wounds that afflict her as a woman. The deeper Teresa advances in Divine Love and the closer she draws to the heart of Divine Intimacy, the more she is challenged to identify and heal the self-doubt and self-loathing that diminish her.

Overview of Teresa's Dark Night of the Feminine

Building on John's images of the previous four-fold typology of the dark night, the night of the feminine depicts a continuum of spiritual growth in which Teresa is brought to another level of alienation and fragmentation to be healed and made whole. Her soul experiences the spiritual violence directed against, and internalized by, women, and God's suffering of her violation as a woman. Teresa's battle now is an internal one. Spiritually, she confronts the roots of women's oppression in historical conditions of deprivation and marginalization: the struggle for faith in a world where the God of faith may be a betrayal of all a woman stands for; bodies that bear the brutalizing of the receptive and guileless in disproportionate number; the humiliation and domination of unequal relations; and the subjugation of women by the forces of control, greed, and lust. This intensification of suffering precludes a breakthrough into a new life of integration and affirmation, in which Teresa recognizes and claims her inner authority and refutes those who do not understand—or who intend to stop—her path.

Her soul's agony in the night of the feminine forces Teresa to confront and transform the violation of divine mercy and compassion in thought, word, and deed. God's endless capacity for benevolence, suffering, and gentleness stands in stark contrast to all that Teresa does to deny and oppress her nature. A woman's felt experience of her rejected humanity becomes Teresa's recognition of being brought to her own nothingness, as she embodies a divine-human suffering and a divine-human injustice interpreted through her own life experience. Teresa's trials are her own personal battle, but they also represent the pain of all women. Having once glimpsed her image in the divine mirror, Teresa cannot turn back on herself. She can never be free from having known the potential of the spirit and the great wonders that await her on the other side of everything partial and conditioned.

The night of the feminine is an inflow of God; it is God's desire to incarnate and restore in her the dignity and empowerment of her womanhood. It is thus an embodied dark night that takes Teresa back to the beginning—to a refiguring of the ground upon which she stands. It is a restructuring of a woman's being that takes place at a primary level—at the outflow of all our religions and spiritual traditions and definitions of the self. Teresa is taught not to transcend her doubt, persecution, aloneness, and worthlessness, but to feel and inquire into the nature of these emotions, to question and resist them fully, until she is able to realize the breakthrough that leads to dignity and self-worth. She is not to leave behind, forget, reject, or deny her pains, but to invite them in and offer them over to transformation, as Julian's sufferings are transfigured by Christ's dying love into "badges of honour."

In a life marked by frequent physical illness and immense inner fortitude, Teresa directed her exuberant energies to transform the inferior spiritual status of women. In her role as mother founder of seventeen women's monasteries, she reformed the Carmelite order to which she belonged and encouraged her religious sisters to transcend the stereotypes that afflicted a woman's self-awareness, ability to grow spiritually, and remembrance, knowledge, and love of God.

Heroic and Brave Night

Characteristics that distinguish the dark night of the feminine from the dark night proper are subtle and varied, because its most significant distinguishing feature—its embodied aspect—may be confused with St. John's work and appear to be another purification of the senses. Inseparably related to the whole transformative process the soul undergoes, a woman's suffering is further intensified by this confusion of signs. Feelings of pain, anguish, and loss associated with purgative contemplation are magnified. More radical still, the night of the feminine is the tearing up of the foundation upon which women's debasement has been constructed. Because the night of the feminine digs down into women's abused humanity and into the violation of women's divinity, its trials and pains extend from the rarified dimensions of consciousness into the deepest substratum of cellular memory. The pain of being "woman" that Teresa tries to transcend cannot be transcended in the feminine night. The detachment of the senses, considered to be a hallmark of spiritual maturity, is inoperable in this realm. A woman is not able to reject, suppress, or mystically override her soul wounds, but is compelled to feel them at a deeper level and to bear them until they bring forth the birth of her full humanity. Thus the feminine night is the gestational ground of the un-saying of "woman." In becoming nothing and letting go of all that identifies her, "she is emptying out the 'content' of the term 'woman' in the same way that the mystic empties out the content of the term 'God,' thus leaving it open—as a space of the unspeakable—to the possibilities of the 'truly other.'"[28]

This mystical emptying out of the term "woman" purifies and heals all the divisions within and outside us that prohibit the vulnerable, gentle, intimate, and loving from being received in our world. In a way perhaps unimagined and unnamed in the society to which Teresa belonged, the night of the feminine involves a bodily engagement with all of creation. In numerous texts, Christian mystics repeat the ancient formula of the "imitation of Christ" in both his incarnation and his death on the cross. While the human personality and the body are no doubt deeply affected by this, there is little explicit development of an embodied mysticism in these texts. Yet I contend that Teresa and many other women mystics of the medieval period were working out precisely the psychosomatic wholeness of embodying the mystery of the incarnation in the female body.[29] Our women mystics were challenged by their experiences of freedom to honor and accept the responsibility and awe of being integrated, spiritually whole women. In the dark night of the feminine, the reciprocity between human and divine is lived out and brought to consciousness, and the violence inflicted on the body of God in the female person and in the whole of creation is experienced.

In suffering the wounds of the world, women's natural intimacy is transformed. A certain naïve and intuitive connectedness with life is branded by the fire of women's pain and forged into word through women's mystical consciousness. The night of the feminine reorders being itself and leads to a new realized intimacy of God-women-creation. It is a new revelation of our incarnation in matter, and of the holiness of bodies—women, men, and all sentient life. It is a heroic and brave night, when the soul of women voluntarily gives up her natural and intrinsic intimacy with God to turn toward the world, suffer the marks of women's crucifixion, and heal the ancient fracture in our hearts. Women's dark night of the feminine heralds the lifting up of creation to a *realized intimacy* of the utter sanctity and beauty of life.

Feminist Spirituality as Dark Night

In seeking to understand the struggles contemporary women face, it is helpful to reflect upon them in light of Teresa's experience. Although the circumstances and context of Teresa's life vary widely from most women's lives today, the spiritual *processes* involved in her transformation of consciousness, especially in its purifying stages, are remarkably consistent.[30] As a tool of re-imagining, we can conceptualize feminist spirituality and theology as a collective journey into the "unsaying of 'woman'" and through the dark night of the feminine.[31]

As a collective active night, women pass through the sensory part of the soul where the accumulated memory of name and identity is held. Women struggle with a male God and patriarchal language, and with the intensely painful realization that they do not know who and what they are. Everything women have been told and everything they know spiritually does not function as it did before. Women's impasse raises questions about faith, the betrayal felt in the exclusiveness of religions, and the ways in which women have been pushed outside of religious institutions. To become self-reflective of their deepest nature, women have to interpret their reality through language structures that often belittle or silence them. The body, mental, emotional, and soul memory of women's domination, oppression, and silencing is felt. The five exterior and the three interior faculties must be harnessed and directed to women's highest nature.

Women are not alone in this struggle. At the beginning of *The Dark Night*, John depicts the person's efforts in the sensory night as guided by God's motherly cares. "With no effort on the soul's part," John writes, "God is handing the breast of His tender love to the soul, just as if it were a delicate child."[32] In the active night of the feminine, when a woman's soul turns away from pleasing the world on its terms and in its time, when she is aware that she must reject the bartering of her soul, God offers her tender loving kisses, and feeds, touches, and envelops her in caresses. In these moments of illumination, comfort is found in sisterhood, revolutionary rhetoric, and empowerment. As agents in the transformation of unjust and sinful social structures, women assert their right to educational, economic, and religious equality. New theological languages that include women and reform tradition, new metaphors and images for God, and the challenging task of fostering equality for women in all areas of life stir up profound societal change.

These spiritual gifts and delights do not go on forever, however, as the soul must be detached from its mother's care and forge its own path to God. Just when its consolations are most high and the soul is illuminated most brightly, God darkens all this light and prepares the soul to be strengthened. The soul of a woman is drawn into the passive night of the feminine, to that place where all names and images are an affront to the contemplative source she already is but does not yet consciously know or experience. A woman's prayer life wears thin, and although the dominance of patriarchal language and symbols gives way to an inclusiveness and even, in some cases, to new religions or the reaffirmation of one's birth religion, her soul is not at rest. At some fundamental level, at a depth that she cannot see or name, nothing has changed. As a woman she is not yet free.

While previously a woman transcended attachment to patriarchal religions through affirming her spiritual gifts and turning toward women's spirituality, now these consolations appear hollow and empty. Her soul is being separated from everything known, and in this sense from those spiritual things that are more intellective and sensory. A woman turns inward on her spiritual journey. The solace she used to find in her prayer life, sisterhood, or professional and personal accomplishments is taken away. Not only does she undergo a breakdown of everything known and experienced, but also her spiritual will—by which consciousness "inclines toward the good"—is marred by the experience of broken symbols and shattered hopes.[33] A woman's dark night requires a breaking and tearing of thought-patterns and ways of knowing and loving that perpetuate a fundamental falsehood that women *by nature* are less. Because she is unable to integrate her experience of divinity into women's preordained subordination, and unable to disaffect her from prior ways of knowing and being, a haunting dividedness assails a woman's spirit. In this night of the feminine, women are drawn into a mystical process that heals painful memories, restores lost faith, and leads to as yet unspoken, feminine dimensions of consciousness. This

pristine and uncreated word of the feminine restructures one's whole interpretation of reality. Yet bringing women's word into language and symbol is
arduous, wrenching, and fraught with fear. This night of coming-to-speech
is anguishing, for it raises a woman's fear of physical or spiritual annihilation—she *will* be killed—if she dares break the code of women's silencing
and subordination.

Thus, a woman cannot go back to what she was before having seen herself reflected in the mirror of the Feminine Divine, nor can she go forward
to incarnating her new self in form because the fundamental source of
her fractured self-image has yet to be healed. As a result, she now struggles
fiercely with the roots of her oppression. The inability to rest and continual
urges of needing to do more and to be more plague her spirit. In her
anguish and despair, a woman experiences loss of hope and disinterest in
prior ways of being and living. She also may experience a grief that cannot
be assuaged by belief in the future, and a gripping tension that demands
the birth of what authentically represents her true self. From a woman's
perspective, she must confront the purgative process of letting go of all the
images, understandings, and memories that do not name her. She must leave
behind mental and bodily cravings and learn a new way to God through the
loving path of contemplation. Because many women do not see themselves
reflected in God-images and theological languages, and do not feel self-love,
the way is very dark indeed.

To find their original, nonseparated being, women must bring their truth
to speech. Straddling past and future, women give away everything that
violates and suppresses their spirit to cross over to the divine possibility
already impregnated in them. In this passage to the not-yet, they embrace
the wound of being female in this world. They experience in some way
the history of feminine consciousness and the cellular memory of women's
bodies that have been brutalized and dominated throughout history yet
have survived with amazing alacrity and strength. With a resiliency and
a heroism that have given birth to all humans and have fostered creative
relationships with all life, a woman brings forth out of her deepest self the
possibility of divinity again and again. Her soul no longer experiences only
her personal history but "holds every woman before God, women of the
present and women of the past."[34]

Teresa's life helps us to understand why traditional maps of the spiritual journey are not completely effective for women. Unlike the characteristics associated with most descriptions of purgative experiences, Teresa

never feels abandoned by God. Instead, she anguishes over her inability to overcome her sense of worthlessness and to embody her true certainty and strength as a woman. She describes an invisible and internalized abuse that continually subverts her attempts at wholeness. Yet, despite her feelings of desolation and powerlessness, it is God within her who calls her to a mystical feminism—to liberate herself from the violent and punishing way in which we humans treat each other and creation.

The most revolutionary and difficult aspect of the feminine night for Teresa is the immensity of the divine benevolence she receives. Again and again, God refutes Teresa's attempts to ignore or override her deepest feelings, imprinting in her soul something more—a desire to deify herself and her world. In this mystic feminist journey of unsaying, Teresa seems to pass through crucifixion *and* resurrection, to take on all the marks of the *parousia* (presence or arrival), She who returns to lift our world up to its fullest potential. Not an apocalyptic vision of destruction, election, or privilege, it is a revolutionary realization of benevolence and beauty—of the Feminine Divine claim on creation that is imbedded deeply into our cells in love. The night of the feminine incites her conscience to assert the inherent dignity, worth, and holiness of her sisters and all women. The balm that bathes her soul in grace is restorative not only to her, but to everyone she meets and to divinity as well. Her healing *is* God's healing. As painful and radical as the night of the feminine is, it is the supreme experience of love that takes a woman back to the beginning and to the undefiled beauty of her original nature.

In sharing this conceptualization of the dark night of the feminine with others in classes, retreats, or spiritual dialogue, I find it has tremendous resonance in the spiritual lives of women and men who understand the kind of suffering John and Teresa recount, and who recognize the need for deeper healing. It speaks to what has been unspoken: how harshness and rejection of one another afflict our souls.

chapter eight

Subversion in Contemplation
Resistance, Resiliency,
and Dignification

St. Teresa is the perfect example of a woman, who, starting from zero
(by rejecting men's vantage point), interpreted her own experiences
and the world around her. It did not matter that her starting point
was obedience to male authority—the clerics who commanded her to
write—for St. Teresa "started obeying in order to disobey," to do things
her own way, and this is her greatest glory, not only as a woman, but as
a renewer of the language.[1]

The courage of Teresa, Julian, and other medieval women mystics remains
for us today a testimony to the strength of women's spirit. From them
we learn that even the deepest soul wounds are not outside God's activity. As
women risk the journey inward to the core of their beings, to confront their
demons of worthlessness and self-loathing, the Feminine Divine initiates a
transformation that is interior to their own depth. The pain that women
carry—this inner fracture from which they fear they will never be free—is
overturned by the example of the women mystics who were determined
to break down the stereotypes that conscripted them to marginalized roles,
and to thus uncover the original, true self. As an act of resistance against
centuries of anti-female spirituality, this is their most enduring contribution—to take the heroic risk that a life lived on the edge is the best life, for
it disturbs the status quo and claims a place for women becoming divine.

For Teresa, the deep sense of self-worth, mutuality, and dignity that she
finally accepts as her God-given inheritance is hard won. She discovers that
trust of her inner truth and protection of her dignity are the most difficult
aspects of the spiritual path for women. The experience of Divine Love,
which spills over as love for others and eventually leads to self-love, no
longer allows her to remain suppressed. Like Sophia, who cannot ultimately

137

be possessed or owned, no external agent, neither men nor the church, can keep Teresa from her ministry. For Teresa to be finally incapable of being subjugated—to be resistant, resilient, and dignified—struck fear in the organized forces of church and state. Because she recognizes that her prayer life is also political, she provides us with contemporary lessons in her commitment to the rights of women and to religious, social, and political reforms.

This affirmation of herself as a *woman* and her strong conviction in women's dignity and worth is passed on by Teresa to her monastic sisters. Affirmed by God as holy and good in her sexual identity, Teresa resists and repudiates the warnings of her confessors about self-deception, and their attacks against what they thought of as the dangers of women asserting authority. Brought to new frontiers of spiritual understanding by her intimate companionship with Jesus, Teresa no longer labors under a suspicion of subordination or inferiority. She obtains her freedom. This turning inward toward the true self—the self that is undefiled and free—becomes a vantage point of seeing from God's perspective. "The fact remains," writes Constance FitzGerald, "that Teresa was so affirmed as a woman by this 'Master of Wisdom'. . . that her view of herself changed, and she began to see women from the perspective of God."[2]

Teresa's search for a language to express what Antonio Pérez-Romero calls "her new, wild, and uncharted territory"—Teresa's personal transcendent experiences—took enormous courage "because she had to follow a voice higher than that of any man."[3] Without help or encouragement, and often facing the strictest ridicule and condemnation, she "conquered this territory, and charted and interpreted it, using feminine eyes, outlook, speech, and writing."[4] In the fiery crucible of her own agonizing struggle to bring into speech what she deeply knew and experienced, Teresa transmutes her personal desire for mystical union into a social commitment that champions women's worth and dignity. Her life was a studied attempt to obey and disobey, as she taught her sisters to value the mystical life over religious authority, and to develop inner certainty through divine grace. Overflowing from a radical encounter with truth, contemplative prayer led these women to forge new spiritual lineages and to champion mystical practices that fostered the transformation of the social and ecclesial order. Intimately they knew, and often practiced in subversion, that contemplation conceals an explosive force of positive social transformation.

In their efforts to bring mysticism into the mainstream of women's lives, reject the strict asceticism that bound women's monastic communities, and uphold the value and primacy of direct experience over the intellectual monopoly of "men of letters," Teresa and her sisters unleashed a revolutionary power. These women realized that the source of their wisdom, strength, creativity, and spiritual equality arose precisely because of their abandonment to the wellspring of contemplation. Upholding tradition, but at the same time demanding a moral accounting of institutional sin, women mystics pioneered a protofeminist transformation of the social and political climate of Europe. Like the Taoist philosophers Lao Tzu and Chuang Tze, women mystics discovered that weak conquers might, humility overcomes pride, and purity of heart overturns hierarchy, orthodoxy, and law.

Spiritual Climate of Teresa's Spain

As one of the few socially sanctioned escapes from anti-female cultures, for many medieval women the decision to become nuns was not solely spiritual but also included an equally compelling protest against dominant social and cultural norms. Graphically represented by the walls of the monastic enclosure, the attraction of solitude and silence had a far greater and more expansive symbolic and psychic dimension. Freeing women from stereotypical gender roles as wives, mothers, and caregivers, the monastery protected women from marriage and the real threat of psychological and sometimes bodily death. It also gave women access to study, knowledge, and learning normally reserved for males, and provided them with authority and prestige unthinkable to the majority of their nonreligious female contemporaries. Denied formal learning, women mystics nonetheless legitimized their teachings based on prayer, spiritual wisdom, and holy visions. Through church-sanctioned obedience, the transmission of their religious writings, formation of monastic houses, and development of new spiritual lineages were fostered, giving voice to women's religious, spiritual, social, and political concerns.

Large shifts in cultural history were working themselves out during the formative period of medieval women's mysticism. In Teresa's Spain, the forces of Renaissance humanism and Reformation thought were vying for dominance and control, as the full thrust of the Catholic Counter-Reformation was being played out during her lifetime. Most compelling was the gradual shift toward greater lay participation in reading scripture and the democratization of worship that characterized the idealism of Luther, Erasmus, Agrippa, and others. At the beginning of the sixteenth century, Christian humanists defended the rights of women to study scripture and participate in evangelical democratization. The new religiosity that swept Europe deprivileged Latin as the language of religion, thus removing the male priests' monopoly over its interpretation. New religious thinking also demystified official or orthodox knowledge, "the elaborate intellectual construction that had conspired to make religion the special preserve of the hierarchy—and its representatives—the theologians. By proclaiming that everyone—even uncultured women—could have direct, experiential, and powerful knowledge of the Divinity,"[5] these new religious movements were depriving the traditional church of its centuries-old exclusive claims to control religion and the practices of the faithful.

According to Pérez-Romero, the traditional Catholicism of Teresa's day looked at mysticism with great suspicion, and imposed certain unwritten guidelines that it must follow to be tolerated. Included among these conditions was that mysticism had to be worked out within the framework of traditional church hierarchies. For most of its history, contemplative prayer had been viewed as an esoteric way followed by cloistered friars and nuns. In light of this history, it was perceived as a very arduous path, followed by members of contemplative orders capable of maintaining a life of strict asceticism. Mystical pursuits must be contained within the walls of convents and monasteries, along with the maintenance of church sacraments and rituals. But in the religious renewal that swept through sixteenth-century Spain, contemplative prayer "burst through the walls of convents and monasteries, and was adopted as a lay path."[6] Practitioners outside the established hierarchy were claiming to reach mystical union with the divine, and to have found an experience that was "profoundly liberating, curative, and empowering."[7]

In her book *Teresa of Avila and the Rhetoric of Femininity*, Alison Weber recounts how Cardinal Ximenez Cisneros effected radical change in early-sixteenth-century Spain by advocating the translation of scripture and spiritual texts into Spanish and distributing them to religious houses. "The accessibility of works of St. Catherine of Siena, Saint Claire, Saint Juana de Orvieto, Gerson, and St. John Climaco in the vernacular," Weber writes, "meant that many more women were inspired to participate in the wave of new evangelism."[8] The quality of this mystical knowledge of the divine seemed to downgrade or even dismiss the authority and importance of the Christian tradition, and of speculative, theoretical, and nonexperiential knowledge. "It was upon these latter kinds of knowledge," Pérez-Romero contends, "that the traditional hierarchical Church based its authority, primacy, and supremacy."[9] Thus as Cisneros's reform swept through Spain, groups of laity and religious (men and women) began to meet in private homes. Because they held in common the belief that scripture could be understood through the Holy Spirit without the mediation of clerical authorities, they came increasingly under suspicion by the church. Given the derogatory name *alumbrados* (Illuminists), the movement also was distinguished by the number of *conversos* and women in its ranks.

Two years after Teresa was born, Weber continues, "a confluence of events—the death of Cisneros in 1517 and the beginnings of Luther's rebellion in the same year, the growing suspicion of Erasmian anticlericalism, and the intensification of anti-*converso* racism—moved the Inquisition to repress what it could only define as a native protestantism in the making."[10]

The Threat of Prayer

The constant interplay of disclosure and concealment that marks Teresa's life and texts attests to her personal involvement in the religious questions sweeping through Europe. The deep division between theologians attached to universities and spiritual men of prayer splintered Christian thought and practice, and found its way into the more subtle aspects of Teresa's spiritual life. On one side, the theologians and intellectuals "distrusted prayer, and spoke deprecatingly of the mystical life, especially when promoted among women."[11] Ever conscious of heresies that might disturb the hierarchical church or royal ideology, Teresa (along with John of the Cross, Ignatius of Loyola, and other mystics) was under suspicion all her life. "The spiritual men, on the other hand," writes Kieran Kavanaugh, "looked down on theologians as professionals in the letter of the law but lacking in spirit; they grimaced at any mention of the competence of these men in spiritual matters and declared them to be inept in the business of guiding souls."[12] As we have seen, many of Teresa's spiritual directors and confessors were incapable of guiding her soul, subjecting her most sacred experiences to concerns unrelated to the movement of the spirit in her. So frightened had the church powers become, that contemplative prayer was feared as the possible downfall of the Christian republic, and as grounds for closing universities and books. Kavanaugh's understanding of the conflict, found in the introduction to Teresa's *Collected Works*, is worth quoting at length:

> The intellectualist tendency, spearheaded by the schools of Salamanca and by Dominican theologians, was definitely assumed and imposed

as the norm of the Inquisition. Two of the more notorious among the theologians were the formidable Dominican, Melchior Cano, and the Archbishop of Seville and Supreme Inquisitor, Fernando Valdes. Cano taught that the practice of mental prayer was a danger not only for the church but for the Christian republic as well. . . . He reasoned that since it is impossible to devote oneself to both the active and the contemplative life, colleges and universities would have to be suppressed, books closed, and studies annihilated if all were to dedicate themselves to prayer.[13]

In 1559, Fernando Valdes published an index of forbidden spiritual books written by contemporary Spanish authors and well-known classical writers. Many of these texts were among Teresa's favorites. Despite the Inquisition and the index, however, Teresa does little to conceal her belief that mystical prayer is the superior path to perfection. To combat the prevailing mood, contemporary scholars contend that Teresa develops a distinctive literary style as a foil to the inquisitional temperament. She uses in her writings a "rhetoric of femininity" to depreciate her wisdom and exercise her authority, alternately depicting herself as a weak and foolish woman or as a prophetic voice in the spiritual wilderness.[14] The journey inward toward self-knowledge and divine union emboldens Teresa, freeing her to claim that in prayer God is found very deep within one's soul. "Within oneself," she writes, "very clearly is the best place to look; and it's not necessary to go to heaven, nor any further than our own selves; for to do so is to tire the spirit and distract the soul, without gaining as much fruit."[15] As she deepens her commitment to contemplative prayer, she simultaneously strengthens her resolve concerning the importance, power, and goodness of her message to change the status of females and remedy social injustices. The fire burning inside her could not be contained within the relative barrier of stone walls. As she turns her burning sight toward the rights and sufferings of others, Teresa champions the social good as a necessary obligation born of deep and surrendered contemplation. Recognizing the heavenly gift she receives through prayer, she finally leaves aside the critique of learned men, "for the soul sees that in an instant it is wise; the mystery of the Blessed Trinity and other sublime things are so explained that there is no theologian with whom it [the soul] would not dispute in favor of the truth of these grandeurs." Later on, in the same text, she also confirms: "I know through experience that what I say is true."[16]

In numerous ways, Teresa extols the virtue of her way of prayer and emphasizes that it is the superior path to perfection. She speaks of the power of inner prayer to obtain such freedom in the soul "that everything I see her below seems loathsome when compared to the excelling and beautiful qualities I beheld in this Lord."[17] She elevates contemplation over the monopoly of the intellect, because nothing is impossible in God, even "that the Lord makes a little old woman wiser, perhaps, in this science than he [the Dominican Garcia de Toledo] is, even though he is a very learned man."[18] Against the threat of the Inquisitors, who take away her books and suppress her authority, Teresa insists that God—only God (not men)—teaches her everything on the mystical path. Betraying a fierce independence of thought and conviction, Teresa even dismisses the power of these men to name and control her inner life: "It would be pretty bad for my soul if there were something in it [her writing] of the sort that I should have to fear the inquisition; that I thought that if I did have something to fear I'd go myself to seek out the inquisitors; and that if I were accused, the Lord would free me, and I would be the one to gain."[19]

In her *Way of Perfection*, Teresa tackles the Inquisitional threat directly, maintaining her right to authorize her contemplative teaching on prayer. "Well, what is this Christians," she chides, "that you say mental [interior] prayer isn't necessary?"[20] Teresa even urges her sisters to not pay any attention "to the fears they [men] raise or to the picture of the dangers they paint for you."[21] And with a humorous aside, she says: "Hold fast, daughters, for they cannot take from you the Our Father, and the Hail Mary."[22] Kavanaugh comments: "Here the censor, quick to catch the point, intervened and, going a step further than his usual method of simply crossing out the passage, wrote in the margin: 'It seems she is reprimanding the Inquisitors for prohibiting books on prayer.'"[23]

Men of Letters and the Subversion of the Intellect

It is no secret that institutional power in medieval church and state was closely tied to control over literacy and the dissemination of information. Women were kept ignorant of the language that men of letters read and discoursed. Not only did Teresa of Avila not read Latin, the language of most theological texts, but she was also banned from reading vernacular books by the Index of 1559. In her anguish over this loss of her great love of reading, Teresa takes her woes to Jesus, who tells her to forget the edicts of men, for all she needs to learn will be taught to her from an interior source. "The Lord said to me," Teresa recounts in her *Book of Her Life*, "don't be sad, for I shall give you a living book. . . . Afterward, . . . I received so much to think about and such recollection in the presence of what I saw, and the Lord showed so much love for me by teaching me in many ways, that I had little or almost no need for books. His Majesty had become the true book in which I saw the truths."[24] This theme of interior wisdom as a truly superior way of knowing becomes a central theme in Teresa's life and teachings.

Perhaps it is easy to dismiss Teresa's insistence on the primacy of infused knowing as solely the result of cultural and religious prohibitions against women's education in Spanish society, or to insist that, had women had access to academic and intellectual resources, they would have preferred the scholarly to the mystical life. Without a doubt, women's writings would have taken on a different character had they been filtered through the language of academic knowledge. There is no way to know with certainty what Teresa would have communicated or how her writing would have differed had she possessed a formal theological education. But it is clear that she was very aware of this battle waging between intellectual and spiritual men, and placed herself solidly on the side of spiritual wisdom.

While Teresa did not disparage or dismiss scholarly learning, she saw from her contemplative vantage point that mystical knowing is not the stepchild of the rational mind, but a superior type of knowing that informs all other forms of knowledge. As receptive, nondual, and unself-interested, Teresa considered mystical knowledge to be the surest and most true perspective, for it alone mirrors reality itself. As participatory knowledge, mystical knowing implies that there is a reciprocal relationship between the capacity to be vulnerable, intimate, and loving and the ability to perceive new meaning, value, and interpretation. There is ample evidence to suggest that Teresa was only too aware of the distraction—and often the destruction—that was a product of the academic schools of her time. Among these we have to include not only the great movements for reform and illumination, but also the incredibly dark and cruel reasons used to conscript theology in the service of inquisitions, crusades, witch burning, wife beating, and other violent sides of human nature. Visionary knowledge, infused contemplation, and silent words from God, while needing to be measured against scripture, confessors, and learned authorities, had an advantage over official and intellectual knowing. For Teresa, mystical knowing was rooted in humility (which guards against the pride and fanaticism that fuels harsh decisions and extreme movements); it was pointedly concerned for the "other" and not for the self alone; it was passive, nondual, and receptive; it was centered in the heart, and thus taught a form of knowing that was loving, compassionate, and merciful; and it was devoid of desire for honor, wealth, social status, or esteem.

The protests made by Teresa and other women mystics that they were ignorant, illiterate, or unlettered concealed a double message that was in part real and in part a rhetorical strategy. From an official perspective, these disclaimers protected Teresa from the Inquisitional authorities. But they also promoted her bold insistence on the subversive value of experiential knowledge. Keenly aware of the "great illusion in which we walk and the blindness we suffer," she chides priests and kings to see how paltry their desire for great domination is in comparison to the exalted gifts found in the highest states of infused prayer.[25] "Oh, how fit a state this is for kings!" Teresa writes. "How much more worthwhile it would be for them to strive for this stage of prayer rather than for great domination! What righteousness there would be in the kingdom! What evils they would avoid and have avoided! In this stage one does not fear to lose one's life or honor for the love of God! . . . In spite of what I am, I experience great consuming impulses to tell these truths to those who are rulers. O my God!"[26]

Teresa's attempt to create a language that would be worthy of her experience also is a source of anguish. Painfully aware of the difficulties in translation between mystical insight and the written text, she labors to bring into speech her mystical experiences and commentaries on scriptures, acts of teaching and preaching prohibited by men. "For a long time," she confesses, "even though God favored me, I didn't know what words to use to explain His favors: and this is no small trial. For it is one grace to receive the Lord's favor, another, to understand which favor and grace it is; a third, to know how to describe it."[27] Confused and seduced by patriarchal language and intellectual categories to abandon and reject her way, Teresa cautions her sisters that to succumb to the language of letters is the deepest form of self-betrayal that can only lead to pain. In the *Way of Perfection*, Teresa confides in her sisters to leave behind common language and the foreign words of men: "God is your business and your language. Whoever wants to speak to you must learn this language; and if he doesn't, be on your guard that you don't learn his; it will be hell." Nor should they be concerned that they sound illiterate or hypocritical.

> If they should think you're unsophisticated, what does it matter? If they take you for hypocrites, it matters even less. You will gain in that no one will want to see you except the one who understands this language . . . for to begin to speak a new language would cause no small amount of harm, and all your time would be spent in learning it. And you cannot know as I do, for I have experience of it, the great evil this new language is for the soul; in order to know the one, the other

is forgotten. The new language involves a constant disturbance from which you ought to flee at all costs, for what is suited to this path that we are beginning to discuss is peace and tranquility of soul. If those who speak with you wish to learn your language, though it is not your business to teach anyone, you can tell about the riches that are gained in learning it.[28]

Because mystical language was a powerful tool of personal authority, Teresa came under increasing pressure to repudiate her visions. At one point, fearing that the devil is leading her astray, Teresa's confessors even instruct her to use a cross to drive away her visions of Jesus. She acquiesces. Overcome with remorse by this act, Teresa turns again to prayer, where she finds comfort in Jesus, who tells her "to tell them that now what they were doing was tyranny. He gave me signs for knowing that the vision was not from the devil."[29] FitzGerald contends: "This challenges Teresa to accept her own humanity but also the integration of many seeming contradictory elements in her life: outer obedience with inner freedom and certitude; conflict and opposition with genuine maturation; personal autonomy and strength with fidelity and surrender in relationship; inner light with inner darkness."[30]

We have seen in Julian, as well, an emphasis on the power and importance of spiritual language over the book of learning. Julian's convictions about her locutions (silent words from God—her inner voice) resemble what Teresa of Avila has to say about her own experiences of such silent words from God. These silent words "are very distinctly formed, much more clearly understood than if heard by ear, of themselves convincing that they come from God, carrying authority, producing sudden changes in the soul, persisting in the memory. All these are indeed Julian's beliefs about the 'words formed in her understanding.'"[31] Through the "eyes of the soul" Teresa learns everything. In her visions, locutions, and infused prayer, a higher form of language is impressed upon the intellect "with such clear knowledge that I don't think it can be doubted."[32] It is radically experiential and so profound that it "is a language that belongs so to heaven that here on earth it is poorly understood, no matter how much we desire to tell about it, if the Lord does not teach us by experience."[33] Through the various mediums of knowing that Teresa employed—visions, locutions, bodily illness, soul suffering, prayer, meditation, fasting—she tapped into a participatory knowing, which was an "unknowing" that pierced through and informed everything.

Democratizing of Contemplation

Given the religious and political climate, Teresa's insistence that her way of prayer was superior to that obtained through officially sanctioned methods controlled by an elite priestly class was a bold and dangerous stand. In *The Book of Her Life*, she recounts and acclaims mystical prayer as the way to salvation. By establishing her contemplative teachings as a faster and more reliable way to achieve divine knowledge, Teresa authorizes a female lineage of contemplatives and subverts men's monopoly over spiritual affairs. The emphasis she places on the deeper states of passive contemplation reverses women's subordinate roles and democratizes mysticism. Teresa's four degrees of prayer are a direct path to God and a deeper penetration into the mystery of the receptive nature of the divine, where God and the soul share a mutuality and equality of energies and being. In the intimate friendship she shares with God, Teresa gradually learns to take authority away from external agents or social contracts—church, priests, book learning—and places it instead in a woman's inner life. Infused prayer not only has spiritual potency, leading the devoted soul to the marriage bed of its Beloved, it also has social and political ramifications.

In defense of her way of prayer, Teresa is consistent and careful to emphasize its passive character. As detailed in previous chapters, this receptive or passive prayer symbolizes everything that is suspect to church-sanctioned orthodoxy. True knowing comes directly from God. It is not subject to the authority or censorship of men. God and only God, like a great and loving mother, teaches Teresa everything about the mystical life and the journey of perfection. Further, the soul learns in surrender, without any effort on its part. "An infant doesn't understand how it grows nor does it know how it gets it milk," she instructs, "for without its sucking or doing anything, often the milk is put into its mouth. Likewise, here, the soul is completely ignorant. It knows neither how nor from where that great blessing came to it, nor can it understand."[34]

This resting in God, in which the soul can *do* nothing on its own but receive the gift of love, heals the split stamped into a woman's soul that she is merely an imperfect male who can never do enough to repay her debt or to reclaim her corrupted, forbidden nature. In direct refutation of church prohibition against women teachers, Teresa spends the beginning chapters of *The Book of Her Life* telling how her way of prayer leads to Christian salvation. By establishing contemplation as the heart of women's freedom and salvation, Teresa reclaims women's right to name themselves as equals in love. The person who achieves the great delights that result from diligent practice of her way of prayer discovers the gift of her own being. In finding her true self-image in the image of her divine Beloved, Teresa encourages others to obtain the total purity, liberation, peace, equality, intimacy, and mutuality that God bestows on her intimate friends.

For Teresa, the wisdom received in these passive nights of prayer is unimaginable, and cannot be gained by official ideology or the language of scholastic theology. It is the true source of women's strength, empowerment, confidence, and will toward justice. In this democratizing of contemplation, Teresa encouraged *conversos* to join her monasteries, counseled male confessors and spiritual friends, and opened wide the horizon for women to pursue a life of wisdom, teaching, and social change. "She did all the forbidden things," writes Pérez-Romero. "She taught and expounded the Christian mysteries, and gave authority to her discourse, contributing to religious culture; and she founded convents where her nuns could follow her path, carving out spaces where females could put their talents into practice, thus creating female culture or intellectual communities."[35]

Dignification of Women

As women mystics in societies acutely suspicious of females and contemplation, Julian and Teresa confronted their subordination and disempowerment as women. This confrontation becomes one of their most enduring contributions, in which they reveal the soul wounds that generate moral weakness and failure, and the contemplative processes that move them from fragmentation to wholeness, dignity, and empowerment.

If the goal of the mystical life is to become divine, something that Julian and Teresa both longed and prayed for with fervor and intention, then whatever impedes that realization is against ethics. The ethic of perfection that fuels our mystics' longing is dynamically related to and culminates in an ethic of dignification. To love as God loves requires a healing of the wounds that fracture self-love and divide a person against herself. In becoming divine, women mystics must suffer the reign of self-violence, of an internalized social self-hate. Julian and Teresa cannot share in the fullness of an integrated intimacy without accepting their self-worth and equality in the eyes of God.

As discussed above, Julian conceptualizes this journey through Jesus Sophia, the motherhood of God. The subtlety and nuance of her awareness and critique of women's status are illustrative of the importance Julian places on the empowerment that comes from embracing women's vision of reality. In Teresa, however, we have traced a distinct women's battle with spiritual oppression. In her negotiation of the soul's journey, Teresa draws away from conventional definitions of women's spiritual benefits as well as from traditional women's roles. As she matures in her spiritual life, Teresa confronts a deeper and more radical fracture that inhabits her consciousness, and battles to recognize the misogyny that is at the bottom of her self-doubt and feeling of worthlessness as a woman. This brokenness is further instigated by the assault on Teresa's spiritual life by powerful male confessors intent on keeping her subordinated, but is healed as she passes through the dark night of the feminine and into the blinding love of dignity and communion, alone with her Beloved.

Through the freedom Teresa obtains by being chosen by God, she turns her attention to the situation of her world, in which she played a dynamic role. As mother founder, Teresa traveled widely, bought and sold property, reviewed legal documents, encouraged and supported her newly established monasteries, and battled those who tried to discourage or derail her intentions. She had a keen nose for business affairs, and for the folly of men. She was equally astute about her own shortcomings and blind spots.

> It [my soul] deplores the time when it was concerned about its reputation and deplores the deception it suffered in believing that what the world called honor was honor. It sees how this belief about honor is the greatest lie and that all are involved in it. . . . The soul laughs to itself over the time when it esteemed money and coveted it. . . . What is it we buy with this money we desire? Is it something valuable? Is it something lasting? Oh, why do we desire it? Miserable is the rest achieved that costs so dearly. . . . Oh, if everyone would consider it unprofitable dirt, how harmoniously would the world proceed, how many lawsuits would be avoided! What friendship there would be among all if there were no self-interest about honor and money! I think this absence of self-interest would solve all problems.[36]

In her later works, Teresa introduces the theme of the empowerment and dignification of women through highlighting the great perfection and virtue that her nuns were able to achieve. Teresa wants her sisters to achieve spiritual discipleship, as she herself aspires to be an apostle who brings souls to God.[37] Her longing to have her petitions of mercy and justice heard ignites her texts; at the same time Teresa is acutely aware of the negative judgment levied against her and her sisters. "Is it not enough, Lord," she writes, "that the world has intimidated us [women] . . . so that we may not do anything worthwhile for You in public or dare speak some truths that we lament over in secret, without Your also failing to hear so just a petition? I do not believe, Lord, that this could be true of Your goodness and justice, for You are a just judge and not like those of the world. Since the world's judges are sons of Adam and all of them men, there is no virtue in women that they do not hold suspect."[38]

Teresa's attempts to make actual an ethics of perfection and ennoblement are most apparent in *The Book of Her Foundations*, in which she chronicles the formation of her monasteries. She wishes to lift up human reality to reflect the experiences of love, mercy, and compassion that she perceived in her mystical visions. Against the harsh treatment of women and girls, Teresa would pit the final test of love, in which she was taught by Love itself the worth God bestows on women. Through her community of sisters, she repels the injustice and violence against women and resists the social order by harvesting her mystical knowledge for political purposes. In response to the cultural preference for males, Teresa extols the virtues of women and the shame of parents who do not know of "the great blessings that can come to them through daughters or of the great sufferings that can come from sons."[39]

An astute observer and critic of the social order, Teresa chafed under a system in which money, honor, and prestige were seen to be the heights of sophistication. She contrasted this ignorance with the truth of the soul's equality in the Divine Heart, and she actualized this insight by recognizing that "lineage and social status mattered not at all in the judgment of God."[40] Teresa describes a number of women who desired to be monastics and were whipped and punished by their families, or who disfigured themselves in order to avoid marriage. The conversion of one of these women, Catalina Godinez, gave Teresa "a new definition of lineage" that passed from the material and economic to the spiritual.[41] Teresa recounts how after Catalina Godinez read the inscription on a crucifix, "the Lord worked a complete change in her. She [Godinez] had been thinking of a marriage that was being sought for her, which was better than she could have hoped for, and saying to herself, 'With what little my father is content, that I become connected with an entailed estate; I am thinking of becoming the origin of a new line of descendents.'"[42]

In addition to contributing to the renewal of the Carmelite Order, Teresa also helped *conversos* by admitting them into her monasteries on the basis of their piety and suitability for the religious life, accepted their financial and logistical support, and afforded their families the social prestige and religious consolation that derived from endowing religious institutions.[43] Replacing the material basis for prestige and wealth with a spiritual one, Teresa would have agreed with Julian that all our sufferings would be turned into honors.[44] The radicalness of this insight bore heroic deeds in her. Teresa's contemplative life led her to be a champion of social and religious reforms, and to set the foundation for a new social order in which all were to be equal. Constance FitzGerald contends:

> Her fearless struggle to destroy concern for honor and wealth, and therefore uphold the value of the person over money and ancestry, her unswerving struggle for the recognition of women's rights to deep interior prayer and therefore to significant service in the Church at the time of great ecclesial danger and turmoil: these constituted the framework on which she built her renewal of the Carmelite Order in the sixteenth century Church, as well as her teaching on prayer, wholeness, and union with God.[45]

Intimacy and love for the world exerted a powerful influence on healing the roots of violence that generated suffering and diminished Julian and Teresa as women in society and church. In effect, identification with Jesus' suffering face and mothering love becomes the force that compels them toward healing the wounds that inhabit their consciousness, as well as the spiritual and social pains of others. From mystical intimacy, Julian and Teresa discover God's equality of love, as they reach out to uphold this ethic of loving the world into being. But deeper still, they confront the primacy of dignity as an ethic that must become part of the social good. It is not enough to experience the heights of mystical union; this experience must become the fire that burns away the dross of inferiority, self-loathing, and doubt. Julian and Teresa risk bearing the divinity of the world. The ethics of perfection, as they journey toward becoming divine, culminates for them in an ethic of dignification, in which they assert their spiritual authority as the impetus for church and societal reform. "There are many more women than men," Teresa confides, "to whom the Lord grants these [spiritual] favors. This I heard from the saintly Friar Peter of Alcantara—who said that women make much more progress along this path than men do. He gave excellent reasons for this, all in favor of women; but there's no need to mention them here."[46]

Part Three

Embodied and Engaged Contemplation

chapter nine

Women's Body as Mystical Text

For he [God] does not despise what he has made, nor does he disdain to serve us in the simplest natural functions of our body, for love of the soul which he created in his own likeness. For as the body is clad in cloth, and the flesh in skin, and the bones in the flesh, and the heart in the trunk, so are we, soul and body, clad and enclosed in the goodness of God. . . . That is to say, there is no created being who can know how much and how sweetly and tenderly the Creator loves us.[1]

In this and the following two chapters I attempt to write from women's divinity, from the undefiled place of women's holiness and dignity. Not as seekers on the way but as women who are found; not as victims but as women who have the strength to transform themselves and the world. This type of vision has a prophetic edge to it. It can never remain in the purely ethereal or personal realm, but always spills over into a concern for the world and its injustices, troubles, and woes. This vision is an insight into what breaks our hearts open and calls us to something greater than we believe ourselves capable of being. Some may consider it highly ideological or rare. But I find that only when we express what profoundly touches us, do we actually find what is most human in us.

There are limits to my rendering. First, the perspective I take here is not primarily psychological or theological, but mystical. I begin from the premise expounded by Julian, Teresa, and other mystics that the core of the person is always one with its divine source. From a mystical vantage point, to be "awake" is to be aware and always striving for the greatest actualization of this unity. It is my intention to engage with vital questions concerning our responsibility for, and love of, the world: How is women's presence on earth, on the level of body, society, and world, a labor toward and living out of this profound ontological unity? How do our actions honor, or commit crimes against, the mystical interdependence of life? What kind of impact does violence against women exert on this interior communion, this loving dance of spirit and matter? How does it expand or contract the consciousness of divine presence on earth? Further, as an indivisible extension in time and space of this primary spiritual communion between women and God, what metaphors and images assist women in re-imagining the holiness of the female body?

A second premise is that no explanation, metaphor, vision, or description can be exhaustive. My attempt to write about the mystical implications of women's embodiment is one contribution to fostering women's agency in the world. It represents a partial view, only one way of seeing and knowing the great potential that awaits us. I put a magnifying glass on a specific type of reading—a mystical reading—that keeps attention focused on the process that honors and furthers the reciprocal longing between divinity and humanity.

Mysticism, of course, is always imbedded in a concrete historical context. My third premise, therefore, is that this mystical interpretation is not meant to exclude or deny the historical, cultural, or theological debt owed. But the complex interrelationship of social, cultural, and religious issues imbedded in mystical discourse prohibits more than a partial development in such a short space. Whether females and males are constituted differently has been argued from both sides. My intention is to find ways of reading the mystical as a serious source of theological reflection on women's bodies without sentimentalizing or essentializing them. The mystical is always searching for a prior unity that is hidden in, and embodied by, the diverse and magnificent variety and differences that make up creation. The idea that mysticism advances unity at the expense and necessary awareness of our differences is to misapprehend what "oneness" means. As a quality of consciousness and a state of heart that perceives the indivisible stream of life energies as holy and worthy of awe, oneness is the animating force of everything. It is a challenge for the rational mind fed on subject-object thought to maintain the irreducible paradox of oneness and diversity in balance with each other. In singling out the body of women as mystical, I do not exclude male bodies or the bodies of other life forms, but hold them in this unity. Each body defies universalization; each body in its uniqueness and particularity is the presence of the sacred. Due to the history of crimes against females, however, women are frequently trapped in cultural matrices that encourage and perpetuate contempt for female bodies. It is thus crucial to women's *full presence* on earth that they understand, in order not to undermine, how divine revelation expresses itself in and through female bodies. Reading God's presence through the body of women is the writing of women's divinity in the world.

Symbolic Representations of Women's Body

Women live with an intuitive, if unrealized, sense of the mystical. They consistently display qualities of consciousness depicted as divine or holy: interdependence, mutuality, intimacy, pathos, moral outrage, passionate pain, righteous anger, caring, courage, compassion, and unself-interested love. They also participate in life processes and roles associated with awe, mystery, magic, and transcendence: biologically through menses, pregnancy, birth, and lactation; as midwives, mothers, clergy, and caregivers; and as visionaries, shamans, mystics, prophets, and saints. Yet most women, even those who have made a conscious choice to pursue an awakened life, do not imagine themselves as spiritually integrated with their bodies. The deeply ingrained division between spirit and flesh is so profoundly identified with females that it has maintained a pervasive influence on women's lives, despite the work of spiritual feminisms, goddess traditions, and other philosophies that affirm the sacredness of the female body.

Bringing the intuitively mystical into conscious awareness necessitates a new reading of the body as the site of an embodied mysticism. Contemporary scholarship emphasizes how experience of our bodies not only is filtered through its material existence but also is organized by cultural representations of them. The material body is thus one of those discursive practices that is "not universal but [has] historical specificity. It is itself a sign imbued with meaning that can be glossed."[2] Western representations of the body perpetuate an antiquated suspicion of the flesh and, by association, of the female person. Throughout this history, despite cultural and religious variations, women's bodies have been effectively desacralized, treated as biologically inferior, morally corrupt, and wantonly carnal. Mikhail Bakhtin argued that two antithetical representations of the body—the classical and the grotesque—structure discursive norms in Western culture. These two bodily representations never existed except as cultural norms, but they nonetheless provoked or promoted an idealized or debased relationship to the body.

In medieval culture, the classical body was male, harmonious, unified, proportionate, spiritual, and pure; it was free of pain, limitation, or decay. Women and other marginalized social groups and classes were associated with the grotesque body and its material orifices, fluids, and filth. As representative of the grotesque body, women were disproportionate, heterogeneous, profane, sinful, congenitally impure, and deserving of punishment. Despite its association with the lower bodily functions, the grotesque body depicted in numerous mystical and literary texts also had the capacity to regenerate. It was unfinished and open to the world, by contrast with the classical body, represented as sealed and formally perfect.[3]

Yet neither of these cultural representations accounts for another and more potent mystical reading of women's bodies. In oral, native cultures all over the world, spiritual traditions existed (and still do today in selective areas) that honored female embodiment. Through veneration of the goddess, ritualizing of female biological processes, and respect for the maternal productivity of the earth, women were associated with divine female power. Spiritual feminists, especially those working in goddess traditions, have retrieved and expanded on this ancient tradition of female sacredness. Countering negative cultural stereotypes, they affirm the closeness of the divine in the natural processes of women's body. It is a worldview in which the biological functions of the female body are both metaphors and manifestations of a divine fecundity imaged as female. In goddess feminism, "a woman's embodied finitude is holy in that it belongs to the intramundane processes of divine creativity: there is no division of the spiritual and the profane; all is related in the universe, and none stands apart from nature."[4] By associating women's embodied finitude with the sacred, women become the locus and medium of the holy. Their participation in the natural processes of divine creativity also signifies their capacity to make the divine intimately present in our world. As Meinrad Craigheid writes, "we may apprehend the incarnate presence of the holy in all of creation. Through them God our Mother communicates with us through her body, within her own mysterious creation."[5]

This sacral reading of the female body begins from a different premise than the one promoted in classical Christian thought. It functions from a primary vision of goodness, wholeness, and dignity seeking to be expressed and met. The female body is not a defiled spirit or a carnal object needing to be tamed, but is integral to the flourishing of creation. As a miracle of atomic, cellular ingenuity, the female body "marks the passage of the sacred through the world in the numinosity of her experience of its continuous change: conception, birth (not only babies), ageing or decay, death, rotting, and rebirth in to non-human life forms."[6] This generative, coequal, and mutual interdependence of spirit and body expresses a fundamental good-ness that Western society and women have learned to reject. Although the labor of becoming divine is played out daily in women's lives, the wisdom of women's bodily holiness is effectively absent from dominant cultural discourses. Unnamed and ignored, an entire level of interpretation, caring, and responsibility is prevented from restoring a vision of bodily-spiritual wholeness to our collective consciousness.

Spiritual feminists have contributed enormously to our understanding of the ways in which the divine is made present through female immanence. Broadly defined, "immanence" refers to the presence of the sacred within the world and its inhabitants. It is a concept primarily directed to the world in which we live, insofar as it is through life on earth that we participate in the spirit. "Transcendence," by contrast, is a term used to distinguish the divine from creation and to maintain an ultimate difference between the two. As a response to the excessive transcendence of Western patriarchal theologies, spiritual feminists bring a much-needed correction to centuries of false and painful depictions of women's bodies as debased spirit. At the same time, spiritual feminists also are critiqued for confusing the boundaries between God and creation, and for perpetuating the claim of private revela-tion over against institutional religious forms.

A mystical reading of women's body expands on the work of spiritual feminists by paying special attention to the interplay of the transcendent or mystical aspects of female embodiment. I use the concept of transcendence in a particular way: as a sign not of divine distance but of divine closeness. Here transcendence is understood from the perspective of immanence; that is, it signifies how the body is always seeking to communicate its divine origins. Through mystical processes and spiritual insights continually break-ing into awareness, the body writes its own divinity into the world. From an undivided, undefiled place of women's holiness and dignity, the body represents the possibility of restoring human connectedness with the entire cosmos. In reading women's body as a mystical text, I refer to the multiple voices, meanings, and layers of consciousness that demarcate and signify women's spiritual power. Here, the body can be read not only as a cultural representation of idealized or gross materiality but also as an extension into space and time of self-deification, of the power to make present through the body the spiritual signs, ethical concerns, and unitive visions of reality inscribed upon it from a person's deepest core or divine source.

Unlike other cultural representations of the body, the metaphor of women's body as revelatory or mystical is not a disguised form of essentialism designed to universalize women or to apply a standard by which all women are measured. It is not a description of women's essence, but an interpretation of women's body as the site of an embodied contemplation. As noted in chapter 2, recent scholarship has shown that mysticism also is a culturally constructed discourse that is susceptible to control by power elites, gender identities, clerical authority, and institutional censorship. Yet, stubborn refusal to succumb to metaphorical reductionism is always present in mystical texts. At the same time that mystics consistently acknowledge their experience of divinity as truth, they also employ poetic imagery and metaphors to describe that reality which language is only partially capable of representing. In the ineffable space between metaphor as representation and experience as truth rests a moment of grace. In my reading of women's body as mystical text, this slippage between metaphorical reading and experiential fact cannot be stabilized. Irresolvable ambiguity *is* disclosure.

Women's body, thus, both conceals and reveals the mystery of embodiment. There is something distinctively female in the act of the mystical that bears within itself and labors to bring the divine into the human sphere. It is this seamless flow between body and spirit, life and divinity that makes actual—brings into form—the unity or oneness that is deeply felt and fiercely known. Awareness of this constantly occurring communion between God and the soul is critically important to women's development of a body-affirming consciousness. So powerful is this interior communion that it is fair to say that a conscious realization of the mysticism of embodiment is its own distinctive spiritual path.

To script the text of women's wholeness is to read women's full embodiment as a sign of the mystical. Women's bodies function not simply at the biological or material level, but as the site in which and through which women experience the presence of truth and awe. The body is always seeking to communicate its divine origins through the multiple textuality that *is* women's full presence. This understanding of the mystical body is well documented in Eastern religions, which have sophisticated vocabularies to describe the various manifestations of chi, *prana*, chakras, and other etheric or energy fields that intersect with and animate the physical body. These energetic expressions of mind-body communion also include spiritual states of consciousness, advanced meditative practices, and other types of spiritual or soul powers, as well as their corresponding physical sensations, feelings, and emotions. To imagine women's body as a mystical text implies the full embodiment that constitutes their presence—biological, psychological, emotional, intellectual, spiritual and so forth—is the act of inscribing women's revelation in the world. Every day, women write the body of divinity through the text of their bodies.

We see this strategy operating in the women mystics. Beneath the anti-body rhetoric rooted in medieval thought and internalized in their texts, these women were effective in partially transforming anti-female discourses by re-reading the body as a place of the holy. Against the loathing of female flesh, they pitted their own bodies, choosing and praying for various forms of suffering and self-discipline as a method of personal autonomy and control. Despite protestations against the flesh, the body is central to their spiritual power, as that which feels, visions, hears, enraptures, suffers, mourns, loves, and is loved. Imaginative and intellective visions, auditory signs, levitation, stigmata, and other spiritual consolations solidified their spiritual authority and self-deification. Extravagant methods of self-discipline that were designed to regulate the female body (including mantric prayer, vigils, fasting, and flagellations with iron chains or hair shirts) paradoxically consolidated women's power. These "technologies which, in the hands of a powerful church, were meant to limit severely the autonomy and authority of women became for the mystics a source of self-determination, virtually the only one available to women during this period."[7]

Such intense experiences of rapture, suffering, and beauty prepared them to be persons of authority, which derived not from belief in external teachings or sources, but from God's presence directly experienced within the self. For them, authority was bearing witness in one's body—bearing witness in one's body was revelatory.[8] God was not a substitute for an impoverished or passive self. Rather, God functions in their lives and texts as women's ventriloquist, as the speaking subject or voice of their unspoken desires, sufferings, and truths. Profoundly practical, dialogic, and analytical, we find in Teresa, Julian, Hildegard, and others an attentive concern for what is most human: the encircling embrace that holds the entire cosmos in love. Theirs was not a superficial interpretation that succumbed to an excessive spiritualization of their lives and world events. Instead, they learned to take seriously and respect a deeper level of understanding that was working itself out even in the most domestic of human affairs. As Teresa reminded her sisters: "The Lord walks among the pots and pans." They show us that the hardest aspect of the spiritual life is the recognition of one's goodness, equality, and mutuality with divinity. It is not loving others but self-loving and self-dignity that is the most painful for women to achieve. But without this self-love, women cannot honor, preserve, and protect their deepest mystical capacity. Only women can name and claim this for themselves. No relationship, religion, or institution can give it to them. It is an inner realization that comes from touching the depths of women's capacity to be a living embodiment of divine indwelling.

In protest to cultural and theological norms of women's discourse, our women mystics acted courageously to interpret the scroll God was inscribing on the tablet of their souls. They were attuned to the subtle signifiers of a divine self-communication continually expressing itself through multiple layers of meaning. They studied their bodily signs from the perspective of a unitive worldview. Visions, spiritual gifts, worldly problems, ethical concerns, soul sufferings, and physical pains were probed for insight into God's concern on earth. The labor of reading and applying these signs to the quest for holiness occupied their life-long efforts to live up to the promise already given. They practiced silence and solitude, worked out their suffering, and understood intimacy as the most profound gift of prayer. They *chose* to be attuned to the subtle movement of the spirit within them. The women mystics mapped how body excesses and worldly pains can affect the spirit, wounding and damaging the soul, just as the spirit can transcend, overwhelm, or break through into body awareness. Every day was not ecstatic, but a slow working out of their mystical capacity to restore human connectedness with the whole cosmos in God. To do this required a turning inward to hear, in the silence of a still heart, the secret teachings that infused one's whole being with love. Here is finally a freedom that cannot be taken away. Here is a vision that cannot be erased. In this temple of meaning, suffering and joy combine to form an integrated holiness, the holy of holies within one's own flesh.

Body as Hierophany

In her book *The Body of God,* Sallie McFague radicalizes our notions of the body. She develops a new way of imagining and expressing divine transcendence and immanence that includes the entire universe and all creation as a sacral body. God does not stand outside creation as the external ruler, nor is God reduced to an appearance in one particular time and place. "In the universe as a whole," writes McFague, "as well as in each and every bit and fragment of it, God's transcendence is embodied."[9] This does not imply, however, that God is wholly contained in or reduced to the world. Rather, for McFague, the model or metaphor of the universe as God's body "is a rich, suggestive way to radicalize the glory, the awesomeness, the beyond-all-imagining power and mystery of God in a way that at the same time radicalizes the nearness, the availability, the physicality of divine immanence."[10] McFague's work illustrates that God and creation are related in vulnerability, responsibility, and caring. God is at risk in the bodies of the world.

When we apply McFague's metaphor to women's bodies, we can say divinity is already imbedded in the bodies of women, engendering healing and igniting holiness from within. God loves women's bodies; anoints them as good and holy; preserves their dignity and purity; feels their violation and wounding; and draws them again and again to healing and fullness. Women's bodies represent the divine transcendence expressing itself through women's full presence that neither reduces transcendence nor glorifies immanence, but places them in reciprocal communion. As representatives of Feminine Divine transcendence—Shekhinah, Sophia, Mary, Sapientia—women are so wholly *other*, they are concealed within the concealed; their beauty, strength, and mercy can never be fully seen or expressed. But as representatives of Feminine Divine immanence, women are so wholly *with us* that they are the breath of our breath, wound of our wound, and love of our love. Like Hildegard's keen sense of feminine fecundity, we can envision the integration of transcendence and immanence "not as a force propelling the world from without but as an ambience enfolding it and quickening it from within."[11] Healing, loving, and longing are not the activities of a God outside us, but a divine activity always operating within us.

Women express in their cellular embodiment a revelation of the elusive and mysterious communion of spirit and matter. "If," as McFague writes, "God is physical"—if women's body is God's body—then through the beauty, vulnerability, pain, laughter, maternity, sexuality, and joy of women's bodies, transcendence (spirit) and immanence (matter) unite. From this perspective, we can suggest that one goal or purpose of women's embodiment is to give birth to the potential union already incarnate in us. It is to lift up the world to the unity and freedom that is already present, but unrealized and unclaimed. If women represent the capacity to realize and make actual this nascent or unrealized oneness, then they have a stake in uniting the divisions of the world. As an expression of *both* transcendence *and* immanence, infinity *and* finitude, divine *and* human, women's embodied presence is a hierophany—from the Greek *hiero-* (sacred) and *phainein* (to show)—a term designating the manifestation of the holy.

Claiming women's body as God's body implies a conscious assignment as such, a recognition of a hidden or possible dimension usually unnamed or unseen by what is normally designated as secular or natural (as opposed to supernatural). Like Teresa's depiction of the soul's mixture of natural and supernatural states of consciousness that together compose a higher realm of unity, so, too, can women's bodies be understood as a complex and interdependent psychosomatic, biospiritual communion. Here, the body is read as a multifaceted text operating on multiple levels and dimensions of meaning: as biological, physiological flesh; as a canvas upon which cultural definitions and constructions are drawn; and as unseen, ethereal, or mystical "bodies" or realms of consciousness—including those designated as spiritual, mental, emotional, energy, and soul—that constitute the whole person.

There are certain challenges inherent in the metaphor of women's body as the body of God. Expressing an incomprehensible paradox between presence and limitation, every hierophany, by virtue of expressing the sacred through a concrete form, ceases to be absolute. To assert that women's bodies are revelatory is to also insist that in making itself manifest, the sacred limits itself. Women's bodies, as all other living forms, do not capture the totality of the sacred; they are not wholly divinized. Representations of the female body as sacred do not deify women or imply that women claim such designation. Rather, it is a way to approach and understand the integral, undivided, and holistic plurality that constitutes women's lived experience. It involves an interpretive shift in which women recognize their potential to become transparent vessels of sacred power in and through their bodies.

In this way, the body of the mystical text becomes transposed into the female body. Like the mystical text, women's body cannot be explained or determined away; it is a work of art—a masterpiece—and a poetry waiting to be read. Rational thought cannot contain it; reason cannot name it. Women's body defies description; its luminosity and awe cannot be possessed. It is not understood by those outside or afraid of the circle of vulnerability. It is elusive, offering glimpses of something other, something wholly unknown yet tangibly present. Like the poetic, which binds together seen and unseen with an effortless flow of words, women's body—its "otherness"—*is* a mark of holiness. But, in anti-body cultures, women represent

the rejected closeness of God. This pervasive denial of the spirituality naturally expressed through women contributes to a kind of cultural invisibility
in which women labor under a misbelief that they are not seen. Under this
illusion of cloaking, women are encouraged by economic and cultural mar-
kets to expose and exaggerate their physical body, and are exhorted to do
everything possible—even selling their bodies or souls—to convert another
person into lover, partner, confidant, or friend. Instead, from a mystical vantage point, it is precisely because women's sacred intimacy *is* experienced
and seen that cultures have a stake in perpetuating gender stereotyping
designed to keep women ignorant of their great worth, and to project them
as human cargo in the marketplace of economic exchange.

Yet, "there is something in the sacredness of the other, untouchable and
at no one's disposition, that must plunge us into a powerlessness; the common, sacred power can be derived only from there."[12] Then women's *otherness* "is no longer the shame of being denied subjecthood, but a sign of the
spiritual power of female being."[13] Women's spiritual strength and energetic
fecundity make the body a powerful site of holy resistance and emotional
receptivity. Women's faces are undeniably windows into the sacred; they call
forth an obligation and a mystery that only can be grasped in all their excessive, yet simple, grace. This claim of women's divinity initiates the mending
between sacred and profane—that binary opposition that underlies Western patriarchies and keeps our world bound in chains, offering homage
to an antiquated and punishing narrative of sin. External agents cannot
impose women's claim of bodily integrity, a sacredness of self that cannot
be scapegoated, pushed down, or defiled. It is a spiritual intention that must
grow inside the soul of women. It is the realization of the obligation and
the empowerment that derives from the inseparable operation of women's
divine humanity.

Theology of Women's Spiritflesh

Women contain the salvific potency and enlightening potential of being
bearers of the holy. They know and understand She who is "not the Remote
One, but the One Who is involved, near, and concerned."[14] Like women
who care for the concerns of the world, "God does not stand outside the
range of human suffering and sorrow," writes Abraham Joshua Heschel.
God's concern "denotes, not an idea of goodness, but a living care; not an
immutable example, but an outgoing challenge; . . . no mere contemplative

survey of the world, but a passionate summons."[15] Heschel describes pathos (compassion, and suffering with) not as a psychological condition, but in its theological implications, signifying how God is engaged to Israel and has a stake in its history and destiny. Applying Heschel's understanding of pathos as a metaphor for women's being in the world, we can say: Like God, who is engaged to Israel, women are wed to creation, being the guardian of its life-giving function and the creatrix of human birth. Women thus have an immediate stake in its wellness, integrity, and destiny. Women have a covenantal relationship with the flourishing and preservation of the body of God in creation. Their concern is not confined to the purely personal, or even to the child itself, but to the whole life-giving function—to the love for the world that makes the world an intimate place.

Women's becoming divine is never a solely privatized affair of achieving union with God, but obligates a new way of being in the world. The female body portends a way of speaking and knowing what has not been known or has never been communicated. Only as a woman approaches her own spiritflesh in amazement and respect, with the gratitude offered the holy, does she discover the gift of her prophetic presence. In honoring her embodiment, she makes present the divine intimacy in her that seeks its counterpart in human intimacy, and the divine vulnerability that longs to be touched, felt, and known. Certainly birth provides one of the most compelling images of this mysterious adoration of spirit and flesh, this reciprocal communion by which a woman's body bears the coming into presence of new life. Inside their own bodies, women substantiate and nourish another body, one who they do not yet know but nevertheless love. Perhaps it is not too bold to say that women are charged with bearing the divinity of the world. I wonder if every mother does not secretly believe that her child will be born holy—will be the new prophet, sage, lama, or redeemer who exposes and heals the pains of the world.

I believe the women mystics we have studied profoundly understood how a realized embodiment is a higher form of spirituality. In their writings we find traces of a feminist incarnational spirituality premised on divine-human generativity and benevolence. The women mystics read the signs of the spirit through the pains and triumphs of their bodies in order to learn how to self-deify and thus convert others to living more fully in the sacred. Despite rhetoric that chastised or castigated the female body, it was precisely the feminized body (represented positively as receptive, open, surrendered, and intimate) that was the site of the highest mystical consciousness.

Whether biologically female or male, the feminized body was depicted as constitutively mystical. As recipients of intellective or tangible visions, locutions, levitations, illnesses, or mystical touches, the sacred was written in the "weakness" of female flesh. Both male and female mystics depicted body and soul through female images and metaphors; they recognized how the feminized body is sensitive to and affected by both positive and negative experiences of spirit and world. What they feared, suffered, and longed for, as well as what brought joy, contentment, and hope, were the silent effects of a deeper self-communication. Further, the feminized body assumed and internalized the care and suffering of the world—in order to transform it—in a way that the male body did not. Precisely for their greater receptivity and pliability, females and feminized males are often despised as outcasts in anti-body cultures.

Teresa, Julian, Hildegard, and others were especially aware of how, through the body, what is unifying or holistic is made spiritually present or available. In suggesting the importance of bodily signs in reading the ineffable, the body becomes a temple of the holy. It is a cipher or code to understand the mystery of divinity and matter, the vulnerability with which life exposes the holy, and the celebration of lifting up consciousness to its highest level of awareness. The body, then, is more than body, but not because it is merely matter and thus finds value only as it cedes value to the transcendent Other. It is more than body because in and through the body ever more subtle, sensuous, and intangible levels of consciousness are encoded. The body, therefore, is another revelation of divinity. It seeks to communicate its divine origins; what draws it toward happiness or sorrow; what debases or elevates its inherent dignity. Daily life events, emotional upheavals, physical pains and joys, as well as soul suffering and happiness, are the sensual expressions of deeper and more hidden realizations.

In a reversal of the biblical notion that women suffer as punishment for their sins, the women mystics recognize that women bear the divinity of the world in a real and metaphorical way. They illustrate for us today how women are empowered to transform the structures of consciousness in which sin dwells, and are charged with the alchemical transformation of matter into spirit. Every woman is conduit, translator, prophet, redeemer, and mother of the sacred into the world—she who is female power to create and generate change. From their intense practice of prayer, the women mystics experience how spiritual changes in their body effect changes in the world and vice versa. They possess the holy power to heal, transform, reconcile, rebuke, redeem, and liberate others from pain and sin. Through their willingness to experience suffering and bliss, women break down the barriers between sacred and profane. They are able to travel back and forth across the sacred-secular divide, to unite in their body and soul the worldly division between God and creation, and spirit and matter.

Embodied Contemplation

Contemplation is always a revolutionary act. It subverts the daily tedium and searches for the kernel of meaning hidden at the center of each thing. It is thus not the talent of a spiritual elite, but the deepest core of silence present in all of us. Its radicalness is also the quest for normalcy and everyday quiet. But for women, especially those who labor to raise children, work, and tend to families, contemplation often becomes a subversive choice. Bombarded daily with conflicting cultural commitments and media images ascribed to females, most women probably do not identify themselves as mystics or believe they are capable of leading a contemplative life. However, unlike our spiritual predecessors, women today do not need to confine themselves to a cloister or cloak themselves in religious clothing to live in a contemplative way.

The stone enclosure that literally marked the boundaries of the medieval monastery is transposed from the concrete into a state or quality of con- sciousness. To be enclosed in the monastic sense is to devote oneself to God. In a modern context, this ancient purity of heart refers to the discovery of the divine as the one relationship fundamentally essential to one's life and lives out of *its* source. Far from being alienating, the simplicity of this inten- tion is transformative. A woman's relationship to the world is shifted from being primarily other-directed, to focusing on an interior solitude from which flows the richness and pleasure of all relations.

Two interwoven themes or archetypes were critical to the formation of the women mystics: solitude and sexuality. For women to be able to practice an embodied contemplation, we need to transpose these ancient archetypes into a contemporary form.

Solitude

Each woman contains within herself an inner monastery where she and her beloved divinity are alone. Here she is enclosed in a sanctuary where God and the self are one. No one is allowed to disturb this primary relationship, this bond of intimacy that makes all other intimacies what they are and long to become. So vital is this solitude to a woman's full presence in the world that the attainment of the center point of stillness is critical to her spiritual growth. Yet, a woman's being is defined as a self-for-others: she who is relational; she who is available; she who is caregiver, helpmate, and mother. "She is constituted by a variety of other people's desires; at worst she is a pornographic non-subject, a screen of flesh for male sexual projects."[16] Her spiritual center is distracted by the numerous roles she is called to perform, the many commitments imposed on her and others that she internalizes and demands of herself. To find the monastery within is to discover the place of rest out of which all other relations flourish and grow. To be with one's beloved, in the center of one's heart and soul, is to finally claim women's right to be alone.

Solitude is solace; silence is food. They are necessary for the nourishment of the whole person, and for the actualization of the deepest possibility of a spiritual life. To live at the center of one's being requires practicing life in our inner monastery where we are undisturbed by the noise, demands, and busyness of the world. Silence allows no other speech to enter the enclosure where God and self are one. It washes away the harsh, violated, lashing speech that humiliates and shames. Silence is a balm that soothes whatever has falsely named and blamed women; it flows out of an untarnished beauty into the beauty of every woman's face and presence. In stillness, women celebrate their "unnaming" in order to be renamed as beloved. Freed from false identities, women find a new openness and intimacy. Silence recharges and restores the powerful yet fragile awareness of life's radical awe. It is the electrical current that ignites the divine spark at the center of our being.

Solitude is more than a withdrawal from other people, just as silence is more than the absence of speech. It is an interior state of consciousness in which women protect and preserve the integrity of self from unwanted intrusion. Far from being an escape from the world, solitude establishes women in the world in a new way. It provides an inner resiliency and power that grows from the core of women's self-integrity. It is the antidote to patriarchy and the liberation that overcomes bondage, disclosing the wide expanse of joy that is a woman's true self. Solitude is both a hermeneutic (an interpretation) and a method of women's achieving mystical humanity. It is the interpretive experience that women need in order to overcome the difficulty of "living for others, whether partners, husbands, children, or ageing relatives." Confusing selflessness with love, women "frequently subordinate their own identity and self to the needs and interests of other people."[17] Women give away their solitude, and thus they give away or forcibly are robbed of their most urgent healing and curative resources. Out of this first relationship with God, every other relationship is seen in the light of its own incandescence.

Solitude provides the freedom to stand alone and not to succumb to the crowd. Commenting on Thomas Merton's "Philosophy of Solitude," Lawrence Cunningham writes that Merton argues for "the solitary [as one who] avoids the temptation to succumb to the thinking of the group and the passion for conformity to society. Hence, the authentic solitary can take up, assuming purity of intention and clarity of purpose, the prophetic task of disagreeing completely 'with those who imagine that the call to diversion and self-deception is the voice of truth and who can summon the full authority of their prejudices to prove it.'"[18]

Sexuality

To be human is to have a generative, creative impulse that expresses itself through the body in various sexual, artistic, and intellective ways. This procreative capacity is always bound to spirit, as it emerges from the deepest core of the person. Sexuality is thus one of the main areas of women's reclamation of holiness. Central to feminist concerns, sexual autonomy is usually analyzed in terms of biological or social choices and freedoms. But there is another type of sexual autonomy tied to the mystical understanding of intimacy and is the fruit of solitude. In Christian monasticism, for example, the relationship of the vowed religious to Jesus Christ involves a "total affective involvement" and a "psychological-spiritual exclusivity" analogous to the marital relationship with another person.[19] Referring to the pure love of divine union, the soul is celibate, *caelebs* (single or unmarried). The "virgin" soul, a common theme in medieval mystical texts, also depicts consecrated celibacy in a symbolic sense as the soul's purity. Empty and without image, the soul is as free as when it was uncreated. Naked of all things, and having nothing in common with anything, she receives into herself nothing less than the divine in all the splendor and vastness of being. Meister Eckhart employs this image to make a distinction between the soul as a married person, and as a virgin who is a wife. Married people are "possessively attached to prayer, to fasting, to vigils" he writes, "and to all kinds of exterior exercises and penances." "Pledged to possessiveness," married souls "produce little fruit" of the spirit. Yet, a "virgin who is a wife is free and unpledged, without attachment; she is always equally close to God and to herself." Her emptiness is fecund and she gives birth to many fruits of the spirit that are "neither less nor more than is God himself."[20]

As we transpose these spiritual concepts into our present context, a symbolic celibacy can free us to recover the simple health of one's inner life. Related to the soul's freedom to preserve solitude with God, symbolic celibacy does not represent the foreboding asexual presence we might imagine, but is the lively birthing place of the holiness of relations. We are all sexual beings, whether we are actively sexual or celibate. Women's right to interior solitude is the discovery of the deepest possibility of human friendship and love. This freedom to sustain the paradox of solitude and sexuality is a spiritual path for women today, as its draws from the wisdom of contemplation the resources necessary to be open to the wonders of pleasure and happiness, and deeply faithful to our relationship with our ultimate source. We discover that beneath and more prior to our sexual exploits and the unholy way we treat our bodies, we are still an untarnished solitude—"single of men"—in the sanctuary where God and the soul are alone. We are free to enter and to leave the chamber of intimacies with God. We come and go as silently and as naturally as the wind on a warm day in May.

As sexual beings, our creativity and passion are not separate from the mystical or contemplative, but expressions of the mutual interpenetration, co-equality, and co-intimacy that exist between spirit and body. In this sense, deep relationships flow out of contemplation, as contemplation flows out of solitude. As one of the most powerful mediums through which women uphold the sanctity of the flesh and the mysticism of the sensual, sexual love can be viewed as a type of infused contemplation. Here there is fusion—an intimate dance of spirit and body—and receptivity to the mystery of cells and to the generosity of the body that cannot be forced or controlled, for then it borders on the possessive or pornographic. Whether sexual intimacy is lived out through physical intercourse, spiritual love, or unimagined expressions of human creativity, it overflows from our core of goodness and generosity in "loving imitation of how God loves."[21]

A realization of the relationship between mystical solitude and the body is especially important for women who have succumbed to painful sexual extravagances, been abused or raped by male partners, or had their integrity violated by allowing, or being forced to use, their bodies as objects of male sexual pleasure. Women who have suffered through physical violence or humiliation (and even women who do not have extreme sexual histories) often describe themselves as "tainted," "impure," or "unworthy of love." These deeply painful feelings extend into women's spiritual self-image and capacity to believe in God's love for them. Feeling that acts of sexual violence or exploitation have permanently corrupted their innocence or purity and effectively aborted any possibility of living a spiritually meaningful life further contributes to women's despair. Yet, the central insight of a mystical anthropology—that the core of our being is untouched by sin and belongs to God—can be enormously healing in these circumstances. Thomas Merton exemplifies this mystic stance when he wrote that "at the center of our being is a point of nothingness which is untouched by sin and by illusion, a point or spark that belongs entirely to God, which is never at our disposal, . . . and is the pure glory of God in us."[22] No pain, error, or violation can penetrate the inviolable sanctuary of unconditional love.

If we truly recognize the power and responsibility of never being separated from God, even as we grieve over treacherous acts of betrayal, then we will understand that a woman's most insidious internalization of cultural "sin" is to believe in or contribute to her own desacralization. One of the great mother wisdoms feminism teaches is the power of resistance to large religious and social forces that permit the female body to become merely a commodity, a thing to be bought and sold, or a pawn for the commercial enterprises of other women and men. It is, thus, this vision of the seamless communion of spirit and matter that we call "the body" that obligates women to practice personal benevolence and spiritual justice. By the nature of what it means to be embodied sexual beings, women are compelled to protect and love the integrity of their bodies, and to preserve, defend, and honor their holiness. Their own flesh cries out to mend the split between spirit and matter, and to abolish the stunning punishment women inflict on their bodies. The shocking statistics that cite the vast number of women who starve, punish, cut, sculpt, or otherwise inscribe violence on female flesh indicates the urgency of our times. Rather than the body and spirit being opposed, and the flesh needing to be tamed and controlled, women's sexuality is a sanctuary of the holy.

Women's body is the house of holiness. Behind the hidden and inexpressible God of classical theology, women touch the unveiled divinity in the daily acts of generosity they perform: the creating, feeding, laboring, nurturing, caring, loving, and birthing that mark most women's lives. They know and embody something of the pure Other that cannot be possessed or claimed. More silent, more elusive, more intimate than the hidden and inexpressible God, this unveiled divinity speaks "feminine"—a language of intimacy. Our material culture, blinded to the unseen, turns unveiling into a disrobing, a taking off of clothes—or even a putting on of a required cloth—in order to expose, judge, or constrain the content of women's body itself. It is up to women to claim as their own the essential core of purity that they possess and that men and history attempt to wrest/rape from them.

Perfectly or imperfectly, women's body expresses divine love laboring to be made fully conscious and fully embodied in us. It is divine eyes that struggle to see, divine mind that labors to know, and divine heart that longs to love in the midst of human greed, temptation, betrayal, cruelty, and loss of hope. It is this conscious bearing that compels us toward humility, reconciliation, and redemption, from which we are never free and which calls our hearts to relieve each other's suffering and distress. It is this primary imprinting, this stamping of our being with divine being, that leads us to the doorway of freedom and truth. In honoring women's sexuality, symbolic celibacy is a restorative image that prepares women for a "more human love . . . [which] will resemble that which we are preparing with struggle and toil, the love that consists in this, that two solitudes protect and border and salute each other."[23]

chapter ten

Seeing through God's Eyes

Women's Spiritual Rights

Is there anything sacred, holy, left in the world? . . . Sacred is not just a substitute for "ultimate" or "absolute." It also implies salvation for the one who will respond to it and be introduced into it. And so I ask once more: Is there anything that is ultimate and incapable of being manipulated, anything that makes an ultimate demand on human beings in the form of promise and fulfillment? . . . In our own age, there can be little doubt that the defense of human rights represents for many of us something sacred—something that makes ultimate demands on us and holds out the promise of salvation.[1]

In his commitment to the liberation theology of the poor, Jon Sobrino sounds a passionate plea to wake up from our materialistic slumber and work toward the establishment of a loving and caring community on earth. At the heart of Sobrino's liberation theology exists an inseparable relationship between an ultimate concern for the world and the nearness of divine love. Like Sobrino and other prophets of peace, Mohandas K. Gandhi recognized as well how the quest to identify and alleviate suffering in this world *is* God. In campaigning for the dignity of India's people, Gandhi wed his nonviolent experiments in truth to the glaring political wounds of his day: segregation of India's lowest caste, the "untouchables"; mass poverty and hunger; foreign political control and corporate greed; and the plight of women. Part of Gandhi's brilliance rested on his unshakable faith that the most deeply practiced spiritual life was the moral impetus for radical social transformation. No separation existed between working for truth in everyday life and the highest spiritual attainment. "What I want to achieve," he wrote, "what I have been striving and pining to achieve these thirty years—is self-realization, to see God face to face, to attain Moksha."[2]

This divine injunction to measure our own success or failure—even our own salvation—against the commitment to divine love and to the alleviation of the suffering of others is painfully apparent in the violence against women rampant in every part of the world today. In countries around the globe, the deplorable treatment of women tells us that God's presence and revelation in females continues to be tortured, humiliated, neglected, ravaged, and starved. Further, the majority of these travesties is carried out by males on populations of females with wanton disregard for the sanctity of their lives, and often with an intentional purpose to desecrate women's holiness. Not only do women suffer the consequences of a "virulent misogyny [that] exists to varying degrees beneath the fragile surface of our societies,"[3] they also witness the contempt dominant political powers have for the mass numbers of the world's children—all born of women—who die from malnutrition, are permanently crippled by disease, are sold into slavery, or are slain in war.

Feminist scholars contend that the atrocities committed against women are profoundly connected to the destruction of animals and earth, the treatment of the most fragile and vulnerable of the world's people, and the militarization of the planet. Of added significance, feminists assert that the inability of the international community to secure the health, safety, and integrity of the world's women is evidence of a collective human sin against God's female presence on earth. This failure by the global community to protect women's bodies has resulted in every imaginable and unimaginable atrocity, wrenching our hearts and rendering us all complicit in the tragedy that afflicts far too many lives today. The sanctity of life is indelibly stained by extreme acts of destruction against the collective female body and cries out for an adequate response. How can we not find this of ultimate concern?

Human Rights in Context

The furthest frontier in feminist activism rests with a woman's spiritual rights, and her right to claim herself as representative of the divine in every area of life. Throughout history women have ceded these rights to male power elites, and to religious professionals who owned and dictated women's relationship with God. In order for women to achieve equality and dignity, legal solutions, religious concessions, or economic advancement is not enough. Women must claim their right to full spiritual equality and work toward its advancement. This demand for justice rises up from a woman's deepest center, where she is one with her divine source. It is, in its most eloquent spiritual form, a claim for human rights.

According to international definitions, human rights are a special class of rights that one has simply because one is a human being. The source of these rights is derived from the moral nature of humans. "Violations of human rights deny one's *humanity*," Jack Donnelly writes. "They do not necessarily keep one from satisfying one's needs." We have international covenants on human rights to commit the world community to those "things 'needed' for a life of dignity, for a life *worthy* of a human being, a life that cannot be enjoyed without these rights."[4] Up until the middle of the twentieth century, the rights of a human person were the rights granted by his or her government. This theory of rights was shattered in the aftermath of World War II and the horrors committed against humanity in Nazi Germany, Stalinist Russia, Hiroshima, Nanking, and other holocausts of war. In response to these atrocities, the Universal Declaration of Human Rights (passed by the United Nations in 1948 without a dissenting vote) asserted international human rights law as a higher standard of law than the state. As defined by the Universal Declaration, human rights flow from the "dignity and worth of the human person" and are prior to and more important than the dictates of nation, state, or group.

In the human rights arena, where advocates combat the gravest forms of cruelty and shame against their fellow citizens, the notion of individual rights is always measured against a prior and more serious deprivation. Every expression of a right begins with a personal journey of consciousness raising. In order for a person to claim something as a human right, he or she first must be able to recognize and name what it is that is deprived; and, further, how the right that is withheld is fundamental to "the inherent dignity of the human person." Human rights claims always emerge from the failure of granting or enforcing this fundamental moral equality of being human. In the American civil rights movement of the 1960s, for example, the demand for equal treatment before the law became an issue of human rights because Black Americans were structurally prevented from achieving the inalienable rights granted to all citizens by the constitution. Excluded from full participation in society by racism, socially sanctioned violence, and segregation, Black Americans fought for their basic right to dignity as persons and for equal treatment before the law.

As the civil rights movement demonstrated, rights that are denied or withheld are seldom if ever returned voluntarily by the authority or institution that asserts a prior claim of power. Thus, every demand for a human right requires a corresponding duty or obligation placed on other persons or institutions to implement and enforce formal changes in social behaviors, institutions, and laws. Rights and duties are interrelated; human rights claims ultimately compel an obligation that the presence of another life makes on us. From a secular viewpoint, we humans make a claim on each other to uphold our duty to the moral good of society. From a religious perspective, it is God or Spirit who obligates us to perform merciful actions in the world.

International human rights covenants recognize three broad areas of rights: "first generation" civil and political rights, "second generation" social, cultural, and economic rights, and "third generation" environmental and developmental rights. Liberal Western democracies have tended to stress individual civil rights and political liberties. Social democracies, developing nations, indigenous cultures, and women's groups place greater emphasis on second and third generation rights, including rights of education, food, health care, employment, child care, or stewardship of the earth. Despite the inclusion of all three areas of rights in the Universal Declaration of Human Rights and the numerous declarations, covenants, and conventions endorsed by the United Nations, there is a tendency in the international community to polarize these differences and to approach them as conflictual, rather than as interlocking rights.

There also is concern, especially among feminist activists, that an emphasis on individual human rights does not protect the world's marginalized cultural and social groups. Since much of the violence against women is embedded in larger socioeconomic and religious issues, women's rights advocates are especially attentive to the relationship between a woman's dignity and her physical and social well-being. Others contend that the fundamental belief that human rights inhere primarily to the individual is a safeguard against cultural and religious domination or supremacist ideologies. The fact that individuals may hold human rights as a member of a community or protected social group but the group cannot hold or exercise these rights against the individual is cited as evidence of the moral value of the person. "Families, for example," Donnelly contends, "are protected by a number of internationally recognized human rights, but from a human rights perspective . . . families may not exercise their rights in ways that infringe on the human rights of their members or any other persons. For instance, families may not deny their members freedom of religion or the right to political participation, nor may they discriminate on the basis of sex."[5]

Beyond these tensions and distinctions, however, we can say that all definitions of human rights have a spiritual basis to them, whether explicitly or implicitly referring to human nature, divine covenant, or natural law. For this reason, the understanding of human rights is designed in each of its forms to address in a global forum what can be called the spiritual dimension of life.

Women's Rights Are Human Rights

Like the Universal Declaration of Human Rights, the Convention on the Elimination of All Forms of Discrimination against Women, adopted in 1979, is founded on an essential faith in the dignity and worth of the female person. The culmination of more than thirty years of work by the United Nations Commission on the Status of Women, the Preamble to the Convention explicitly acknowledges that "'extensive discrimination against women continues to exist,' and emphasizes that such discrimination 'violates the principles of equality of rights and respect for human dignity.' As defined in Article 1, discrimination is understood as 'any distinction, exclusion or restriction made on the basis of sex which has the effect of nullifying the recognition, enjoyment, or exercise by women . . . of human rights in the political, economic, social, cultural, civil or any other field.'"[6] The Convention is concerned with women's civil, legal, and reproductive rights, as well as with the impact of cultural factors on gender relations. These articles focus on women's rights in public life, including the right to vote, to own and inherit property, to receive an equal education with males, to choose their spouses, and to be free from sexual trafficking, and they revise penal codes that discriminate against women.

Despite its broad understanding of the extent of gender-based discrimination against women worldwide, the Convention "does not specifically confront violence against women, nor does it mandate nations to report on the issue or adjust their national legislation to address it."[7] The United Nations adopted two additional general recommendations in 1989 and 1991 to correct these omissions; they recommend that countries ensure that adequate laws be enacted to protect women from family violence and abuse, rape, sexual assault, and other gender-based violence. As nonbinding recommendations, nations may choose not to follow them, while others, including the United States, have yet to ratify the Women's Conventions. Deeply ingrained sexism embedded in cultural, religious, and traditional practices worldwide continue to remain an obstacle to women's right to live in dignity. Universal in theory, human rights inadequately address the unjust and discriminatory laws women face in almost every country of the world. The feminization of rights and the feminization of violence are inseparable challenges for the global community.

"Much of the struggle over women's rights has been a struggle over what is public and what is private. How far," questions Melissa Gillis, "should human rights concerns be extended to the 'private' realm of family or religion traditionally beyond the scope of state regulation but where women face the greatest likelihood of violation?"[8] The right to privacy in the home, for example, is often confused by a false dichotomy and an unequal distribution of power between men and women in the public and the private spheres. Most nations provide protections to keep the "private" realm free from social or state interference. However, the power that men exert over women as heads of households is reinforced by cultural taboos and legal precedents against invading the sacrosanct domain of male authority. Without question, patriarchal cultural values, religious beliefs, and moral codes are implicated in the violent treatment of women worldwide. Even our most sacred documents of compassion and justice, like the Talmud, the Christian Bible, and the Qur'an, do not adequately uphold the full dignity and equality of women. A better glimpse of how the privatizing of freedom can actually be a form of male institutional oppression can be briefly traced in the sphere of religion.

In its 1981 "Declaration on the Elimination of All Forms of Intolerance and Discrimination Based on Religion or Belief," the United Nations upheld a person's "right to freedom of thought, conscience, and religion." Religious human rights address "the inherent right of a person in public or private to worship or not to worship according to one's own conscience, understanding, or preferences; to join in association with others of like faith; and to change one's religious identity—all without hindrance, molestation, or discrimination. Religious human rights require the equality of all religions, as well as irreligion, before the law."[9] Broadly affirming the inviolability of individual faith and religious liberty, the tension implicit to the private versus the public sphere is, however, only hinted at but not resolved. The Declaration asserts that no one shall be subject to discrimination "by any State, institution, group or persons, or person on the grounds of religion or other belief," but it does not extend its reach, for example, to gender-based or sex-based discrimination *within* religions or interfere with internal religious structures or politics. It also affirms, as does the Universal Declaration, an individual's personal freedom of conscience, but it does not *explicitly* address the right to be free from oppression and exploitation *within* a religion that violate international human rights covenants. Although religions today are some of the most ardent advocates for human rights, "for most of human history," Robert Traer contends, "religious leaders resisted what we today describe as fundamental human rights . . . being more concerned with enforcing their authority and with the welfare of the community, rather than with rights of their followers—especially if recognizing these rights meant permitting dissent."

> Religious people who today support human rights need to acknowledge humbly that their traditions and teachings have long been used to deny many contemporary civil and political rights and that, until recently, support for human rights has come more consistently from secular political and cultural movements than from religious constituencies."[10]

Movements within the World Council of Churches, the Second Vatican Council (1962–1965), and Jewish organizations were among the contributions religions made to the theory, law, and activism on religious rights.[11] During Vatican II, for example, John XXIII's *Pacem in Terris* legitimized human rights discourse for the first time as a church teaching. In its document on religious freedom, *Dignitatis Humanae*, Vatican II continued the development of its doctrine of the dignity of the human person as the foundation of "the right to religious freedom." Yet religious freedom was understood as inhering in the church absolutely, but to its members only analogically, as a partial comparison. Because the church, as the Body of Christ, holds the sacrament of freedom, "'human rights have validity within the church,'" Aloysius Pieris writes, "'in an *analogical* way.'"

> The analogy is based on the fact that the church's fundamental rights, in contrast to the general human rights, do not precede the church. For, while men [*sic*] exist before the State, Christians do not exist before, or independent of, the church. *The human rights of religious freedom, can, therefore, not hold in the church, which is the community of the faithful and hence the community of one faith.*[12]

The denial of religious freedom within the church is arrogated to the church only if the church is understood "as the embodiment of a supernatural right to dominate every human sphere."[13] According to Pieris, belief in the superiority of church-sanctioned control over human rights is based on a monistic claim lurking beneath Catholic theology but also found in other Christian denominations: "Whereas people endowed with fundamental human rights exist before the state exists so that they could continue to enjoy such rights within the state, the same is not true of Christians, in that they do not preexist the church and are not independent of the church, which is the given sphere of salvation for them."[14] A similar case based on their distinctive theologies and worldviews could be made for Islam, Judaism, and others of the world's religions.[15]

I witnessed an explicit version of this struggle in one of my classes on Catholic spirituality. A female student had written a research paper historically refuting the church's stance against women's ordination. The entire class was animated around the discussion as many students expressed anger, disbelief, or pain. Since I was also teaching a class on the theologies of nonviolence that semester, I posed the question of why women in the church did not take a collective stance of nonviolent protest against this violation of women's equal human dignity. By refusing nonviolently to participate in an unjust structure, women would be upholding the spiritual tenets of their religion. I was surprised by the reaction I received, in part because most of these women students self-identified as "liberated," "lapsed" or "nonpracticing" Catholics, and were not ardent churchgoers. Responses such as "The Pope would condemn me," "I am afraid that I would go to hell," and "I fear the danger of committing a mortal sin" alerted class participants to how easy it is for individuals to relinquish human dignities when threatened by moral authority, divine punishment, or mortal sin. In internalizing these threats, the cycle of fear is perpetuated, thwarting the person's ability to speak out against or resist violations of intrinsic human rights.

Contemporary proponents of rights within the churches, such as Jon Sobrino, thus appeal not to the juridical authority of the institutional church but to the covenantal community of the body of Christ. "We begin to see," writes Pieris, "that the *authority* of the church, by Christ's intent, is dependent on its renunciation of *power*."[16] Religious freedom, freedom of conscience, and freedom to uphold the fundamental dignity of personhood is guaranteed by the spirit of Christ, and one's fidelity to the covenant founded on love and mercy. Here, rights and responsibilities intersect. Only as one accepts one's inherent right to be loved as the beloved does one recognize the responsibility to claim these human rights for oneself and others. Thus, this *spiritual* grounding of rights at the heart of liberatory praxis and liberation theologies takes priority over other interpretations of human rights.

Because women's rights are profoundly intertwined with religious beliefs and cultural prejudices that debase and marginalize them, our current definitions of human rights do not go far enough in uprooting the underlying causes and implications of violence against women. In order to evaluate this issue more closely, I propose a category of rights called "spiritual rights." I first define spiritual rights; I then briefly expose worldwide sexual or intimate violence against women. Finally, I explore how intimate violence against women is also soul violence. In the next chapter I propose how these spiritual rights become a basis for, and flow out of, a mystical ethics.

Distinctiveness of Spiritual Rights

Given the primacy of human dignity in the international human rights charters, it is worth asking why a special emphasis on spiritual rights is necessary. As we have seen, international covenants on human rights are derived from the inviolable sacredness of the person, and are intended to form a world consensus that exerts moral authority on nations to uphold and implement the fundamental principle of human dignity. One of the profoundly hopeful aspects of the work of the United Nations rests on its belief in the extra moral impact the individual person is granted—by virtue of being human—to exercise over any institutional structure, whether that is a nation-state, religion, or other cultural entity. Working through political, social, and religious means, the Universal Declaration upholds this global consensus of the sacredness of human life.

Spiritual rights, as I define them here, are built upon the pioneering work of international human rights advocacy; they are meant not to replace but to add to human rights norms. In spiritual rights, the Western emphasis on freedom of conscience and freedom of the individual as a legal entity is upheld, but it is always tempered by and subservient to the person who is embedded in an interdependent web of relations. The sanctity of the person is tied to the theology of theistic religions, as it is the person who is made in the image and likeness of God or is God's vice-regent on earth. An even greater identity is made in the religious philosophies of the Indian subcontinent, where, for example, *atman* (soul) *is Brahman* (God). Even when personhood is defined in radically different ways in the world's religions, human life on earth is sacred. The person's quest for her or his divine source commands an understanding that justice is unjust if it lacks compassion and mercy. The rights of indigenous peoples, the poor, women of diverse races and ethnicities, and other economically and culturally marginalized groups make a divine claim on the global community to fulfill what Sobrino calls "the promise of salvation." Bringing a new hermeneutical perspective to global suffering, spiritual rights ask us to see each other and all creation from a divine perspective. Because the highest calling of the person is to have fullness of being, spiritual rights address what prevents or violates this pursuit.

As the common element in all human cultures and traditions, the spiritual dimension of life is intertwined with and underlies all other rights. It thus requires an additional level of analysis and interpretation. It recognizes that spirituality is life itself; thus, a life of dignity is inconceivable without spiritual integrity and freedom. While many religions do not have a word corresponding to the term "spirituality," they nonetheless affirm the holiness of life and the realm of the "spirit." Today, spirituality is used in secular and religious contexts, and is applied across and within traditions, as well as in interfaith and intermonastic settings. "Thus spirituality has become a kind of universal code word to indicate the human search for direction and meaning, especially in times of crisis, widespread uprootedness, and confusion."[17] Our relationship with God is not separate from our moral values and concerns for the world, but profoundly interrelated to them. As the most fundamental of human experiences, spirituality calls us to a conversion from self-centeredness to compassion, mercy, and love. Deeply embodied in human experience, spirituality evaluates life situations from the perspective of what is a more profound and more noble reality that encloses and embraces us.

This addition of a specific category of spiritual rights provides a way of thinking about human dignity from a slightly different perspective. Derived from "a belief that recognizes within other people the presence of the divine through which a person attains full humanity," spiritual rights place the expressly spiritual as a recognized right interdependent with and interrelated to civil and political rights, and economic and social rights.[18] This sentiment is summarized in its African context by the "concept of *Ubuntu*, which asserts that each person is endowed with inner energy . . . [that] is a force or presence in us originating in God. This inner energy is one's dignity and personality. Thus a human being is not only a physical body, trapped in the material reality; a human being also . . . is given to serve the purposes of God in the world."[19] This spiritual or mystical dimension honors the fundamental unity and mystery of life, and recognizes that only a specific intention to evaluate rights violations through the lens of interdependence and mutual respect is adequate for the development of planetary dignity and right human relations. It questions with utmost seriousness the implications of our failure to prevent the severing and wounding of *presence*—that seamless relationship between body and spirit that *is* life. It demands an accounting of how human acts of violence tear at our hearts, lay waste to our souls, and lead us to the brink of despair. It asks how these travesties against the spirit of life contribute to our collective grief and afflict us in ways that even now we have yet to feel, name, or understand.

Spiritual rights are, thus, attentive to a certain quality of consciousness and a certain depth of heart that heal and transform. An indivisible relationship exists between the attainment of planetary responsibility and the necessity for spiritual practices, prayer, and meditative solitude. Some of the world's most eloquent global thinkers—Mohandas Gandhi, Abraham Heschel, Martin Luther King, Dorothy Day, Thich Nhat Hanh, and others—recognize that rights are the political expression of the deepest core of freedom already granted by the spirit. Their advancement is indelibly tied to religious values that teach and practice compassion, equanimity, nonviolence, and peace. Every commitment to advancing human dignity also involves a necessary awareness and transformation of hidden states of consciousness that perpetuate acceptance or silence in the face of the inferior status of "the other" or violence directed at another's life. A right always involves growth in consciousness, which in turn obligates the right holder to combat the inferiority, self-hatred, or lack of self-worth that demoralizes personal integrity and crushes one's ability to resist. Similarly, on the side of abusers and those thus obligated to effect remedy, there must exist an inner repentance, or coming to terms with the shame and sorrow one feels and the suffering and pain one has caused. This, too, involves engagement with the spiritual issues of life.

The inclusion of spiritual rights into the vocabulary of rights reminds us not to "forget the existence of mental and spiritual violence as well as the fact that physical violence can harm and destroy not only the body but also the human spirit."[20] As Teresa of Avila poignantly reminded us five centuries ago, women must prevent "being subject to a man in the outside world; a man who often kills their bodies, and God forbid, could also kill their souls."[21] Violence to the spirit extends to include violent uses of language and the metaphors and images we hold of God and creation. Spiritual rights, however, are not alone concerned with the negative impact of violence, but with what Gandhi called *satyagraha*—the "soul-force" that empowers the life-affirming strength and moral resilience necessary for the conversion of the human heart and the creation of new cultural transformation. It is this spiritual core of the person that provides the ultimate strength of character to uphold the sacredness of life and to resist dehumanizing violence. "Spirituality can be a chief source of resistance against cultural violence as it draws on all that is just and life giving in people's traditions, and critiques those parts of tradition that are death dealing in women's lives and the lives of their communities and lands."[22]

Like spirituality, spiritual human rights must be holistic and cosmic, connecting our bodies, our spirits, and our communities in the search for a more just, humane, and meaningful direction for our lives. This transformation "only comes partially and slowly as small pieces of our cultures are lifted up and reshaped to affirm life-giving values and spirituality."[23] As a solution to global apathy or ignorance, women and all others deprived of fundamental rights must be seen through God's eyes—from the perspective of divine love and compassion—as one human family. Our personal and global integrity depends on it.

Intimate Violence against Women

> Unremitting and interminable the obscenity and brutality of violence suffered by women are named, only to occur, again and again and again. Will it never end? The pain permeates the being of all women when we confront the unrelenting evil done to women in war and in times of so-called peace.[24]

In today's global community, violence against women remains one of the most intractable violations of women's human rights. In various forms it persists in times of peace as well as times of conflict. Women are beaten in their homes by husbands and other intimate partners; raped and sexually assaulted during war by soldiers; raped in refugee camps by other refugees or the military; and targeted for sexual trafficking, often leading to death, by bands of predators around the globe.[25] In a global community that has yet to take concerted and direct action to ameliorate the suffering of women worldwide, sexual violence against women occurs simply because they are female.

Traci West calls this "intimate violence." These varied forms of violence are directed at the "sexual violation of a woman's body and constitute intimate violence regardless of whether the assault occurs within a chosen relationship of intimacy or not."[26] Male-perpetuated partner or stranger rape, domestic or sexual abuse, genital mutilation, incest, forced prostitution, and torture are wielded as an attack against a woman's bodily and spiritual integrity, and are targeted toward a woman's intimate connection with her self or her relationship with her community and her divine source. Since physical and spiritual inviolability is a cultural sign of women's integrity—and a free gift of divinity that must always be freely given—violence against women also is violence against the spirit of God in them. Because sexual violence desecrates what is most intimate in women, there is no separation between sexual violence against a woman's body and violence against her soul. The right to guard her *being* from penetration by violent aggression is granted by the inviolable dignity of her person made in the image and likeness of the divine. All forms of intimate violence attack what is most sacred in women.

Recent statistics provide a shocking view of worldwide abuses committed against women in all countries around the globe.

- The World Health Organization reported in 2002 that up to 70 percent of female murder victims are killed by their male partners.
- In Rwanda alone, approximately 500,000 women were raped during the 1994 genocide and an estimated 5,000 pregnancies resulted from those rapes.
- In its 1997 report, the UN Family Planning Association estimated that over 120 million women worldwide have undergone some form of genital mutilation and at least 2 million girls per year are at risk of mutilation.
- The United States government estimated in 1999 that one to two million women and girls were being trafficked annually around the world for the purposes of forced labor, forced prostitution, servile domestic labor, or involuntary marriage.[27]
- More than sixty million girls are estimated to be "missing" from the world today as a result of sex-selective abortions and female infanticide as of 1999.
- Up to 200,000 women were estimated to have been forced to serve as "comfort women" in military brothels of the Japanese Imperial army during World War II.
- Women and children make up some 80 percent of the world's millions of refugees and other displaced persons.[28]
- In the United States, a woman is beaten every eighteen minutes; three to four million are battered each year, and four thousand are beaten to death by their partners.[29]

In addition to explicit sexual acts of violence against women, economic, racial, and social inequalities contribute to the untold tragedy of millions of women around the globe. Because of traditions within societies, women are allocated less food in developing nations, where 50 percent of all women and 60 percent of pregnant women suffer from nutritional anemia, resulting in dire consequences for newborns' and mothers' health. Each year, almost 600,000 women (or 1,600 per day) die in pregnancy and childbirth. These women leave behind at least a million motherless children.[30] Women, who are half of the world's population, also make up 70 percent of the world's poor and perform two-thirds of the world's work. But they receive only one-tenth of the world's income and own only one-one hundredth of the world's property.[31] Lest we think that American women have achieved economic equality with men, we must realize that in the United States women still garner less in wages for similar jobs, earning 73 cents for every dollar earned by men.

So rooted is this male privilege over females in human societies that even a cursory glance at this list reveals that an inseparable link exists between violence against women, the inequality of women's power, and ownership of women's sexuality. Through legal codes, state-enforced norms, and religious consensus, women around the world still belong to, and are the property of, men. The male person as representative of a male God or Higher Power is authorized and valorized by cultural habit and religious decree to have control over the bodily and spiritual production of females. Often dependent on male family members for physical protection and sustenance, women in our world community are vulnerable to dowry murder, *sati* (in India, socially sanctioned suicide whereby the widow throws herself into the funeral pyre of her husband); reproductive violence; and other brutal social crimes. Domination and dependence of females are reinforced by male physical violence and ultimately violence over the most vulnerable and sensitive aspects of a woman's humanity—her sexual and spiritual integrity. In her study of the societal function of mass rapes, Ruth Seifert concludes that rape "regulates unequal power relationships between the sexes: it serves to maintain a certain cultural order between the sexes or—when this order becomes fragile—to restore it."[32]

Women as Objects

Intimate violence is designed to depersonalize women's bodies, rape their souls, and destroy their resistance. This acceptance of sexual violence against women in the domestic sphere is reflected in the shocking statistics that dehumanize and objectify women's bodies. Every year, some three million women in the United States alone are smacked, punched, kicked, scalded, burned, stabbed, shot, or sexually tortured by the men who say they love them. Domestic violence is magnified elsewhere in times of national or regional war, where women are targeted for rape as a deliberate policy of warring parties, and are sexually abused by the opposing side as a method of war. The objectified and raped female body functions to demoralize and punish the enemy. Studies of war crimes against women in Bosnia-Herzegovina, for example, indicate that soldiers did not fear being punished for sexual violence because women—like other objects—are spoils of war and therefore sexually available to them in times of conflict. "As a member of the highest military court in the United States explained, a rape in a war zone has no relation to available women or prostitutes. That means that in the 'open space' of war, many men simply prefer to rape."[33]

Ownership of Women's Bodies

Intimate violence against women is violence against their bodies. Most analyses of sexual violence and "femicide point out that such male violence against women and children is motivated by proprietary control and jealousy which are deeply ingrained in [the world's] cultural, political, and religious traditions and self-understandings."[34] Sanctioned ownership over females reflects a cultural recognition of women's vital importance to life that is inversely connected to the degree to which this cultural need is disowned or disguised. Often, the more valuable women are to social well-being, the more cultural controls are placed on them, and the less likely it is that their contributions are acknowledged. Patriarchal societies and religions, for example, assert rights over the production of women's bodies but disown the sacredness of their bodies. Frequently, male assertion of ownership and control over women is justified as a means to protect women's purity or to imply care or concern. But, in fact, such protection comes at a steep price because care afforded to females in these cases is at the whim of an obligation ascribed to the male "owner," and not an inherent entitlement or right of the female who is "owned."

Violence against Women's Spirit

Violence against women's bodies is also violence against their spirits. Physical abuses are spiritual abuses; spiritual violence perpetuates and underlies physical violence. Torture, rape, and other physical punishments are "intended [not only] to brutalize the body but also to intimidate the soul, until a state of total dependence [is] created."[35] Based on a desire to degrade, humiliate, objectify, possess, or murder the spiritual power or soul force that is female, intimate violence against women also can be understood as a profoundly mystical issue. Insofar as woman's body is God's body, male intimate violence against women attempts to make God a defiled woman. Rape destroys or attempts to destroy the bodily and spiritual integrity of a woman; it tears apart the capacity for intimacy that is holiness itself, making of intimacy a pornographic act designed to take away the humanity of another person. While violent aggression—rather than sexuality—is often cited as the motivation for rape, it is also violence against the sexual being that women spiritually represent. It is an act of rage against women's divinity, against what is whole, intimate, or pure. So radical is the effect that violent sexual acts have on women's body and soul that rape is viewed as "a massive attack on female subjectivity that goes so far as to destroy it. If one suppresses and silences this experience, it means that, in a cultural context, women's experience and therefore women's subjectivity is extinguished."[36]

Women's Humiliation Is Cultural Humiliation

The inscription of women's bodies is so central to cultural and national identity that throughout history rapes, forced pregnancies, and other sexual abuses have traditionally served as a means to attack the enemy's population. In many cultures a group's meaning is denoted by the female gender, through whose person, body, and life the community is created and perpetuated. This means that "the rape of the women in a community can be regarded as the symbolic rape of the body of this community. Against this background, the mass rapes that accompany all wars take on new meaning: by no means acts of senseless brutality, they are rather culture-destroying actions with a strategic rationale."[37] The rape of Native American women, for example, is the story of the violent destruction of their bodily integrity, the destruction of cultural and national sovereignty, and the desecration of the earth. Traditionally, Native women usually were not subordinate to men. While stereotypes persist that Native women were dominated by males, many societies were matrilineal and violence against women and children was unheard of or rare. However, "Paula Gunn Allen argues that Christian colonizers realized that in order to subjugate indigenous nations, they would have to subjugate the women in those nations. . . . They had to convince 'both men and women that a woman's proper place was under the authority of her husband and that a man's proper place was under the authority of the priests.'"[38]

Silence as Suffering

Violence against women is barely mentioned in the casualty count of wars, often relegated to a footnote or dismissed as a normal part of war. Sexual violence was not even listed as a war crime under the Geneva Convention until evidence of mass rapes in the countries of the former Yugoslavia were brought to the world's attention in 1992. This silence in the face of women's suffering has deep roots in cultural constructions of gender relations, and reinforces women's fear of social shunning by husbands, male partners, families, and friends. It also deprives victims of the critical awareness needed to take action against female oppression, and of the tools necessary for healing at these profound depths. It prevents perpetrators—including male rapists and sexual partners, nations, and armies—from coming to terms with their complicity in violating or even destroying the female body by using language that depersonalizes or distances the victims. Here the full impact of one's actions in defiling or eradicating the sacred is shielded from the collective mourning and repentance necessary for healing and forgiveness.

Violence against women violates a woman's fundamental right to achieve spiritual holiness and to live on the earth sensitive to the unity among all beings. It also highlights how women's divine presence and divine concern in the human sphere is forcibly prevented from contributing to the world or eradicated through cultural violence or early death. Through being attentive to women's spiritual rights we can better evaluate the depth and scope of female suffering and directly name the impact crimes against women have on women's souls. From a spiritual perspective, women's human rights claims exceed any national, religious, or institutional authority, being vested in them by their inalienable status as females.

Spiritual Implications of Violence against Women

It is clearly understood today that intimate violence has an enormous impact on women's spirits and self-identity. Women who have suffered from intimate violence experience profound soul wounds that often imperil their inner security, propel a crisis of faith, and estrange them from their most significant personal and community relationships. Further, the shame and humiliation women suffer are all too frequently reinforced by social mores and legal ineptitude, effectively denying a woman's pain, making her complicit in its causes, or casting her out of communal relations. This societal callousness contributes to women survivors' sense of invisibility and perpetuates the self-erasure and suppression of self-hood that even in times of "peace" feminists concede is the greatest detriment to women's full humanity. In having her body "invaded against her will, used as an object by another, or injured by someone she trusted to care for her," a woman suffers defilement.[39] This sense of being unclean, tainted, or impure is a form of spiritual annihilation that renders a woman "homeless in her own body."[40]

In damaging her personal integrity, intimate violence threatens a woman's sense of control over her own life and her ability to love and be loved. The pain violence inflicts is far deeper and more profound than the physical injury itself. It scars her soul, damaging a woman's faith, hope, love, and trust. It blocks her ability to connect with deep reservoirs of vulnerability and generosity, not in supplication to male demands, but as the source of her own quest for meaning and fullness of being. The effect of these hidden scars in women's hearts and souls cannot be measured in material or monetary terms. These wounds profoundly affect a woman's capacity to fulfill her highest spiritual potential. Harboring such suffering, a woman's world and relationships are radically unsafe, her heart is unstable, and her ability to love and be loved, impoverished. Women survivors of abuse struggle against a tide that threatens to overwhelm or drown them in grief, shame, or guilt.

Because women are socialized to bear the responsibility of relationships, women survivors of intimate violence frequently blame themselves for causing it. The complicity of society in blaming the victim and perpetuating her shame contribute to the intense anger survivors feel or fear. In addition, religious teachings on forgiveness, compliance, and love can compound the emotional pain of women and girls afflicted by violence, many of whom are encouraged by their clergy or families to be more tolerant or forgiving of their abuser, especially if he is a husband, father, or other close relation.[41] This betrayal of trust extends to God, leading survivors to question why God has allowed this to happen, or why God is punishing them for sin. Traci West, in her study of black women's experiences of sexual violence, writes, "It may seem that God is not able to feel women's woundedness and deprivation, or that God deliberately chooses to ignore them because the woman deserves to suffer."[42] A sense of being abandoned or rejected by God further damages a woman's fragile hope of healing and requires renewed effort to restore her faith in God's indwelling spirit.

In her study of global torture, *The Body in Pain*, Elaine Scarry recognizes that "pain comes unsharably into our midst as at once that which cannot be denied and that which cannot be confirmed. Whatever pain achieves, it achieves in part through its unsharability, and it ensures this unsharability through its resistance to language."[43] At the same time, women's outrage against attempts to permanently silence them through violent acts of pain can empower survivors to resist and retrieve previously unknown or suppressed resources of female power, compassion, and strength. A woman's particular suffering is also all women's suffering: it is the pain of feeling God's presence and simultaneously experiencing God's absence in the world. It is the inner realization of divine love—whatever denounces love wounds the heart of each and every one of us lovers.

We cannot assimilate fully the extent of the suffering women experience worldwide. But we can understand that God has a divine concern with the integrity of women and the honoring of the holy in them. As women demand their inherent right to spiritual dignity, they become powerful forces for social transformation. The source of their resistance is not only social, economic, or cultural but also mystical: that fount of mercy, power of determination, and spirit of courage women bring into the world. In honoring women's mystic presence, we must do everything possible to refute the death-dealing politics and subjugating cultural norms that contribute to global female violence, and commit our hearts to the flourishing of the Feminine Divine in women and girls.

chapter eleven

Love of the World

An Ethic
of Ultimate Concern

Think of the phoenix coming up out of ashes, but not flying off. For a moment we have form. We can't see. How can we be conscious and you be conscious at the same time and separate? Copper when an alchemist works on it loses its copper qualities. Seeds in Spring begin to be tree, no longer seed. Brushwood put in the fire changes. The snow-world melts. You step in my footprint and it's gone. . . . Predestination and freewill: We can argue them but they're only ideas. What's real is a presence, like Shams.[1]

I began this book writing about a kind of American pragmatism that becomes mere sloganism and dulls us to the profound implications of a spiritually sensitive life. It also conceals a thinly disguised cultural materialism that appropriates our world as a commercial enterprise with no intrinsic worth of its own. By placing a higher value on what has the latest currency in the marketplace, we denigrate the majesty with which life confronts us. In whetting our attraction to material comfort and benefit, we are diverted from the terrible barbarism being unleashed on the world today. Perhaps even more disturbing, a materialistic mind-set also permeates the religious dimension, permitting and justifying prejudice and hatred—racism, sexism, homophobia, war, violence, and pain—perpetrated in God's name. In its extreme forms, materialism, whether cultural or spiritual, becomes a collective trivialization of the wonder and tragedy of life. As it condones the rape of the earth's natural resources, it pits those who have too much against those who do not have enough. In a global economy, women are doubly repressed by this ideology, as producers for its advancement and commodities to be owned.

Into this mix, contemplation comes as a breath of pure air, reminding us that we find true freedom and happiness in the simplicity of self, and not in the accumulation of desires. The problem is that women need to discover a contemplative way of living that comes out of their own experiences and that is integrated into their own lives. In a way, they have to be mystics, willing to search beneath the superficial distractions and ideologies that pose as cultural sophistication today to bring out their inner spiritual freedom. It is not enough that women discover a mystical approach, but they must apply the mystical to free whatever of the feminine or female is repressed or oppressed in them; and then further, to link women's prophetic authority to social transformation.

Important, too, is that the contemplative ideal as practiced by the women mystics is also a model of resistance, which sees the worth of things not in their attraction for self-advancement or gain, but in their simple furtherance of the depth of the soul. This means that contemplation is often at odds not only with dominant cultural norms but also with religion, and even with its spirituality. To the extent that they, too, are tools of suppression, religions domesticate the kind of deep engagement that "penetrates beneath the surface of a [person's] life to get behind the façade of conventional gestures and attitudes which [one] presents to the world."[2] Even as its various forms of prayer may emerge out of a religion, contemplation does not belong to religion, being its prior and more holy animating force. It alone is capable of planting the wisdom of solitude within a person's heart. And this, too, is the worth of contemplation as women today navigate the treacherous waters of economic gain and social advancement. At risk in the world of commerce, the lure of achievement and progress often is bought at the expense of women's physical and spiritual health.

The contemplative life cannot offer us what the world tells us we should want; it has nothing to teach us about the demands of earthly accumulation and personal privilege. Contemplation takes us to something more enduring and freeing, away from the illusory self and into the depths of our own hearts. It rejects the false dichotomizing that pervades political circles today and the false optimism that makes a mockery of women's and the world's suffering in order to tend to the soul of creation. In the sublime solitude contemplation offers, women find the courage to protest the commercializing of their bodies, and the strength to resist the stealing of their souls. Oriana Fallaci wrote: "The solitude [I needed] wasn't a physical solitude. . . . It was an interior solitude that comes about from the fact of being a woman—a woman with responsibilities in the world of men."[3]

Contemplation centers the self not in one's religion, family, or nation, but in silence. From this centered point of nowhere, all of our actions and relations come into focus. As women free themselves from oppression, they come full circle, recovering ancient sources of women's wisdom as tools for the betterment of their lives and their relationships. They are prophets who turn their attention to the plight of creation in what is variously termed the postindustrial, postmodern, and postreligious world in which we now live. Yet, despite the fact that all civilizations posit the human as expressly capable of transcendence, this capacity to grow toward divinity is probably one of the most difficult of women's admissions today. If we believe in our potential in the private sphere, talk of it is virtually absent from the dominant political and social realm. It is almost invariably true that in "polite" company we do not admit our desire to be saints. Our technological world has placed the divine at risk and all but made us ashamed of that superior commitment to personal holiness and human dignity that is the heart of every noble civilization. Feminism, at its core, works to uphold the unity of all beings in the circle of creation. It is this reclamation, not only of women's divinity, but also of the whole world's sacredness that is urgently needed now.

Thoughts on a Mystical Ethic

> I am loved by him who is not in this world. . . . Yet I see him who is eternal and yet born, and speak with him and dare to say: I love, for he loves me. I feed on contemplation; I clothe myself in it; united with him I transcend the heavens. And that all this is true and certain, I know.[4]

These words of the Greek monk Symeon the New Theologian are more than metaphor; they represent a provocative attempt to convey the truly real—the most tangible and significant meaning in life. Possessed by an awareness of the nearness and presence of God, the force of Symeon's love is echoed elsewhere by other souls inebriated by ambiguity and awe. The Sufi master al-Hallaj joins a long list of martyred saints who dared to state: *I am God* (*ana al-haqq*, literally "I am the truth"). Not the sign of an inflated, privatized self, but the ecstasy of finally being nothing, this claim of identity cannot be quelled. It flows over into everything, unifying in itself the illusion of separateness like sugar dissolved in water or salt poured into the sea. "We are limbs of Christ; Christ is our limb . . . and I, the poorest creature," praises Symeon, "am the hand and foot of Christ."[5] In meeting another human being, we have the opportunity to sense the image of God, the presence of the holy.

This concern for the whole earth and its inhabitants as one interdependent family is rooted in a deeply contemplative, prayerful attitude. Contemplation builds an inner hermitage in the person's core—a holy respite free from everyday antics and daily distractions—where one does not flee from the world but rather finds it anew. As a return to the center point of love, contemplation touches an inexhaustible ocean of compassion from which all external works of mercy are generated. This relationship between ethical action and contemplative prayer is explicitly stated in Teresa of Avila's *Meditations on the Song of Songs*. "Martha and Mary," she writes, "never fail to work almost together when the soul is in this state [mystical marriage]. For in the active (and seemingly exterior) work the soul is working interiorly. And when the active works rise from this interior root, they become lovely and very fragrant flowers."[6] Fruitful action, action that does not create harm, violence, or pain, arises from nonaction—from a person's capacity to be free from self-interested gain.

The authority of a contemplative ethic arises out of a mystical connection to the whole family of creation. This means that the depth of our being is in solidarity with the depth of all beings. The divine spark in the center of our soul is sustained by and has a stake in the flourishing of all other souls and life forms. It also recognizes that our spiritual life is profoundly affected by and dependent upon the spiritual integrity of every other life. We are never free from the suffering and the happiness of the world. The understanding prevalent in many religious traditions, that there is truly no individual enlightenment without the enlightenment of all beings, is mystically true. "The ultimate goal of the Kabbalist," Abraham Joshua Heschel writes, "is not his own union with the Absolute but the union of all reality with God; one's own bliss is subordinated to the redemption of all."[7] Heschel's realization is elsewhere echoed, as in the Mahayana Buddhist vow to relinquish individual enlightenment until all sentient beings are free. Conversely, the idea that we are elected or chosen to achieve salvation at the expense of, or with indifference to, others is contrary to the vision of a mystical ethic.

While this mystical sensitivity and ethical stance toward the dignity of all beings cannot always be achieved, its vision, nonetheless, can be used as a unifying model of interpretation, analysis, and decision-making. In this unitive state of consciousness, we can say: all beings are reflected in my being;

all suffering is my suffering; all mercy is my mercy. This *capacity* for mystical sensitivity is a fact intrinsic to what it means to be human: we are made in the divine image; we are interdependent with all beings; we are bonded together in love. An ethic of ultimate concern moves out of contemplative states of consciousness—among them prayer, meditation, development of virtues, and silence—in order to leave behind conventional views and behaviors and to bring the divine vision into the human sphere. Within the vessel or enclosure of enlightened states of awareness, God's longing for our redemption takes root and grows. Contemplation is both source and fruit of spiritual virtues, the former leading to the attainment of humility, compassion, and detachment of soul, while the latter overflows into concern for the happiness and betterment of all beings. This mystical core of transcendence within the human being mirrors and strives to plant the seeds of justice and love in all relations. Through the heart of the person seized by God, individual consciousness is universalized—one loves and feels from the perspective of the whole—and expands out from a personal, salvation ethic to include a wider social, contemplative ethic.

This contemplative ethic is founded not in "should" and "ought," or abstract principles of theological analysis or the law, but in silence and awe. It is not an ethic derived from external codes of conduct but, more fundamental and radical, is one already inscribed in the spiritual structure of the world. This ethical intimacy with God is present in our action and suffers our non-action; it is forever involved in the flourishing of life on earth. Against the vast expanse of God's ever-present compassion and mercy, human tragedy and glory is felt in the most intimate part of the soul. Often contrary to our own will or knowledge, our soul is united in empathy with the suffering and happiness of others. Human compassion for the immeasurable sensitivity of life draws us closer to each other and to God; just as human harm divides and fragments our hearts. In the interior stillness where God speaks directly to our soul, one to one and heart to heart, the authenticity of the person is tested and honed.

A mystical ethic is, in essence, a mothering one; it embraces the world as a mother's body surrounds and nurtures life within her womb. Metaphors of pregnancy and birth help convey how each day we bear—lay our bodies down for—the spiritual renewal of life. And when this offspring of our flesh (or mind or heart) is born, this bodily-spiritual integrity, this connection to Life, is never severed, even unto death or after death. We, who are born in intimacy with our mother/God, know something of her/Her suffering, and have a stake in the healing of souls. Drawn together in the piety of creation, we are never free of this reciprocal and indivisible closeness to the divine spirit in us. It is merely a mental sleight of hand—the realm of illusion and conditioning—that situates the separated, individualistic self at the center of reality. No, the reality is more majestic than that: within our own mind is also Enlightened Mind, Christ Consciousness—a fully realized and fully awakened state. The intensity of this realization compels us to *feel* what we rationalize, objectify, or ignore, and to bear these emotions in a deeper ground of equanimity and solitude.

Our Mother Pietas (Piety) leans down toward earth, drawing all creatures into Her nourishing fold. Like St. Hildegard's depiction of Sapientia and Caritas, Pietas represents the mutual indwelling of the Feminine Divine in the world and the world in Her. In its medieval usage, piety did not "carry the superficial religiosity that it does at present in English. Rather," Ewert Cousins explains, "piety was a profoundly relational virtue, the ancient Roman *pietas* that provided the root of intimate relations in the family, in the clan, and in the state. It included love, devotion, affection, reverence, kindness, fidelity, and compassion." With this in mind, we can realize the significance of the word "piety" in conveying the familial bond that was exemplified in St. Francis's communion with all of creation. "When he considered the primordial source of all things, he was filled with even more abundant piety, calling creatures, no matter how small, by the name of brother or sister, because he knew they had the same source as himself."[8]

Our Mother Pietas fosters an "ethics of Shekhinah" and an "ethics of Sophia" that reverse the powers of the world, making the weak mighty and the lowly high. As the presence of God's indwelling, the kabbalists tell us that Shekhinah is outcast in the world. By dwelling among us, she willingly goes into exile from her divine origins and suffers isolation and the tragedy of the human condition. Involved in the perilous state of the world, Shekhinah is the embodiment of the highest form of love—mother-love—and only through Her can we find our way back to God. Similarly, Sophia plays an active part in our destiny, calling aloud in the streets, demanding that we free ourselves from ignorance (Prov. 1:22). Sophia is both teacher and what is taught, instilling in us a moral concern based on "an inexhaustible sweetness and purity, a silence that is a fount of action and joy," Merton's praise proclaims.

> It rises up in wordless gentleness and flows out to me from the unseen roots of all created being, welcoming me tenderly, saluting me with indescribable humility. This is at once my own being, my own nature,

and the Gift of my Creator's Thought and Art within me, speaking as
Hagia Sophia, speaking as my sister, Wisdom. . . . We do not hear [Her]
mercy, or yielding love, or non-resistance, or non-reprisal. We do not
hear uncomplaining pardon that bows down the innocent visages of
flowers to the dewy earth. . . . Sophia crowns [God] not with what is
glorious but with what is greater than glory: the one thing greater than
glory is weakness, nothingness, poverty.[9]

The ethics of Shekhinah and Sophia does not and cannot ignore sin or
evil, but rather situates all moral action in the primacy of unconditional
mother-love. Sin-based theologies founded upon an originating violation
that is rectified only by movement toward an undisclosed future, is contrary to Her blessing, which affirms the original sinlessness of creation. The
notion of one god and one truth that situates itself over against all "others,"
and struggles to preserve its singular identity and power, is a distortion of
Her compassion and mercy. The ego structures that undergird a religion's
quest for dominance and superiority violate Her cooperative relationality,
which brings all to Love. She loves us even when we do not deserve love;
She desires us even when we are undesirable; and She longs for us even
when we deny our own longing.

Mother Pietas reveals divine compassion as the inner structure of the
world, and intimacy—mutuality, closeness, and affection—as the inner
structure of the human being. Divine mothering love is not a stage in the
history of the world, but the liberatory inner structure of history. Given the
solidarity of all human beings in Her indwelling presence, mysticism is not
only a self-realization of the individual soul, but always a prophetic com-
mandment as well. In this meditation on the heart-breaking glory of our
world, three images come to mind: bearing the intimacy, love, and holiness
of the family of creation.

Bearing the Intimacy of the World

Intimacy is a central metaphor in the writings of the women mystics we
have studied. Whether identified with God's suffering, or with compassion
for all sentient beings, the women mystics move from beginning experiences of mystical union to a deeper, ontological intimacy between the
depth of their souls and God. The communion between God and the soul
is "so intimate a friendship" that everything is shared equally and the soul
experiences not only its own will, but God's will. Teresa of Avila reflects
on how difficult it is for a soul joined with God "to see the many offenses

committed so continually against His Majesty . . . that I believe that only one day of that pain would have been sufficient to end many lives."[10] For those who are possessed by God's presence in the world, human sin strikes at the very core where God and the soul are one.

In Julian, Teresa, and other mystics, intimacy rejects a static moral order in favor of a relational ethics, which derives its authority from a primary encounter with God's suffering and pathos for us. In their personal mystical revelations of the suffering face of Christ, our mystics would find resonance with Emmanuel Levinas on the importance of the face, and would no doubt agree that "a face imposes itself upon me without my being able to be deaf to it or to forget it, that is, without my being able to suspend my responsibility for its distress."[11] It is always in relationship to the wounded face of the other that the women mystics are pierced to the core of being in solidarity for the suffering others of our world. This intimate and intensely relational love of God draws the person into direct experience of the existential reality that is at the core of Buddha's Four Noble Truths, Jesus' passion on the cross, or God's pathos for the world. Rumi captures its poetic essence:

> We are the mirror as well as the face in it.
> We are tasting the taste this minute
> of eternity. We are pain
> and what cures pain. We are
> the sweet, cold water and the jar that pours.[12]

Awareness and compunction lead to healing, and a desire to embrace the collective longing and pain of humanity in spiritual love. Teresa writes how God showed her the experience of hell so she would understand the urgency of an ethical response to take action to mend spiritual wounds. "I notice that if we see a person . . . with a great trial or suffering, it seems that our own very nature invites us to compassion; and if their trial is great, we ourselves become distressed. . . . No heart can bear it without great pain. . . . This awareness also makes me desire that in a matter so important we don't grow satisfied with anything less than doing all we can on our part; let us neglect nothing, and may it please the Lord that He be served by giving us the grace to do all we can."[13] This ability to feel and identify with the depth of another's wound generates an ethic of mutuality and compassion, a desire to share in and bring healing to the sorrows of others.

At the highest states of mystical consciousness, intimacy—as the collapsing, fusing, or annihilating of boundaries—*is* understanding and action. In true intimacy, subject and object disappear. Two become one, an experi-

ence the Vietnamese Buddhist monk Thich Nhat Hahn calls "interbeing,"
a nondual state of reality. The fusion of love between God and our souls is
intrinsic to our deepest nature and is mirrored in the intensity of our desire
for relation and understanding. This powerful drive for unity recognizes and
upholds the friendship and deep affection the whole human family feels for
each other and for all species and creative life forms. Chinese philosophers
also "gave clearest expression to this intimacy of beings with each other in
its splendid concept of *Jen*," Thomas Berry contends, which means "love,
goodness, human-heartedness, and affection. All beings are held together in
Jen, as in St. Paul all things are held together in Christ. . . . For this reason,
there is, in China, the universal law of compassion. This law is especially
observable in humankind, for every human has a heart that cannot bear to
witness the suffering of others."[14]

An ethics of intimacy evaluates our religions and our lives through a different lens. In seeing with the eye of Wisdom, the person as historical subject
is momentarily suspended outside of time, place, and individual awareness
in order to grasp reality from the vantage point of the whole. This momen-
tary collapsing of distinction between self and other, human and divine is
a fact intrinsic to the mystical dimension of consciousness. Subverting the
tendency to claim absolute and final truths, mystical intimacy recognizes
that truth is tested out in daily existence, when the self melts away and both
God and the world are undone. It brings us into deep association with creation, tears down the walls of segregation and exclusion, opens our hearts
to the mysterious patterning of life's wholeness, and teaches us not to turn
away from suffering and pain. There is no liberation for one without liberation for all. In this sense, contemplative ethics is an extended meditation
on the question of integration, of joining the fragmented human self into
wholeness, a wholeness that in turn teaches us about the interconnectedness
of the world.

Bearing the Love of the World

The mystics' affirmation of the goodness of creation requires a different attitude toward the world, an attitude that can be described by what Hannah
Arendt called *amor mundi*, love of the world.[15] Julian of Norwich enshrines
this mystical love for the world in her reflection on the motherhood of
Jesus: "He is our clothing, who wraps and enfolds us for love, embraces us
and shelters us, surrounds us for his love, which is so tender that he may
never desert us."[16] By associating the qualities of unconditional love and

mercy with the mother figure, Julian conveys a more embodied, physical sense of the healing of sins and the unity of creation. Because the mother's service is "nearest, readiest, and surest," writes Julian, "we are brought back by the motherhood of mercy and grace into our natural place, in which we were created by the motherhood of love, a mother's love which never leaves us."[17]

Dorothy Day, the American Catholic activist, also challenges us to transform social injustices and personal despair into an integrated theology of love. Her quest to embrace the world in the arms of love begins with a very personal struggle to reconcile God's love for the world with human apathy and ignorance concerning the *depth* of another's pain. Imprisoned in her twenties for civil disobedience, Day identifies with the anguish of prisoners she meets and those other unknown and unidentified faces around the globe: "I reflected on the desolation of poverty, of destitution, of sickness and sin. . . . I would never be free again, never free when I knew that behind bars all over the world there were women and men, young girls and boys, suffering constraint, punishment, isolation and hardship for crimes of which we are all guilty. . . . I was the mother whose child had been raped and slain. I was the mother who had borne the monster who had done it. I was even that monster, feeling in my own breast every abomination."[18]

Describing a childhood experience in *The Story of My Experiments in Truth*, Mahatma Gandhi also poignantly reflects on the power of spiritual love. He took it upon himself to confess to his father the stealing of a bit of gold from his older brother. On a slip of paper he confessed his guilt and asked to be adequately punished for it. He recollects:

> I was trembling when I handed the confession to my father. . . . He read it through and pearl-drops trickled down his cheeks, wetting the paper. For a moment he closed his eyes in thought and then tore up the note. . . . I also cried. I could see my father's agony.
>
> Those pearl-drops of love cleansed my heart and washed my sin away. Only he who has experienced such love can know what it is. . . .
>
> This was for me an object lesson in Ahimsa [Love and Non-Violence]. Then I could read in it nothing more than a father's love but today I know that it was pure Ahimsa. When such Ahimsa becomes all-embracing it transforms everything it touches. There is no limit to its power.[19]

In Julian, Day, and Gandhi, suffering is for love; we are made for love; our sins are held in love. It is love that makes sin so painful, not punishment.

Love cannot bear the punishment of the lover. All of these mystics held that this sublime forgiveness is not natural to the human person, but is a graced infusion of God's love that illuminates and transforms the human heart. Out of this mystical love, moral behavior bursts forth in a torrent of desire. It is love for the world, the foundational love of all creatures that unleashes pure action and thought. Love engenders wellness and flourishing, and is resplendent in the cycle of birthing, growing, and replenishing that brings forth the diversity of creation. Straight out of the divine heart, again and again, we are compelled toward healing the fracture in consciousness that wounds love.

While a mystical ethics can be read as a repetition of the preoccupation with the salvation of the individual soul, this would be a misreading of the primary impetus of its concern. For it is not individual freedom mystical ethics desires alone, but to use this freedom in service of others. If one thing marks a world mystical ethic, it is the importance of loving the world into being, celebrating its flourishing, and working to mend its fractures and wounds. "The important thing," cautions Teresa, "is not to think much but to love much."[20]

Bearing the Holiness of the World

Holy, holy, holy . . . the whole earth is full of God's glory. (Isa. 6:3)

Mysticism, if it is anything, reveres and works to sustain the sacredness of the world. Never free from the glory of the unitive vision of reality, the mystic is defined as one who *feels* something of the wound God feels in our human ignorance and sin, and *touches* something of the love God pours upon us. On the frontiers of consciousness, she or he lives with a trouble in the soul that perhaps others do not yet feel or cannot yet see. Enraptured by a love for God and creation, it is spiritual love—a love with no self-interest—in us that celebrates the earth's joys and beauty, and works to transform conditions that breed poverty, war, and violence.

Our souls reverberate with the tragedies inflicted on life, even if we cannot name them, do not see them, or have been anaesthetized to their pain. Fired by praise and thanksgiving in the crucible of God's glory, we labor to restore the divine image in creation. Like St. Francis, who felt the imprint of the world's violence in his body, we cannot help but be consumed by events that wound our world. Yet, a mysterious relationship exists between the assumption of pain and the rejoicing that comes from recognizing our spiritual capacity to transform consciousness. One night, after suffering bodily torments for months, Francis begs God to look upon his infirmities so he may bear them patiently, and receives an alchemical vision of the earth transformed into gold. At once, he hears the spirit within him speak: "Tell me, brother: if anyone were to give you for your infirmities and tribulations such a great and precious treasure that, if the whole earth were pure gold, . . . yet you would consider all this as nothing . . . in comparison with the great and precious treasure given to you, surely you would rejoice greatly?"[21] Francis responds that this would be a very great treasure, indeed. Upon arising the next morning he composes his famous hymn on all creatures, "The Canticle of Brother Sun," and taught his companions, chanting "*Altissimo, omnipotente, bon Signore*"—Most high, omnipotent, good Lord—"Praised be You, My Lord, with all your creatures."

Like his spiritual father Francis, St. Bonaventure was praying one day at Mount La Verna in the Italian countryside. On the same hill where Francis had his vision of the six-winged Seraph, Bonaventure also was graced by a Seraphic illumination in the form of Christ crucified, afterward composing his glorious prose *Itinerarium mentis in deum* (The Soul's Journey to God). Envisioning all creatures as reflections of the power, wisdom, and goodness of God, he sees the world as "vestiges" or footprints of the Trinity, and the spiritual journey as a meditation on Christ's presence in the world, in the mind of God, and in the Trinity itself. This "Franciscan attitude," Ewert Cousins writes, "involves two basic elements: (1) a sense of reverence derived from the fact that the world is sacred as God's expression of himself; (2) a sense of intimacy with the physical universe: the inorganic, vegetative, and animal realms. Reverence alone is not enough; we must feel ourselves part of the family of creatures. It is this family consciousness that crowns Francis' attitude toward nature."[22]

In the love canticle of Francis or the gentle prose of Bonaventure, the mystic mind writes out of divinity, seeing it everywhere. This world is God's world. Samsara is nirvana; emptiness is form, and form is emptiness. Separation is our illusion; it is our willful ignorance and rejection of the immense beauty that surrounds us. The progress of a soul is not measured in terms of personal freedom, but is directed to something immeasurably noble: the bearing of divinity with God and for each other. Our hearts are too attuned to the shimmering beauty of God's presence to transcend the world's tragedies, pains, and sorrows. We have to bear them, enclosing them within the womb of mercy and inexhaustible ocean of peace until they, too, are transformed.

What does this mean to us that the great minds of human civilizations have experienced and felt God's imprint everywhere in creation? Perhaps their vision is best understood through exploring the symbolism of the word "bearing" as a way to comprehend the immensity of divine presence. Bearing the divinity of the world means to: (1) *birth* deeper dimensions of divinity and ourselves. Each time we make a choice for openness, love, compassion, and humility, we divinize the world. Every effort we make to bring happiness and peace to others restores our hope. In contemplation, we become living embodiments of the unity of transcendence and immanence; we are the potential birthplace of God in the world; (2) *produce* by natural growth in an organic process. This bearing of divinity does not come about through imposed or forced change. But it overflows from that center point of rest where, as Meister Eckhart wrote, "my eye and God's eye are one eye and one seeing, one knowing and one loving."[23] By so doing, we bring enlightened action and Teresa's "heroic deeds" to support the ongoing good-ness of creation; (3) *support* or hold the divine. Through right speech, truth-ful action, loving kindness, and generous speech we labor toward uniting all the divisions in us that contribute to harmful thoughts and violent actions against each other. This involves a conscious commitment to mindfulness, gentleness, nonviolence, and love. "To create fundamental change, we, the members of society, have to transform ourselves. If we want real peace," Thich Nhat Hanh writes, "we have to demonstrate love and understand-ing so that those responsible for making decisions can learn from us;"[24] (4) *sustain* the contemplative vision through commitment to prayer, meditation, and other spiritual practices and processes. Equally it must be upheld by a commitment to sustained social transformation that betters the lives of all beings. In learning the difference between transient desires and true needs, we discover a deeper and more lasting generosity and humility; (5) *suffer* or endure the failures and beauty of the created order. Because the world itself is the body or site of awe, realization of its stunning magnificence breaks our hearts. In suffering there is always that immensity that is forever beyond suffering; in suffering is another kind of joy. The anonymous author of *The Book of the Poor in Spirit by a Friend of God* says:

> My opinion is that he who is a true friend of God is never without suffering. He always suffers. And this takes place in four different ways. He suffers in his actions, and he suffers in his will; a third suffering is in his spirit and a fourth in God. And each suffering fosters a particular joy. . . .

The third suffering of a friend of God occurs in his soul when the spirit is seized by the divine spirit. God's garment of love is so wrapped around her that she relies on it and this bond becomes so pleasant that she finds everything else unpleasant. If the friend of God meets anything which does not spring from the Holy Spirit it causes him pain. And all that he sees and hears, all that is not divine, pains him and causes him suffering. . . .

The fourth suffering . . . is a suffering in God. This takes place when all unlikeness falls away from the spirit through grace. . . . God gives His heart and His powers in return, and the heart of the soul is now no longer merely human but godlike. Thus the heart always lives in an ardour of the divine fire and is penetrated by it so that she becomes weak through love. . . . When God is the working and man the suffering being, then all is made quiet within him. Man is absolved from punishment and guilt, for, when God reveals Himself to the soul, all must give way. . . . Nothing can reign there save God.[25]

(6) *bring* or carry gifts of the spirit to each other. In bearing the divine we become a host for spiritual gifts: freedom, reconciliation, faith, forgiveness, and hope. We *become* what we bear; the more we give ourselves away, the more spirit lives and works through us; (7) *resist* in body, mind, or heart the desacralization of the world, and actively work toward justice, fairness, and mercy. Spiritual resistance is our soul force, which overflows from the practice of nonviolence in thought, word, and deed; (8) *sow* or transmit peace, goodness, and compassion. As gardeners and sowers, we plant the seeds of devotion in all those we meet. Our job is to give away the self so new life can grow. In this sense, each day presents a new responsibility and a new opportunity to spread and harvest seeds of divinity; (9) *possess* as a quality of being. In bearing divinity, we become divine. In practicing the precepts and virtues of the contemplative life, God our Mother bends toward us and we reach up toward Her. This is our true inheritance. As truth is tempered and fired in the forge of our own nothingness, we, too, in bearing the holiness of the world are transmuted and transfigured by love.

A World Ethic of Spiritual Rights

As the experience of oneness with God, mysticism is the radical substantiation of the dignity of the human being.[26]

In light of Dorothee Soelle's wisdom, I return now to the question of spiritual rights raised in the last chapter. Since we humans are not the creators of life, but the beneficiaries of the precious gift of being, we must bring an attitude of humility to all our endeavors. Can we put into practice the sublimity of the mystics' praise of the world? How do we join in solidarity with others to create a climate of right human relations and planetary harmony? I offer seven meditations on a world ethic of spiritual rights.

Divine Element in Human Rights

Spiritual rights not only emphasize the obligation we humans exert on each other to live in dignity and accord, but also affirm that it is finally the Ultimate (that which is Spirit, God, Reality Itself) and not only humans that makes a primary claim on our actions in the world. Violations of human rights harm our bodies but also our souls; they have an impact on both the human and the divine sphere. In concert with human rights scholars, spiritual rights come into play when something essentially noble that defines the person—one's dignity and integrity—is threatened. Any threat of this magnitude, whether directed at the body, for example through violence or war, or at the spiritual core of the person, through injury to the soul, is defined as a violation of spiritual rights. A claim for a spiritual right can be defended when the deepest integrity of the person—what gives a person access to her or his ultimate source—has been systematically prevented, harmed, or destroyed.

From a spiritual perspective, the implications of our actions also have divine ramifications in the world. Genocide, racism, and sexism, as examples, reflect a direct violence against and rejection of God's living presence in the diversity of creation. Crimes against humanity are also crimes against divinity; similarly, whatever protects life contributes to the spiritual flourishing and happiness of all sentient beings.

Primacy of Spiritual Rights

Spiritual rights are not directed primarily to social and cultural implementation of specific freedoms—such as the right to vote, freedom of worship, or right to work, since these are already part of the United Nations charter and guaranteed by most constitutions. Rather, spiritual rights focus on how neglect, denial, or violence against any life form is directed against the integrity of the holy. They are claimed as a necessary demand for the alleviation of harm to the sacred in the person or in creation. Spiritual rights are involved not only with the right to religious practice or freedom, but also with every way in which what is constitutively religious, sacred, or holy is structurally violated, institutionally harmed, or personally prevented.

In this view, spiritual rights are not merely the experiential form of a religious or cultural view legitimized by a privileged religion, but a necessary partner of human rights; and a critic of religions and the social sciences in clarifying the profound implications of our systematic destruction of the sacred. The specific category of spiritual rights is necessary to remind us that harming the sacred unity of life leaves an indelible imprint on the human spirit. This type of wound is a suffering from which none can escape because it creates an indelible stain in the soul of humanity, bringing our hearts to the brink of despair. When exposed to the extremes of pain, we are left bereft of language, for no language can circumscribe, nor render meaning to, the vast silence that remains. In his book *The Survivor: An Anatomy of Life in the Death Camps*, Terrence Des Pres faced the task of rendering intelligibility to a radical suffering that was in danger of being betrayed by the word. In entering into dialogue with Holocaust survivors, "there seemed one language left—a kind of quasi-religious vocabulary," he writes, "which I have used not as a reflection of religious sentiment, but in the sense that only a language of ultimate concern can be adequate to facts such as these."[27]

Trans-religious Nature of Spiritual Rights

Spiritual rights are trans-religious, not rooted in or confined to any one religion, but they can be used to signify the common element of dignity for life found in all religions, the common element of being human. Spiritual rights are prior to and have moral legitimacy over the corporate religious or national politic, vested as these are in individual moral conscience. Spiritual rights thus reach beyond secular or national institutions into church hierarchies and cultures, spiritual lineages and masters, and other specifically religious entities to empower individuals to not give over to religious authorities rights inherent to being human. They also foster an individual's resistance to intimidation or threats by religious authorities of divine punishment to cede intrinsic human rights. This contemplative basis for moral outrage and mystical resistance is evident in the thought of many of the mystics. Howard Thurman calls it the "emancipation of men from all structural limitations, to make a mystical desert outside structure itself in which all can be one . . . 'a pure nothingness.'"[28] Thomas Merton describes it as a "higher light still, not the light by which man 'gives names' and forms concepts . . . but the dark light in which no names are given, in which God confronts man not through the medium of things, but in His own simplicity."[29]

God Is at Risk in the World

"The mystic's concern with the imperative for social action is not merely to improve the condition of society." This ethic is founded on something more elusive and demanding—its refusal to be concretized and its protest against the merely apparent. "It is not merely to feed the hungry," Thurman argues, "not merely to relieve human suffering and human misery. If this were all, in and of itself, it would be important surely. But this is not all. The basic consideration has to do with the removal of all that prevents God from coming to . . . [fullness] in the life of the individual. Whatever there is that blocks this, calls for action."[30] Thurman's emphasis on the relationship between the depths of moral anguish and the mystical imperative for social transformation is the spiritual heart of human rights. The cry that emits from our collective witnesses "is the voice that God has lent to the silent agony, a voice to the plundered poor, to the profaned riches of the world. It is a form of living, a crossing point of God" and humanity.[31]

Spiritual rights give specific advocacy to bring into dialogue the effect human rights violations have on the emotional and spiritual health of the person and by extension on the entire global community. Our most profound feelings of what is just and unjust, moral and immoral, truth and falsehood are indicators of the spirit speaking through us. We are filled with grief, fear, pain, anger, despair, and shame at the great loss and destruction of the holiness of our planet. We cannot and should not suppress this deep emotional anguish, but rather should channel its energy toward reconciliation and alleviation of suffering. It is both a human right and a divine right to be free from spiritual harm.

Equal Partners in Building the World

The right to be a spiritual person means, also, that what is spiritual no longer has to remain, figuratively, in the back of the cultural bus. Spirituality as the language that honors and preserves the sacred in this world has a right to be an equal partner in the maintenance and sustenance of the world. This does not mean that the spiritual trumps other forms of discourse; or that it has privileged access to truth; or that it can be wielded as a disguise for religious dogma or even a religion. It does mean, however, that the quality of consciousness to which "the spiritual" refers is vital to the future of our planet. There is something we all know—perhaps in Gandhi's notion of soul force or *satyagraha*—that tells us whether this or that religion, state, or theology is valid, or whether it ought to be challenged on the grounds of its truth or its justice. This spirit of ultimate concern recognizes that the fate of human rights, and thus the fate of our planet, is not yet decided in our time. By invoking what is more intimate, vulnerable, and sensitive, spiritual rights challenge the capacity of the human heart to truly love.

Dignity of All Beings

The inclusion of spiritual rights paves the way to apply the concept of a spiritual right to the integrity and flourishing of non-human life as well. It takes the discussion of rights away from its traditional human-centered focus and places them as interdependent with the rights of all other sentient beings and life forms in the cosmos. A holistic perspective that explicitly includes the spiritual contribution of all creation—mineral, vegetable, animal, and human—as central to an analysis of the causes of planetary problems is necessary to change violent assertions of human domination and dominion over nature to ones of cooperation and mutual reverence. Through relinquishing our presumption of superiority over the rest of creation, we realize that the human aspiration toward personal holiness is profoundly tied to and cannot be separated from the communion of the Spirit in and through all life forms. Thus, spiritual rights affirm the organic wholeness of humanity with the totality of creation, and recognize that only a world that respects this unity of interdependence can ensure the holiness of all beings. We have much work ahead of us to further this hope of peace and nonviolence.

Divine Planet on Earth

Spiritual rights provide a way of imagining a divine planet in which we take with utmost seriousness our participation in and responsibility for the sacredness of life. It is a gift to be born and to live in the precious diversity of our mother earth. All religions and spiritual traditions honor the unspeakable beauty of creation. Spiritual rights address what prevents us from actualizing a divine community on earth. They seek to make real the vision of one planetary family that is at the heart of all human rights declarations. Spiritual rights break down the division between spirit and matter that has struck at the very core of human dignity and the peaceful cooperation between peoples, religions, and nations. They purposely use a spiritual language rooted in what is most personal as an antidote to the rational words that often make us ashamed of the depth of our devotion and trivialize our passion for each other and our beloved earthly home.

We need the wisdom of silence and contrition to awaken us from a linguistic slumber that modulates the cries of pain that rob us even now of our humanity. We need grandeur and amazement as evidence of our overwhelming gratitude—prayers of praise and thanksgiving, too—to dissolve our hearts in the excesses of divine love. In times such as these we must practice an ethic of ultimate concern that is capable of addressing the joys and sorrows of the world in a "single voice and . . . with one accord" (Zeph. 3:9).

Epilogue

Hymn to
Hagia Sophia

O Hagia Sophia, Holy Wisdom, everything we are and everything we have you gave us. The very air we breathe and the eyes with which we see, you fashioned. The mind that draws these words out of silence and etches them into the tablet of time, you made. You surround us with beauty: the light in the trees at dawn, our companions the saguaro, white-tailed doves resting above the roof, quail and rabbit babies, *ocotillos* and *palo verdes*. You are the Moon, rising like an orange disk to call us; and the starkness of the desert Sun that burns away the dross of women's soul.

Life is nothing more than a longful dialogue with you. Our words are offerings to you; our thoughts are but passing sails on a silent sea, our emotions caught up in the solace of your intimacy. In the violet-misted morning, we call our favorite dove and it is your mystery we see in the soft gaze of her eyes. Her head, tilted on her breast, forms a gentle curve of neck. Our eyes meet. For one moment we rest in the arch of her being; we are inside your very self. For one moment her luminescent beauty is more than we can bear; we are the passion of your presence.

It is you, Holy Wisdom, who peers into our hearts—you hear our deepest longings and know the triumphs of our souls. Your whole creation is a poem of desire: some days we are a verb; on others, an immovable noun. The syntax of our pilgrimage etches traces across life's page and often we do not know how to speak. But we are intoxicated with your beauty and the beauty of our world. We women feel rising up within us, straight from the heart, a poem of whole generations that is just now coming to speech.

Take our breath, Holy Mother. May each inhalation and exhalation be a tribute to your glory. May our hearts burn with the passion of your fire and your holiness. Take our souls and use them to assuage the wounds; may they grow stronger to hold more of your love. Take women's bodies and make them an instrument of your peace; may our actions be worthy of your mercy. Take us and use us, for we long to give our false selves away. You come upon us silently and in such deep interiority that often we do not recognize your call. And this is no wonder, since the sound of your words is so holy and the wisdom of your words is so profound that even the purest soul struggles to hold them and bear them in memory. In silence, all that is clamoring and jarring is stilled, and we are led to the door of your own solitude.

Let us offer ourselves so that our words reflect your Word. We have tried to speak like men and listen like angels, but we are spiritual women. We have tried to put ourselves into the forms of the world, but we are not contained there, beautiful even as they are. We constantly spill over the borderlines and boundaries, and while in the early years of our awakening we lamented, now we are content to be a wandering bougainvillea. Let us no longer try to be unfree. Yes we are free! Something has broken loose and we are finally free to pour out this immensity. All the chiseled words and theories and philosophies have been imbued with an immense love—a fragrance of sound and color that we are caught in and do not want to escape. It is as if the majesty of you, Hagia Sophia, has rained down upon us and has so flooded our senses and cells that we are interior to your radiance. You emerge out of us and we dwell within you. Right now—could it be?—women are finally coming full circle.

This arduous journey—in which we women struggle through increasingly intense periods of darkness—is the mysterious birthing of your revelatory consciousness. Your *full presence* requires a new understanding of our life and who we are. This awakening requires conceptualization—that most difficult wrenching of silence that we now offer—and theological precision, argument and insight. There can be no unconscious and hidden mystical womanity. You want us to be born in full sight, raising ourselves like the Navajos and Hopis raise their newborn babies up to the sun and moon and stars: *Bless me! Bless us! We have come to offer ourselves in honor of our great and holy mother!*

There was a time for fear. But even fear is gone. What use is it anymore? There is nothing else we can do or be, there is no other path to tread, there is no other spiritual life that makes sense—that doesn't leave gaps and holes in our being or hold us hostage to a way of speaking and relating that is a lie, diminishing the very thing that women have fought for all these years. Holy Wisdom has cajoled and prodded, called and sought. She has found us out and left us to lie in our own sorrows and anguish; then she will anoint us and we arise and say *Yes. Yes it is.*

Language is the bridge. We need the words of the past. They provide solace and meaning as each new birth arrives swathed in the great weaving cloth of ancestral lives, those women who thought, wrote, and struggled as we do. Their names and theologies have meaning too, and we can adorn ourselves with garlands of phrase, sound, and poetry to offer this new child the collected wisdom of our souls. But we know, now, that the words will glide over the essence; they will leave it untouched, as they should. For if our journey as women is truly holy, loving, and freeing, we will make meaning with our own terms and in our own time. Our ancestors will allow us to shout and shake at our gods, to walk in the wilderness, to stare blankly upon our own being and wonder: Who am I to be? And when we learn the wisdom of our ancestors and we drink in their love, we can turn away. For they will be with us, cheering us on as we tread the evolutionary path of all pioneers, visionaries, and simple surveyors. We give away the known for that mysterious horizon, for the authenticity of Hagia Sophia's call to us today, to Her voice in the wilderness that beckons: *Leave all and follow Me.*

Notes

Introduction: Low Places Where Grace Flows In

1. Boutros Boutros-Ghali, "Translating the Momentum of Beijing into Action," September 15, 1995, 2. Fourth World Conference on Women; http://www.fao.org/Gender/static/BeiFoll.htm.

2. Preface to the Japanese edition of *Seeds of Contemplation*, March 1965, in *Introductions East and West: The Foreign Prefaces of Thomas Merton,* ed. Richard E. Daggy (Greensboro, N.C.: Unicorn, 1981), 66.

1. *Via Feminina* and the Un-saying of "Woman"

1. Constance FitzGerald, "Impasse and Dark Night," *Women's Spirituality: Resources for Christian Development*, ed. Joann Wolski Conn (New York: Paulist, 1986, 1996), 429.

2. Boutros Boutros-Ghali, "Translating the Momentum of Beijing into Action," September 15, 1995, 2. Fourth World Conference on Women; http://www.fao.org/Gender/static/BeiFoll.htm.

3. Richard Tarnas, *The Passion of the Western Mind* (New York: Harmony, 1991), 441. Cited in Constance FitzGerald, "Transformation in Wisdom: The Subversive Character and Educative Power of Sophia in Contemplation," in *Carmel and Contemplation: Transforming Human Consciousness*, ed. Kevin Culligan and Regis Jordan, Carmelite Studies 8 (Washington, D.C.: Institute of Carmelite Studies, 2000), 281.

4. FitzGerald, "Transformation in Wisdom," 285.

5. See Grace Jantzen, *Power, Gender, and Christian Mysticism* (Cambridge & New York: Cambridge University Press, 1995).

6. *Femina* and its derivative *feminae* in Latin translate more specifically as "woman" or "women, of the woman." While *feminina* also connotes in Latin the female, it infers a sense of the feminine gender. I felt this nuance opened the meaning up to include biological women, the female gender, and also males who identify or support feminist thought and feminine attributes and qualities.

7. For a thorough study of the apophatic traditions of the Abrahamic traditions, see Michael A. Sells, *Mystical Languages of Unsaying* (Chicago: University of Chicago Press, 1994).

8. *Pseudo-Dionysius: The Complete Works*, trans. Colm Luibheid and Paul Rorem (New York: Paulist, 1987), 139.

9. See Ewert H. Cousins, "Fullness and Emptiness in Bonaventure and Eckhart," *Journal of Dharma* 6 (January–March 1981): 59–68.

10. *Pseudo-Dionysius: The Complete Works*, 136.

11. The usage of the term "patriarchal imaginary" is often traced to the work of Jacques Lacan. In Lacan's thought, the Imaginary is a prelinguistic realm in which the child misrecognizes an image of itself as its self. Some feminists contend that this prelinguistic, visual mirror of patriarchal culture creates and maintains a woman's alienated relation to her original or undivided self.

12. Ambiguity surrounds the usage of feminine divine figures within the Western religious landscape. For the most part, there is consensus on the dominance of God as male. However, there are subtleties and nuances within the mystical corpus that, at times, place Sophia or Shekhinah, for example, as equal to God himself [*sic*]. Consult Susan Cady, Marian Ronan, and Hal Taussig, *Sophia: The Future of Feminist Spirituality* (San Francisco: Harper & Row), 1986; Gershom Scholem, "*Shekhinah*: The Feminine Element in Divinity," in *The Mystical Shape of the Godhead: Basic Concepts in Kabbalah* (New York: Schoken, 1991); Peter Schäfer, "Daughter, Sister, Bride, and Mother: Images of the Femininity of God in the Early Kabbala," *Journal of the American Academy of Religion* 68/2 (June 2000): 233; and Jaroslav Pelikan, *Mary through the Centuries: Her Place in the History of Culture* (New Haven, Conn.: Yale University Press, 1996).

13. Elizabeth A. Johnson, *Truly Our Sister: A Theology of Mary in the Communion of Saints* (New York: Continuum, 2003), 23.

14. Ibid., 25.

15. Ibid., 85–86.

16. Ibid., 51.

17. Ibid., 50.

18. Margaret Whitford, ed., *The Irigaray Reader* (Oxford: Basil Blackwell, 1991), 24.

19. See the excellent article by Ann-Marie Priest, "Women as God, God as Women: Mysticism, Negative Theology and Luce Irigaray," *Journal of Religion* 83/1 (January 2003): 1–23.

20. Johnson, *Truly Our Sister*, 106.

21. Priest, "Women as God, God as Women," 23.

22. John J. L. Mood, *Rilke on Love and Other Difficulties: Translations and Consideration of Rainer Maria Rilke* (New York: Norton, 1975), 35.

2. Feminism and Mysticism: Foundations

1. Teresa of Avila, *Meditations on the Song of Songs*, 7.3, 257. All citations from Teresa of Avila are taken from *The Collected Works of St. Teresa of Avila*, 3 vols., trans.

Kieran Kavanaugh and Otilio Rodriquez (Washington, D.C.: Institute of Carmelite Studies, 1987).

2. Arthur Green, "Introduction," in *Jewish Spirituality: From the Bible through the Middle Ages*, World Spirituality: An Encyclopedic History of the Religious Quest, vol. 13 (New York: Crossroad, 1988), xiii.

3. Seyyed Hossein Nasr, "Introduction," in *Islamic Spirituality: Foundations*, World Spirituality: An Encyclopedic History of the Religious Quest, vol. 19 (New York: Crossroad, 1991), xvii.

4. Ewert Cousins, preface to the series World Spirituality: An Encyclopedic History of the Religious Quest, vol. 1 (New York: Crossroad, 1987), xiii.

5. Spirituality implies a personal, experiential dimension—it is lived faith. See Andrew Louth, *Theology and Spirituality* (Oxford, Convent of the Incarnation: SLG, 1978); idem, *Discerning the Mystery: An Essay on the Nature of Theology* (Oxford: Clarendon, 1983); Francis A. Eigo, ed., *Dimensions of Contemporary Spirituality* (Villanova, Pa.: Villanova University Press, 1982); idem, *Contemporary Spirituality: Responding to the Divine Initiative* (Villanova, Pa.: Villanova University Press, 1983); Karl Rahner, "The Spirituality of the Future," in *The Practice of the Faith: A Handbook of Contemporary Spirituality*, ed. K. Lehmann and A. Raffelt (New York: Crossroad, 1986); Margaret Chatterjee, *The Concept of Spirituality* (Bombay: Allied, 1989); Ewert H. Cousins, "Spirituality: A Resource for Theology," *Catholic Theological Society of America Proceedings* 35 (1980): 124–37; Sandra Schneiders, "Spirituality in the Academy," *Theological Studies* 50 (1989): 676–97.

6. Krishna Sivaraman, "Introduction," in *Hindu Spirituality: Vedas through Vedanta*, World Spirituality: An Encyclopedic History of the Religious Quest, vol. 6 (New York: Crossroad, 1989), xvii.

7. Sandra Schneiders, "Theology and Spirituality: Strangers, Rivals, or Partners?" *Horizons* 13 (Fall 1986): 266.

8. See note 27, below.

9. See Wayne Teasdale, "Spirituality as a Primary Resource in Promoting Peace," *Source Point: A Journal of Interfaith Dialogue* 1/4 (March 2003): 3, http://www.source-point.org.

10. Bernard McGinn, *The Foundations of Mysticism*, vol. 1, *The Presence of God: A History of Western Christian Mysticism* (New York: Crossroad, 1992), 24.

11. Ibid., xix.

12. Pat Hawk, *Pathless Path Newsletter* 1/4 (2002): 3.

13. Teresa of Avila, *The Interior Castle* (hereafter IC), 4.1.4, 318, and 4.2.4, 324.

14. Thomas Merton, *Contemplation in a World of Action* (New York: Image, 1973), 36.

15. For a thorough analysis of the pre-religious in monastic consciousness see Raimundo Panikkar, *Blessed Simplicity: The Monk as Universal Archetype* (New York: Seabury, 1982).

16. Meister Eckhart, in sermon 2, *Intravit Jesus in quoddam castellum,* speaks of the "eternal now" as a power in the soul that is outside of time and flesh and in which God is always present. Cited in *Meister Eckhart: The Essential Sermons, Commentaries, Treatises, and Defense,* trans. Edmund Colledge and Bernard McGinn (New York: Paulist, 1981), 179.

17. Sandra Schneiders, *Beyond Patching: Faith and Feminism in the Catholic Church* (New York: Paulist, 1991), 7.

18. See Grace M. Jantzen, *Becoming Divine: Towards a Feminist Philosophy of Religion,* especially chapter 5, "Women's Experience: Source of a Feminist Symbolic?" (Bloomington: Indiana University Press, 1999).

19. Judith Plaskow and Carol P. Christ, eds., *Weaving the Visions: New Patterns in Feminist Spirituality* (San Francisco: HarperSanFrancisco, 1989), 3.

20. Serene Jones, *Feminist Theory and Christian Theology: Cartographies of Grace,* Guides to Theological Inquiry (Minneapolis: Fortress Press, 2000), 26.

21. Ibid., 29.

22. Perhaps the most intense explication of feminist essentialism is found in Mary Daly's writings: *Beyond God the Father: Toward a Philosophy of Women's Liberation* (Boston: Beacon, 1973); idem, *Gyn/ecology: The Metaethics of Radical Feminism* (Boston: Beacon, 1978); idem, *Pure Lust: Elemental Feminist Philosophy* (Boston: Beacon, 1984); idem, *Outercourse: The Bedazzling Voyage* (San Francisco: HarperSanFrancisco, 1992). Of the French feminists, Luce Irigaray has written some of the most provocative studies on women's difference: *Speculum of the Other Woman,* trans. Gillian C. Gill (Ithaca, N.Y.: Cornell University Press, 1974); *Elemental Passions,* trans. Joanne Collie and Judith Still (London: Athlone, 1992); *Thinking the Difference,* trans. Karin Montin (New York: Routledge, 1994); *Between East and West: From Singularity to Community,* trans. Stephen Pluhacek (New York: Columbia University Press, 2002).

23. Jones, *Feminist Theory and Christian Theology,* 35.

24. Schneiders, *Beyond Patching,* 35.

25. Plaskow and Christ, *Weaving the Visions,* 39.

26. Carol P. Christ, "Spiritual Quest and Women's Experience," in *WomanSpirit Rising: A Feminist Reader in Religion,* ed. Carol P. Christ and Judith Plaskow (San Francisco: Harper & Row, 1979), 228–45.

27. In the academic study of mysticism, there is a similar ongoing debate over an essentialist-constructivist stance. Is there a "common core" of mystical experience that is everywhere the same, or is mysticism constructed through the same linguistic and social factors that form all human endeavors? Like the related feminist questions, the mystical one is not completely resolvable. As in many other areas of academic inquiry, mysticism has not been spared the radical de-centering that marks much of postmodern thought, or the critical investigation of the assumption that mysticism, as a category of human experience, is everywhere the same. Steven Katz, in a widely discussed book, *Mysticism and Philosophical Analysis* (New York: Oxford University

Press, 1978), not only rejects mystical essentialism, but also makes a plea for differences and for a "far more differentiated, pluralistic account of mysticism" (p. 6). On epistemological grounds, he also asserts "There are NO pure (that is, unmediated) experiences" (p. 26). Katz' position was countered in a book edited by Robert K. C. Forman—*The Problem of Pure Consciousness: Mysticism and Philosophy* (New York: Oxford University Press, 1990)—that upheld the viability of the pure consciousness position. Yet, while Katz, Forman, and others have debated the validity of mystical pluralism, as a subject of academic inquiry there have been few accounts of the specifically feminine dimension of difference in the mystical traditions until recently. The plea for difference has remained a plea for *religious* diversity, and not for a thorough investigation of a more fundamental difference—gender, racial, and so forth.

28. Carol Lee Flinders devotes a considerable part of her book to this discussion. Consult *At the Root of This Longing: Reconciling a Spiritual Hunger and a Feminist Thirst* (San Francisco: HarperSanFrancisco, 1998).

29. Luce Irigaray, *Sexes and Genealogies*, trans. Gillian C. Gill (New York: Columbia University Press, 1993), 21.

30. Grace Jantzen, *Power, Gender, and Christian Mysticism* (Cambridge: Cambridge University Press, 1995), 58.

31. Jantzen, *Becoming Divine*, 15.

32. Cited in Jantzen, *Power, Gender, and Christian Mysticism*, 26.

33. Ibid.

34. Cited by John H. Cartwright, "The Religious Ethics of Howard Thurman," *Annual of the Society of Christian Ethics* (1985): 90.

35. Gerda Lerner, *The Creation of Feminist Consciousness: From the Middle Ages to 1870* (New York: Oxford University Press, 1993), 115.

36. Dorothee Soelle, *The Window of Vulnerability: A Political Spirituality* (Minneapolis: Fortress Press, 1990), 72. Also, idem, *The Silent Cry: Mysticism and Resistance* (Minneapolis: Fortress Press, 2001), 45–49.

37. Ibid.

38. Deidre Green, *Gold in the Crucible: Teresa of Avila and the Western Mystical Tradition* (London: Longmead/Element, 1989), 183–84.

39. Ursula King, *Women and Spirituality: Voices of Protest and Promise* (University Park: Pennsylvania State University Press, 1993), 106.

40. Constance FitzGerald, "Impasse and Dark Night," in *Women's Spirituality: Resources for Christian Development*, ed. Joann Wolski Conn (New York: Paulist, 1986, 1996), 429.

41. Mary E. Giles, ed., *The Feminist Mystic and Other Essays on Women and Spirituality* (New York: Crossroad, 1982), 36.

3. Goddesses, Mother Jesus, and the Feminine Divine

1. Henrich von Meissen, *Marienleich*, a poem on Maria-Sapientia's eternal relationship with God. Cited in Barbara Newman, *God and the Goddesses: Vision, Poetry,*

and Belief in the Middle Ages (Philadelphia: University of Pennsylvania Press, 2003), 252.

2. Jaroslav Pelikan, *Mary through the Centuries: Her Place in the History of Culture* (New Haven, Conn.: Yale University Press, 1996), 55.

3. Cited in ibid. 291.

4. Susan Cady, Marian Ronan, and Hal Taussig, *Sophia: The Future of Feminist Spirituality* (San Francisco: Harper & Row, 1986), 35.

5. Creation myth from the Ezon (variously written as Ijo, Ijaw) people of southern Nigeria. Mercy Amba Oduyoye, *Daughters of Anowa: African Women and Patriarchy* (Maryknoll, N.Y.: Orbis, 1995), 23.

6. David Kinsley, *Hindu Goddesses: Visions of the Divine Feminine in the Hindu Religious Tradition* (Berkeley: University of California Press, 1988), 30.

7. Ibid.

8. The *Book Bahir* is an important work of Jewish mysticism that appeared toward the end of the twelfth century in Provence, although the date of its original composition is shrouded in mystery. See Peter Schäfer, "Daughter, Sister, Bride, and Mother: Images of the Femininity of God in the Early Kabbala," *Journal of the American Academy of Religion* 68/2 (June 2000). Citation from Gershom Scholem, *On the Mystical Shape of the Godhead* (New York: Schocken, 1991), 148.

9. Unless otherwise noted, all biblical translations are taken from *The New Jerusalem Bible* (New York: Doubleday, 1989).

10. Cited in William C. Chittick, *The Sufi Path of Love: The Spiritual Teachings of Rumi* (Albany: State University of New York Press, 1983), 169. In the same text (p. 165), reflecting the debasement found in most patriarchal depictions of women, Rumi also states, "Whoever is not a lover of God is a woman in meaning—behold then what sort of women are women! Woman is she whose way and goal are color and scent: She is the reality of the ego that commands to evil embodied in the physical constitution of humankind."

11. Translation from Cady, Ronan, and Taussig, *Sophia*, 42.

12. Ibn al-'Arabi, *The Bezels of Wisdom*, trans. R. W. J. Austin (New York: Paulist, 1980), 277.

13. Ibid., 275.

14. Schäfer, "Daughter, Sister, Bride, and Mother," 225–26, 228.

15. Ibid., 233.

16. Ibid., 228.

17. Ibid., 230–31.

18. Ibid., 233.

19. Moshe Idel, "Reification of Language in Jewish Mysticism," in *Mysticism and Language*, ed. Steven T. Katz (New York: Oxford University Press, 1992), 69.

20. Ibid.

21. *The Rig Veda: An Anthology*, trans. Wendy Doniger O'Flaherty (New York: Penguin, 1981), 63.

22. Cady, Ronan, and Taussig, *Sophia*, 25.

23. Ibid., 23.

24. Thomas Merton, *Hagia Sophia,* in *A Thomas Merton Reader,* ed. Thomas P. McDonnell (New York: Image, 1989), 508.

25. Translation from Cady, Ronan, and Taussig, *Sophia*, 22.

26. See Bernard McGinn, *The Flowering of Mysticism: Men and Women in the New Mysticism—1200–1350* (New York: Crossroad, 1998), 17–30.

27. Luce Irigaray, *Speculum of the Other Woman*, trans. Gillian C. Gill (Ithaca, N.Y.: Cornell University Press, 1985), 191. Cited in Laurie A. Finke, "Mystical Bodies and the Dialogics of Vision," in *Maps of Flesh and Light: The Religious Experience of Medieval Women Mystics*, ed. Ulrike Wiethaus (Syracuse, N.Y.: Syracuse University Press, 1993), 32.

28. Jo Ann McNamara, "The Rhetoric of Orthodoxy: Clerical Authority and Female Innovation in the Struggle with Heresy," in *Maps of Flesh and Light,* 10.

29. Barbara Newman, *Sister of Wisdom: St. Hildegard's Theology of the Feminine* (Berkeley: University of California Press, 1987), note 3, 43.

30. Clement of Alexandria, *Paedagogus*, bk. 1, chap. 6, 12, *Ante-Nicene Fathers*, vol. 2; www.ccel.org/fathers2.

31. Caroline Walker Bynum, *Jesus as Mother: Studies in the Spirituality of the High Middle Ages* (Berkeley: University of California Press, 1984), 126.

32. Ibid., 129.

33. Ibid., 131.

34. Cited in ibid., 113.

35. Ibid. Cited in Bynum, *Jesus as Mother*, 117.

36. Ibid., 138.

37. For background on the goddesses of Old Europe, see Marija Gimbutas, *The Living Goddesses* (Berkeley: University of California Press, 1999); idem, *The Language of the Goddess* (San Francisco: Harper & Row, 1989).

38. Newman, *God and the Goddesses*, 36.

39. On Cornelius Agrippa, see "Renaissance Feminism, and Esoteric Theology," in Barbara Newman, *From Virile Woman to WomanChrist: Studies in Medieval Religion and Literature* (Philadelphia: University of Pennsylvania Press, 1995), 231. For insight into the importance of the feminine figure Charity in Hugh of St. Victor and Lady Poverty for Francis of Assisi, consult Newman, *God and the Goddesses.*

40. Barbara Newman, "Henry Suso and the Medieval Devotion to Christ the Goddess," *Spiritus* 2 (2002): 2.

41. Ibid.

42. Cited in Newman, "Henry Suso," 4.

43. Newman, *Sister of Wisdom*, 45.

44. Ibid., 67.

45. Ibid., 64.

46. Ibid., 66.

47. Mechthild of Magdeburg, *The Flowing Light of the Godhead*, trans. Frank Tobin (New York: Paulist, 1998), 5.4, 183; 4.12, 154.

48. Ibid., 5.4, 183.

49. Newman, *God and the Goddesses*, 11.

50. Ibid., 157.

51. Ibid., 11.

52. Michael A. Sells, *Mystical Languages of Unsaying* (Chicago: University of Chicago Press, 1994), 118.

53. Ellen L. Babinsky, "Introduction," in *Marguerite Porete: The Mirror of Simple Souls*, trans. Ellen L. Babinsky (New York: Paulist, 1993), 28.

54. Sells, *Mystical Languages of Unsaying*, 119.

55. Earl Jeffrey Richards, "Introduction," in Christine de Pizan, *The Book of the City of Ladies*, trans. Earl Jeffrey Richards (New York: Persea, 1982), xxvix.

56. Newman, *God and the Goddesses*, 23.

57. Ibid., 24–25.

58. Richards, "Introduction," in *The Book of the City of Ladies*, xxviii, xxx.

59. Cited in Bynum, *Jesus as Mother*, 135–36.

60. Newman, *God and the Goddesses*, 313 and 326.

61. See Grace M. Jantzen's excellent treatment of this point in her book *Becoming Divine: Towards a Feminist Philosophy of Religion* (Bloomington: Indiana University Press, 1999), chap. 5.

62. Bynum, *Jesus as Mother*, 172.

4. Contemplative Feminism: Transforming the Spiritual Journey

1. The first quotation is from Dorothy H. Donnelly, "The Sexual Mystic: Embodied Spirituality," in *The Feminist Mystics and Other Essays on Women and Spirituality*, ed. Mary E. Giles (New York: Crossroad, 1982), 126–27. It is cited and commented on by Ursula King, *Women and Spirituality: Voices of Protest and Promise* (University Park: Pennsylvania State University Press, 1989, 1993), 88.

2. Constance FitzGerald, "Impasse and Dark Night," in *Women's Spirituality: Resources for Christian Development*, ed. Joann Wolski Conn (New York: Paulist, 1986, 1996), 411.

3. See Kathleen Fischer, *Women at the Well: Feminist Perspectives on Spiritual Direction* (New York: Paulist, 1998); Grace M. Jantzen, *Power, Gender, and Christian Mysticism* (Cambridge: Cambridge University Press, 1995); idem, *Becoming Divine: Towards a Feminist Philosophy of Religion* (Bloomington: Indiana University Press, 1999); King, *Women and Spirituality*; Elizabeth A. Johnson, *She Who Is: The Mystery of God in Feminist Theological Discourse* (New York: Crossroad, 1993).

4. Mary Farrell Bednarowski, *The Religious Imagination of American Women* (Bloomington: Indiana University Press, 1999), 5.

5. From Teresa of Avila's *The Book of Her Foundations*, 31.46; this translation taken from Antonio Pérez-Romero, *Subversion and Liberation in the Writings of St. Teresa of Avila* (Atlanta: Rodopi, 1996), 181–82.

6. For a feminist social analysis of women's oppression in North America, consult Iris Young, *Justice and the Politics of Difference* (Princeton, N.J.: Princeton University Press, 1990). See Serene Jones's discussion on Iris Young in her chapter on "Oppression," in *Feminist Theory and Christian Theology: Cartographies of Grace*, Guides to Theological Inquiry (Minneapolis: Fortress Press, 2000), 69–93.

7. See Johnson, *She Who Is*, chap. 12, "Suffering God: Compassion Poured Out"; Phyllis Trible, *Texts of Terror: Literary-Feminist Readings of Biblical Narratives*, Overtures to Biblical Theology (Philadelphia: Fortress Press, 1984).

8. Consult Katie Geneva Canon, *Katie's Canon: Womanism and the Soul of the Black Community* (New York: Continuum, 1995); Emilie M. Townes, ed., *A Troubling in My Soul: Womanist Perspectives on Evil and Suffering* (Maryknoll, N.Y.: Orbis, 1995); Delores S. Williams, *Sisters in the Wilderness: The Challenge of Womanist God-Talk* (Maryknoll, N.Y.: Orbis, 1993); Ada María Isasi-Díaz, *En la Lucha/In the Struggle: Elaborating a Mujerista Theology* (Minneapolis: Fortress Press, 1993); Maria Pilar Aquino, *Our Cry for Life: Feminist Theology from Latin America* (Maryknoll, N.Y.: Orbis, 1993); Elsa Tamez, *Bible of the Oppressed* (Maryknoll, N.Y.: Orbis, 1982).

9. Kathleen Fischer, "Violence against Women: The Spiritual Dimension," *Women at the Well*, 154–74.

10. Jones, *Feminist Theory and Christian Theology*, 71–77.

11. Introduction, *The Collected Works of St. Teresa of Avila*, vol. 1, trans. Kieran Kavanaugh and Otilio Rodriguez (Washington, D.C.: Institute of Carmelite Studies, 1987), 23.

12. See Alison Weber, *Teresa of Avila and the Rhetoric of Femininity* (Princeton, N.J.: Princeton University Press, 1990), for a thorough analysis of her literary style. A similar theme is developed in Pérez-Romero, *Subversion and Liberation*. Also consult Deidre Green, *Gold in the Crucible: Teresa of Avila and the Western Mystical Tradition* (Longmead, Eng.: Element, 1989); Gillian Ahlgren, *Teresa of Avila and the Politics of Sanctity* (Ithaca, N.Y.: Cornell University Press, 1996).

13. For initial development of my usage of the term "dark night of the feminine," see Beverly Lanzetta, "The Soul of Woman and the Dark Night of the Feminine," unpublished paper presented at the American Academy of Religion (AAR) Western Region, University of California, Davis, March 23, 2003. Also found in Beverly Lanzetta, "Julian and Teresa as Cartographers of the Soul: A Contemplative Feminist Hermeneutic," unpublished paper presented at AAR Annual Meeting, Atlanta, Georgia, November 25, 2003.

14. FitzGerald, "Impasse and Dark Night," 411.

15. Ibid., 430.

16. Ibid., 429.

17. Ibid., 427.

18. Maura O'Halloran, *Pure Heart, Enlightened Mind: The Zen Journal and Letters of Maura "Soshin" O'Halloran* (New York: Riverhead, 1994).

5. Women Mystics and a Feminism of the Inner Way

1. *Gertrude of Helfta: The Herald of Divine Love*, trans. and ed. Margaret Winkworth (New York: Paulist, 1993), 96.

2. Antonio Pérez-Romero, *Subversion and Liberation in the Writings of St. Teresa of Avila* (Atlanta: Rodopi, 1994), 77.

3. Grace M. Jantzen, *Julian of Norwich: Mystic and Theologian* (New York: Paulist, 2000), xxii.

4. Julian of Norwich, *Showings*, trans. Edmund Colledge and James Walsh (New York: Paulist, 1978), Long Text (hereafter LT) 2, 177–79. All subsequent citations from Julian are from this translation.

5. Ibid., LT 6, 186.

6. Ibid., Short Text (hereafter ST) 6, 133.

7. Ibid., 135.

8. A number of important works on the Jewish influences on Teresa's spirituality and thought have been written. Consult Deirdre Green, *Gold in the Crucible: Teresa of Avila and the Western Mystical Tradition* (Longmead, Eng.: Element, 1989); Catherine Swietlicki, *Spanish Christian Cabala: The Works of Luis de Leon, Santa Teresa de Jesus, and San Juan de la Cruz* (Columbia: University of Missouri Press, 1986); Gareth Alban Davies, "St. Teresa and the Jewish Question," in *Teresa de Jesus and Her World*, ed. Margaret A. Rees (Leeds: Trinity and All Saints College, 1981); Teofanes Egido, "The Historical Setting of St. Teresa's Life," trans. M. Dodd and S. Payne, *Carmelite Studies* 1 (1980): 122–82.

9. Teresa of Avila, *The Book of Her Life* (hereafter *Life*), *The Collected Works of St. Teresa of Avila*, vol. 1, trans. Kieran Kavanaugh and Otilio Rodriguez (Washington, D.C.: Institute of Carmelite Studies, 1987), 100.

10. Throughout her works, Teresa makes reference to the dignity of women, social injustice, and ecclesial violence. But her most consistent analysis of social reform can be found in *The Book of Her Foundations* (hereafter *Foundations*), in *The Collected Works*, vol. 3. See also Carole Slade, "St. Teresa of Avila as a Social Reformer," in *Mysticism and Social Transformation*, ed. Janet K. Ruffing (Syracuse, N.Y.: Syracuse University Press, 2001), 91–103.

11. Teresa, *Way of Perfection* (hereafter *Way*), in *The Collected Works*, 117.

12. Julian, LT, 183.

13. Ibid., 204.

14. Ibid., 253.

15. Ibid., 320.

16. Teresa, *Collected Works*, vol. 3, *Poetry*, 383.

17. Teresa, *Interior Castle* (hereafter IC), 1.2.9, 292.

18. Teresa, *Life* 29.8, 249.

19. Julian, LT, 56, 288.

20. Teresa, *Way* 21.2, 117.

21. Ibid., 23.5–6, 127–28.

22. Teresa, *Life* 13.1–3, 123–24.

23. Ibid., 11.2, 110.

24. Teresa, IC 6.10.7, 420.

25. Teresa, *Way* 38.6, 187.

26. Ibid., 21.2, 118.

27. Julian, LT, 195–96.

28. Teresa, *Way* 29.4, 147.

29. Ibid., 29.12, 145.

30. Teresa, IC 7.3.11–13, 442–43.

31. Teresa, *Way* 29.7, 148.

32. Ibid.

33. Ibid., 28.2, 140.

34. Teresa, *Foundations* 5.16, 123.

35. Ibid., 5.8, 119–20.

36. Teresa, *Way* 6.3, 62.

37. Ibid., 7.1–4, 66.

38. Ibid., 6.9, 65.

39. Teresa of Avila, *Meditations on the Song of Songs*, in *The Collected Works*, 7.3, 257.

40. Ann-Marie Priest, "Becoming Nothing: Mystical Annihilation as Feminine Being," Unpublished paper presented to Studium, St. Benedict's Monastery, March 21, 2001, 9–10.

41. For an analysis of the distinction between different types of mystical union see Moshe Idel and Bernard McGinn, eds., *Mystical Union and Monotheistic Faith: An Ecumenical Dialogue* (New York: Macmillan, 1989).

42. Junayd, as quoted in Michael Sells, "The Semantics of Mystical Union in Islam," in Idel and McGinn, eds., *Mystical Union and Monotheistic Faith*, 109.

43. Ursula King, *Women and Spirituality: Voices of Protest and Promise* (University Park: Pennsylvania State University Press, 1993), 108.

44. Ibid., 106.

45. Teresa, *Life* 10.8, 109.

46. Pérez-Romero, *Subversion and Liberation*, 77.

47. Michael A. Sells, *Mystical Languages of Unsaying* (Chicago: University of Chicago Press, 1994), 132.

48. Ibid., 145.

49. Marguerite Porete, *The Mirror of Simple Souls*, ed. Ellen L. Babinsky (New York: Paulist, 1993), 82, 158.

50. Ibid., 82, 158.

51. Teresa, IC 6.18, 418.

52. Ann-Marie Priest, "Women as God, God as Women: Mysticism, Negative Theology, and Luce Irigaray," *Journal of Religion* 83/1 (January 2003): 22.

6. Julian and Teresa as Cartographers of Women's Soul

1. Teresa of Avila, *The Interior Castle* (hereafter IC), *The Collected Works of St. Teresa of Avila*, vol. 2, trans. Kieran Kavanaugh and Otilio Rodriguez (Washington, D.C.: Institute of Carmelite Studies, 1987), 1.1.1, 283.

2. John of the Cross, *The Spiritual Canticle* (hereafter SC) 27.5, 518. All citations from John are from *The Collected Works of St. John of the Cross*, trans. Kieran Kavanaugh and Otilio Rodriguez (Washington, D.C.: Institute of Carmelite Studies, 1979).

3. Teresa, IC 6.2.3, 422.

4. Ibid., 1.2.3, 289.

5. For a thorough discussion of the relationship of soul and body see, Caroline Walker Bynum, *Fragmentation and Redemption: Essays on Gender and the Human Body in Medieval Religion* (New York: Zone, 1992).

6. John of the Cross, *Ascent of Mount Carmel* (hereafter AC) 2.12.1–3, 136–37.

7. Julian of Norwich, *Showings*, trans. Edmund Colledge and James Walsh (New York: Paulist, 1979), Long Text (hereafter LT) 57–59, 290–97.

8. Ibid., 56, 289.

9. Ibid., 56, 288.

10. Ibid., 289.

11. Grace M. Jantzen, *Julian of Norwich: Mystic and Theologian* (New York: Paulist, 2000), 170–71.

12. Julian, LT 50, 266.

13. Ibid., 51, 267.

14. Ibid., 51, 274.

15. Ibid., 51, 271.

16. "For Christ and she [Mary] were so united in love," writes Julian, "that the greatness of her love was the cause of the greatness of her pain. . . . For always, the higher, the stronger, the sweeter that love is, the more sorrow it is to the lover to see the body which he loved in pain. . . . Here I saw a great unity between Christ and us, as I understand it; for when he was in pain we were in pain, and all creatures able to suffer pain suffered with him" (LT 18, 210).

17. Liz Herbert McAvoy, "'The Moders Service': Motherhood as Matrix in Julian of Norwich," *Mystics Quarterly* 24/4 (1998): 192. Also consult the excellent essay by Patricia Donohue-White, "Reading Divine Maternity in Julian of Norwich," presented at the Annual Meeting, American Academy of Religion (AAR), Atlanta, November 16, 2003.

18. Teresa, IC, Epilogue, no. 3, 452.

19. Ibid., 7.1.3, 428.

20. Ibid., 1.2.14, 294.

21. Kieran Kavanaugh, "Introduction," in Teresa, IC, 271.

22. Ibid.

23. Teresa, IC 5.1.9, 339.

24. Ibid., 4.1.9, 320.

25. Ibid., 7.2.4, 434.

26. Ibid.

27. Teresa, *Life* 25.17. Translation from Pérez-Romero, *Subversion and Liberation*, 113.

28. Teresa, *Life* 23.1, 200.

29. Teresa, IC 1.1.7, 286.

30. Teresa, *Life* 8.5, 96.

31. Teresa, IC 4.2.3, 323.

32. Ibid., 4.2.4, 324.

33. Ibid.

34. Teresa, *Life* 11.10, 115.

35. Ibid., 14. 5, 135.

36. Ibid., 16.1, 147.

37. Ibid., 17.4, 153–54.

38. Ibid., 19.3, 165.

39. Julian, LT 43, 253.

40. Julian, Short Text (ST) xix, 159.

41. Teresa, *Life* 18.14, 163.

42. Julian, LT 72, 321.

43. Jantzen, *Julian*, 92.

44. Teresa, IC 6.11.2, 422.

45. Ibid., 5.2.14, 347.

46. Ibid.

47. Julian, LT 65, 309.

48. Ibid., LT 8, 190.

49. Ibid., LT 1, 175.

50. Ibid., LT 4, 181.

51. Ibid., LT 6, 186.

52. Ibid., LT 5, 183.

53. Ibid., LT, 204–5.

54. Teresa, IC 6.11.11, 426.

55. Teresa, *Way* 18.1–2, 102.

56. Teresa, *Life* 11.12, 116.

57. Jantzen, *Julian of Norwich*, 60.

7. The Soul of Woman and the Dark Night of the Feminine

1. Teresa of Avila, *The Book of Her Life* (hereafter *Life*), *The Collected Works of St. Teresa of Avila*, vol. 1, trans. Kieran Kavanaugh and Otilio Rodriguez (Washington, D.C.: Institute of Carmelite Studies, 1987) 20.11–16, 177–79.

2. Ibid., 179.

3. John of the Cross, *Ascent to Mount Carmel* (hereafter AC) 1.2.1, 74–75. Translations of all of St. John's writings are taken from *The Collected Works of St. John of the Cross*, trans. Kieran Kavanaugh and Otilio Rodriquez (Washington, D.C.: Institute of Carmelite Studies, 1979).

4. Ibid., introduction to AC, *Dark Night of the Soul* (hereafter DN), 55.

5. John of the Cross, *Living Flame of Love* (hereafter LF) 3.32, 622..

6. John of the Cross, AC 2.6.1, 119.

7. Ibid. In the poem that precedes the *Ascent of Mount Carmel* and *The Dark Night*, John describes the dark night as also "that glad night," "guiding night," "Night more lovely than the dawn," "night that has united the Lover with His beloved," 69.

8. Constance FitzGerald has been the most consistent and prolific writer on this theme of the feminine in John and Teresa, especially in her works "The Transformative Influence of Wisdom in John of the Cross" and "Impasse and Dark Night" in *Women's Spirituality: Resources for Christian Development,* ed. Joann Wolski Conn (New York: Paulist, 1986, 1996); "A Discipleship of Equals: Voices from Tradition—Teresa of Avila and John of the Cross," in *A Discipleship of Equals: Towards a Christian Feminist Spirituality*, ed. Francis A. Eigo (Villanova, Pa.: Villanova University Press, 1988), 63–97; "Transformation in Wisdom: The Subversive Character and Educative Power of Sophia in Contemplation," in *Carmel and Contemplation: Transforming Human Consciousness*, ed. Kevin Culligan and Regis Jordan, Carmelite Studies 8 (Washington, D.C.: Institute of Carmelite Studies, 2000), 281–358. Consult also, Richard P. Hardy, "'Nursing': A Sanjuanist Image," *Science et Esprit* 28 (1976): 297–307; Wendy M. Wright, "The Feminine Dimension of Contemplation," in *The Feminist Mystic and Other Essays on Women and Spirituality*, ed. Mary E. Giles (New York: Crossroad, 1986), 103–19; Deidre Green, *Gold in the Crucible: Teresa of Avila and the Western Mystical Tradition* (Longmead, Eng.: Element, 1989), especially chapter 5, "Teresa and the Issue of Women's Spirituality"; Vilma Seelaus, "The Feminine in Prayer in the Interior Castle," *Mystics Quarterly* 13/4 (1987): 203–14; Roland E. Murphy, *The Tree of Life: An Exploration in Biblical Wisdom Literature* (New York: Doubleday, 1990), 133–49; Emmanuel J. Sullivan, "Mary and the Holy Spirit in the Writings of John of the Cross," Carmelite Studies 6, http://www.icspublications.org.

9. In addition to John's primary usage of Wisdom from Proverbs, chapter 8, and Wisdom, chapters 7–9, he also refers to the books of Sirach and Baruch, and the Song of Songs. According to FitzGerald, this association suggests "that John of the Cross appropriates not only pre-Christian Judaism's understanding of a feminine gestalt of God, Sophia, but he seems to be completely at home with the identification made by New Testament writers of Jesus as Divine Sophia: *Jesus is Sophia incarnate*." FitzGerald, "The Transformative Influence of Wisdom," 437–38.

10. John of the Cross, DN 1.1.2, 298.

11. Ibid., 1.8.3, 312.

12. In "Transformation in Wisdom" FitzGerald names three subversions in John's text—the subversion of our self-image, image of Christ and God, and our relationship to the world. While FitzGerald's study is not about Teresa and she does not use the term "dark night of the feminine," her three degrees of subversion have a similar correspondence to my usage in the text.

13. Teresa, *Life* 9.9, 104.

14. Ibid., 9.3–5, 100–101.

15. Ibid., 21.5, 186–87.

16. Ibid., 4.7, 67.

17. Ibid., 10.8, 109.

18. Ibid., 20.9, 175.

19. Ibid., 20.10, 176.

20. Ibid., 20.11, 177–79.

21. Ibid., 23.11, 205.

22. Ibid., 23.12–13, 206.

23. Ibid., 25.17, 221.

24. Ibid., 25.18, 221.

25. Teresa, *Collected Works*, vol. 2, *The Way of Perfection* (hereafter *Way*) 3.7, 51.

26. Teresa, *Life* 28.18, 245.

27. Teresa, *Way* 21.2, 118; 22.2, 122.

28. Ann-Marie Priest, "Women as God, God as Woman: Mysticism, Negative Theology, and Luce Irigaray," *Journal of Religion* 83/1 (January 2003): 22.

29. See Caroline Walker Bynum, *Fragmentation and Redemption: Essays on Gender and the Human Body in Medieval Religion* (New York: Zone, 1993); idem, *Holy Feast and Holy Fast: The Religious Significance of Food to Medieval Women* (Berkeley: University of California Press, 1988); Barbara Newman, *From Virile Woman to WomanChrist* (Philadelphia: University of Pennsylvania Press, 1995).

30. The question of universal characteristics has been widely debated in academic circles. One of the more current responses can be found in the chapter by Robert K. C. Forman, "A New Methodology for the Study of Religion: A Proposal," in *Doors of Understanding: Conversations on Global Spirituality in Honor of Ewert Cousins*, ed. Steven L. Chase (Quincy, Ill.: Franciscan, 1997), 29–48.

31. Constance FitzGerald in her article "Impasse and Dark Night" was the first (to my knowledge) to apply the categories of the dark night of the individual contemplative to analyze societal impasse. Sandra Schneiders also uses the dark night as a structure within which to frame the collective struggles and transformation of women religious in the post–Vatican II and postmodern period. Sandra Schneiders, *Finding the Treasure: Locating Catholic Religious Life in a New Ecclesial and Cultural Context* (New York: Paulist, 2000), chapters 5 and 6.

32. John of the Cross, DN 1.1.2, 298.

33. Kieran Kavanaugh, Introduction, AC, 47.

34. Chat McKee, "Feminism: A Vision of Love," in *Women of Power Journal* (Summer 1985): 5.

8. Subversion in Contemplation:
Resistance, Resiliency, and Dignification

1. Antonio Pérez-Romero, *Subversion and Liberation in the Writings of St. Teresa of Avila* (Atlanta: Rodopi, 1996), 77.

2. Constance FitzGerald, "A Discipleship of Equals: Voices from Tradition—Teresa of Avila and John of the Cross," in *A Discipleship of Equals: Toward a Christian Feminist Spirituality*, ed. Francis A. Eigo (Villanova, Pa.: Villanova University Press, 1988), 73.

3. Pérez-Romero, *Subversion and Liberation*, 77.

4. Ibid.

5. Ibid., 97.

6. Ibid., 92.

7. Ibid., 93.

8. Alison Weber, *Teresa of Avila and the Rhetoric of Femininity* (Princeton, N.J.: Princeton University Press, 1990), 21–22.

9. Pérez-Romero, *Subversion and Liberation*, 93.

10. Weber, *Teresa of Avila*, 23.

11. Kieran Kavanaugh, Introduction, *The Collected Works of St. Teresa of Avila*, vol. 1, trans. Kieran Kavanaugh and Otilio Rodriguez (Washington, D.C.: Institute of Carmelite Studies, 1987), 30.

12. Ibid., 29–30.

13. Ibid., 30.

14. See chapter 4, note 12.

15. Teresa of Avila, *The Book of Her Life* (hereafter *Life*), in *The Collected Works*, 40.6, 357.

16. Ibid., 27.9, 11.231–32.

17. Ibid., 37.4, 324.

18. Ibid., 34.12, 298.

19. Ibid., 33.5, 287.

20. Teresa of Avila, *Way of Perfection* (hereafter *Way*), in *The Collected Works*, 22.2, 122.

21. Ibid., 21.5, 119.

22. Ibid., 21.8, 120.

23. Kieran Kavanaugh, Introduction, *Way*, 25.

24. Teresa, *Life* 26.5, 226.

25. Ibid., 21.4, 186.

26. Ibid., 21.1, 185.

27. Ibid., 17.5, 154.

28. Teresa, *Way* 21.4–6, 116–117.

29. Teresa, *Life* 29.6, 249.

30. FitzGerald, "A Discipleship of Equals," 78.

31. Introduction to Julian of Norwich, *Showings*, trans. Edmund Colledge and James Walsh (New York: Paulist, 1978), Long Text (hereafter LT) 29.

32. Teresa, *Life* 27.5, 229–30.

33. Ibid., 27.6, 230.

34. Teresa of Avila, *Meditations on the Song of Songs*, in *The Collected Works*, vol. 2, 4.4, 244–45.

35. Pérez-Romero, *Subversion and Liberation*, 161.

36. Teresa, *Life* 20.26–27, 183–84.

37. Teresa, *Interior Castle*, in *The Collected Works*, 7.4.14–15, 449–50.

38. Teresa, *Way* 3.7, 51.

39. Teresa of Avila, *The Book of Her Foundations* (hereafter *Foundations*), in *The Collected Works*, 20.3, 198.

40. Ibid., 15.16, 175.

41. Carole Slade, "Teresa of Avila as a Social Reformer," in *Mysticism and Social Transformation*, ed. Janet K. Ruffing (Syracuse, N.Y.: Syracuse University Press, 2001), 102.

42. Teresa, *Foundations* 22.5, 209.

43. See Slade, "Teresa of Avila as a Social Reformer," 100.

44. "He wants us to know that it [pain or humiliation] will all be turned to our honour and profit by the power of his Passion, and to know that we suffered in no way alone, but together with him, and to see in him our foundation" (LT 28, 227).

45. FitzGerald, "A Discipleship of Equals," 91.

46. Teresa, *Life* 40.8, 357–58.

9. Women's Body as Mystical Text

1. Julian of Norwich, *Showings*, trans. Edmund Colledge and James Walsh (New York: Paulist, 1978), Long Text 6, 186.

2. Laurie A. Finke, "Mystical Bodies and the Dialogics of Vision," in *Maps of Flesh and Light*, ed. Ulrike Wiethaus (Syracuse, N.Y.: Syracuse University Press, 1993), 36.

3. In *Rabelais and His World*, trans. H. Iswolsky (Cambridge, Mass.: MIT Press, 1968), Mikhail Bakhtin writes how the "grotesque body" is represented in a way that degrades and yet regenerates, while the "classical body" is sealed and formally perfect. See an analysis of Mikhail Bakhtin in Finke, "Mystical Bodies and the Dialogics of Vision," 37.

4. Melissa Raphael, *Thealogy and Embodiment: The Post-Patriarchal Reconstruction of Female Sacrality* (Sheffield, Eng.: Sheffield Academic, 1996), 23.

5. Meinrad Craigheid, "Immanent Mother," in *The Feminist Mystic and Other Essays on Women and Spirituality*, ed. Mary E. Giles (New York: Crossroad, 1982), 81.

6. Raphael, *Thealogy and Embodiment*, 41.

7. Finke, "Mystical Bodies and the Dialogics of Vision," 42.

8. See Kristine M. Rankka, *Women and the Value of Suffering: An Aw(e)ful Rowing toward God* (Collegeville, Minn.: Liturgical, 1998), esp. 113–16.

9. Sallie McFague, *The Body of God: An Ecological Theology* (Minneapolis: Fortress Press, 1993), 133.

10. Ibid.

11. Barbara Newman, *Sister of Wisdom: St. Hildegard's Theology of the Feminine* (Berkeley: University of California Press, 1987), 64.

12. Dorothee Soelle, *The Silent Cry: Mysticism and Resistance* (Minneapolis: Fortress Press, 2001), 130.

13. Raphael, *Theology and Embodiment*, 35.

14. Abraham Joshua Heschel, *The Prophets*, vol. 2 (New York: Harper & Row, 1962), 7.

15. Ibid., 4.

16. Raphael, *Theology and Embodiment*, 72.

17. Ursula King, *Women and Spirituality: Voices of Protest and Promise* (University Park: Pennsylvania State University Press, 1993), 108.

18. Lawrence S. Cunningham, *Thomas Merton and the Monastic Vision* (Grand Rapids: Eerdmans, 1999), 78.

19. See Sandra M. Schneiders, *Finding the Treasure: Locating Catholic Religious Life in a New Ecclesial and Cultural Context* (New York: Paulist, 2000), 14–15.

20. Meister Eckhart, Sermon 2, "*Intravit Jesus.*" Translation taken from *Meister Eckhart: Essential Sermons, Commentaries, Treatises, and Defense*, trans. Edmund Colledge and Bernard McGinn (New York: Paulist, 1981), 178.

21. Dorothy H. Donnelly, "The Sexual Mystic: Embodied Spirituality," in *The Feminist Mystic and Other Essays on Women and Spirituality*, ed. Mary E. Giles (New York: Crossroad, 1982), 135.

22. Thomas Merton, *Conjectures of a Guilty Bystander*, cited in Cunningham, *Thomas Merton and the Monastic Vision*, 61.

23. Rainer Maria Rilke, *Rilke on Love and Other Difficulties*, trans. John J. L. Mood (New York: Norton, 1975), 37.

10. Seeing through God's Eyes: Women's Spiritual Rights

1. Jon Sobrino, *Spirituality of Liberation: Toward Political Holiness*, trans. Robert R. Barr (Maryknoll, N.Y.: Orbis, 1988), 104–5.

2. Louis Fischer, ed., *The Essential Gandhi: His Life, Work, and Ideas* (New York: Vintage, 1962), 4.

3. Alexandra Stiglmayer, ed., *Mass Rape: The War against Women in Bosnia-Herzegovina*, trans. Marion Faber (Lincoln: University of Nebraska Press, 1994), 66.

4. Jack Donnelly, *Universal Human Rights in Theory and Practice* (Ithaca, N.Y.: Cornell University Press, 1989), 17.

5. Ibid., 20.

6. Twenty-Ninth Session, Convention on the Elimination of All Forms of Discrimination against Women (CEDAW), June 30 to July 18, 2003; http://www.un.org/womenwatch/daw/cedaw/econvention.htm#intro.

7. Melissa J. Gillis, "A Call for the Feminization of Human Rights," *Church and Society* 88/4 (March/April 1998): 84.

8. Ibid., 86.

9. James E. Wood Jr., "An Apologia for Religious Human Rights," in *Religious Human Rights in Global Perspective: Legal Perspectives*, ed. Johan D. van der Vyver and John Witte Jr. (The Hague: Martinus Nijhoff, 1996), 455.

10. Robert Traer, "Faith in Human Rights," *Church and Society* 88/4 (March/April 1998): 48.

11. For a comprehensive historical overview of the relationship between religion and human rights, see John Witte Jr., "A Dickensian Era of Religious Rights: An Update on *Religious Human Rights in Global Perspective*," *William and Mary Law Review* 42/3 (March 2001): 707–70.

12. Aloysius Pieris, "The Catholic Theology of Human Rights and the Covenant Theology of Human Responsibility," in *Toward a New Heaven and a New Earth: Essays in Honor of Elisabeth Schüssler Fiorenza*, ed. Fernando Segovia (Maryknoll, N.Y.: Orbis, 2003), 337.

13. Ibid., 345.

14. Ibid., 346.

15 See Witte, "A Dickensian Era of Religious Rights," especially the section "The Problem of Conversion," 758–62.

16. Ibid.

17. Ursula King, "Spirituality for Life," in *Women Resisting Violence: Spirituality for Life*, ed. Mary John Mananzan et al. (Maryknoll, N.Y.: Orbis, 1996), 152.

18. Charles Villa-Vicencio, "Identity, Difference and Belonging: Religious and Cultural Rights," in *Religious Human Rights in Global Perspective*, 527.

19. John S. Pobee, "Africa's Search for Religious Human Rights through Returning to Wells of Living Water," in *Religious Human Rights in Global Perspective*, 401.

20. King, "Spirituality for Life," 151.

21. From Teresa of Avila's *Foundations*, 31.46; this translation taken from Antonio Pérez-Romero, *Subversion and Liberation in the Writings of St. Teresa of Avila* (Atlanta: Rodopi, 1996), 181–82.

22. Letty M. Russell, "Spirituality, Struggle, and Cultural Violence," in *Women Resisting Violence*, 24.

23. Ibid., 24–25.

24. Denise M. Ackermann, "The Alchemy of Risk, Struggle, and Hope," in *Women Resisting Violence*, 141.

25. Human Rights Watch World Report 1999, http://www.hrw.org/worldreport99/women/women2.html

26. Traci C. West, *Wounds of the Spirit: Black Women, Violence and Resistance Ethics* (New York: New York University Press, 1999), 4.

27. Human Rights Watch World Report 1999.

28. "Violence against Women around the World," Amnesty International, http://www.amnesty.org.

29. *Women: Challenges to the Year 2000* (New York: United Nations Department of Public Information, 1991), 67.

30. "Worldwide Maternal Mortality Statistics," http://www.gentlebirth.org.

31. *Women: Challenges*, 10.

32. Ruth Seifert, "War and Rape: A Preliminary Analysis," in Stiglmayer, ed., *Mass Rape*, 57. Also see Catharine A. MacKinnon on the relationship of sexualized dominance to violence against women in *Feminism Unmodified: Discourses on Life and Law* (Cambridge: Harvard University Press, 1987).

33. Ibid., 58.

34. Elizabeth Schüssler Fiorenza, "Ties That Bind: Domestic Violence against Women," in *Women Resisting Violence*, 42.

35. Reinhild Traitler-Espiritu, "Violence against Women's Bodies," in *Women Resisting Violence*, 68.

36. Ruth Seifert, "War and Rape: A Preliminary Analysis," 67.

37. Ibid., 66.

38. Andy Smith, "Christian Conquest and the Sexual Colonization of Native Women," in *Violence against Women and Children: A Christian Theological Sourcebook*, ed. Carol J. Adams and Marie M. Fortune (New York: Continuum, 1998), 378.

39. Kathleen Fisher, *Women at the Well: Feminist Perspectives on Spiritual Direction* (New York: Paulist, 1988), 158.

40. Rhonda Copelon, "Surfacing Gender: Reconceptualizing Crimes against Women in Time of War," in Stiglmayer, ed., *Mass Rape*, 213.

41. See Marie M. Fortune's critique of traditional theological responses to women's abuse as inadequate and potentially life-threatening. "The Transformation of Suffering: A Biblical and Theological Perspective," in *Christianity, Patriarchy, and Abuse: A Feminist Critique*, ed. Joanne Carlson Brown and Carole R. Bohn (New York: Pilgrim, 1989).

42. West, *Wounds of the Spirit*, 59.

43. Elaine Scarry, *The Body in Pain: The Making and Unmaking of the World* (New York: Oxford University Press, 1985), 4.

11. Love of the World: An Ethic of Ultimate Concern

1. Jelaluddin Rumi, *Open Secret: Versions of Rumi*, trans. John Moyne and Coleman Barks (Putney, Vt.: Threshold, 1984), 72.

2. Thomas Merton, *Spiritual Direction and Meditation* (Collegeville, Minn.: Liturgical, 1960), 16.

3. Oriana Fallaci, "Conversation with Oriana Fallaci." Cited in Carolyn G. Heilbrun, *Writing a Woman's Life* (New York: Ballantine, 1988), 88.

4. Symeon the New Theologian, "Love Songs to God," in Martin Buber, *Ecstatic Confessions: The Heart of Mysticism* (San Francisco: Harper & Row, 1985), 38.

5. Ibid.

6. Teresa of Avila, *Meditations on the Song of Songs* (hereafter Meditations), in *The Collected Works of St. Teresa of Avila*, vol. 2, trans. Kieran Kavanaugh and Otilio Rodriguez (Washington, D.C.: Institute of Carmelite Studies, 1987), 7.3, 257.

7. Abraham Joshua Heschel, "The Mystical Element in Judaism," cited in Edward K. Kaplan, *Holiness in Words: Abraham Joshua Heschel's Poetics of Piety* (Albany: State University of New York Press, 1996), 72.

8. Ewert H. Cousins, *Christ of the Twenty-First Century* (Rockport, Mass.: Element, 1992), 138.

9. Thomas Merton, "Hagia Sophia," in *A Thomas Merton Reader*, ed. Thomas P. McDonnell (New York: Image, 1974), 506, 508, 511.

10. Teresa of Avila, *The Interior Castle* (hereafter IC), in *The Collected Works*, 5.2.14, 347.

11. *Emmanuel Levinas: Basic Philosophical Writings*, ed. Adriaan T. Peperzak, Simon Critchley, and Robert Bernasconi (Bloomington: Indiana University Press, 1996), 54.

12. Rumi, *Open Secret*, 22.

13. Teresa of Avila, *The Book of Her Life*, in *The Collected Works*, 32.6.

14. Thomas Berry, "The Spirituality of the Earth," in *Liberating Life: Contemporary Approaches to Ecological Theology*, ed. Charles Birch et al. (Maryknoll, N.Y.: Orbis, 1991), 158.

15. See *Amor Mundi: Explorations in the Faith and Thought of Hannah Arendt*, ed. James W. Bernauer (Boston: Martinus Nijhoff, 1987). Also Grace M. Jantzen devotes an extended treatment to Arendt's concept of *amor mundi* in her book *Becoming Divine: Towards a Feminist Philosophy of Religion* (Bloomington: Indiana University Press, 1999), chap. 6.

16. Julian of Norwich, *Showings*, trans. Edmund Colledge and James Walsh (New York: Paulist, 1978), Long Text (hereafter LT) 5, 183.

17. Ibid., LT 60, 297.

18. Dorothy Day, *The Long Loneliness* (San Francisco: Harper & Row, 1981), 78.

19. Cited in *The Essential Gandhi: An Anthology of His Writings on Life, Work and Ideas*, ed. Louis Fischer (New York: Vintage, 1983), 14–15.

20. Teresa, IC, 319.

21. Ewert H. Cousins, *Christ of the Twenty-First Century* (Rockport, Mass.: Element, 1992), 143–44.

22. Ibid., 138.

23. Sermon 12, *Meister Eckhart: Teacher and Preacher*, ed. Bernard McGinn (New York: Paulist, 1986), 270.

24. Thich Nhat Hanh, *Love in Action: Writings on Nonviolent Social Change* (Berkeley: Parallax, 1993), 67.

25. *The Book of the Poor in Spirit by a Friend of God*, ed. and trans. C. F. Kelly (New York: Harper & Brothers, 1954), 229, 236, and 243.

26. Dorothee Soelle, *The Silent Cry: Mysticism and Resistance* (Minneapolis: Fortress Press, 2001), 43.

27. Terrence Des Pres, *The Survivor: An Anatomy of Life in the Death Camps* (New York: Oxford University Press, 1976), vi.

28. Howard Thurman, cited in Alton B. Pollard III, *Mysticism and Social Change: The Social Witness of Howard Thurman*, Martin Luther King, Jr. Memorial Studies in Religion, Culture, and Social Development, ed. Mozella G. Mitchell (New York: Peter Lang, 1992), 84.

29. Thomas Merton, "The General Dance," in *A Thomas Merton Reader*, ed. Thomas P. McDonnell (New York: Image, 1974), 501.

30. Howard Thurman, "Mysticism and Social Action," cited in Pollard, *Mysticism and Social Change*, 65.

31. Abraham Joshua Heschel, *The Prophets*, vol. 1 (New York: Harper & Row, 1955), 5.

Bibliography

Primary Sources

Book Bahir. *The Bahir: Illumination.* Trans. Aryeh Kaplan. York Beach, Maine: Samuel Weiser, 1979.

Christine de Pinzan. *The Book of the City of Ladies.* Trans. Earl Jeffrey Richards. New York: Persea, 1982.

Clement of Alexandria, Saint. *Paedagogus.* New York: Fathers of the Church, 1954.

Dionysius (Pseudo). *Dionysius the Areopagite: The Divine Names and the Mystical Theology.* Trans. C. E. Rolt. London: SPCK, 1983.

———. *Pseudo-Dionysius: The Complete Works.* Trans. Colm Luibheid and Paul Rorem. New York: Paulist, 1987.

Eckhart, Meister. *Meister Eckhart: Essential Sermons, Commentaries, Treatises, and Defense.* Trans. Edmund Colledge and Bernard McGinn. New York: Paulist, 1981.

———. *Meister Eckhart: Teacher and Preacher.* Eds. Bernard McGinn and Frank Tobin. New York: Paulist, 1986.

Gertrude of Helfta. *Gertrude of Helfta: The Herald of Divine Love.* Trans. and ed. Margaret Winkworth. New York: Paulist, 1993.

Ibn al'Arabi. *The Bezels of Wisdom.* Trans. R. W. J. Austin. New York: Paulist, 1980.

John of the Cross, Saint. *The Collected Works of St. John of the Cross.* Trans. Kieran Kavanaugh and Otilio Rodriguez. Washington, D.C.: Institute of Carmelite Studies, 1979–.

Julian of Norwich. *A Book of Showings to the Anchoress Julian of Norwich.* 2 vols. Eds. Edmund Colledge and James Walsh. Toronto: Pontifical Institute of Medieval Studies, 1978.

———. *Showings.* Classics of Western Spirituality. Trans. Edmund Colledge and James Walsh. New York: Paulist, 1978.

Mechthild of Magdeburg. *The Flowing Light of the Godhead.* Trans. Frank Tobin. New York: Paulist, 1998.

Porete, Marguerite. *The Mirror of Simple Souls.* Trans. Ellen L. Babinsky. New York: Paulist, 1993.

Rumi, Jelaluddin. *Open Secret: Versions of Rumi.* Trans. John Moyne and Coleman Barks. Putney, Vt.: Threshold, 1984.

Teresa of Avila. *The Collected Works of St. Teresa of Avila.* 3 vols. Trans. Kieran Kavanaugh and Otilio Rodriguez. Washington, D.C.: Institute of Carmelite Studies, 1987–.

————. *The Complete Works of St. Teresa.* Trans. and ed. E. Allison Peers. London: Sheed and Ward, 1979.

————. *The Collected Letters of St. Teresa of Avila.* Trans. Kieran Kavanaugh. Washington, D.C.: Institute of Carmelite Studies, 2001.

Secondary Sources

Ackermann, Denise M. "The Alchemy of Risk, Struggle, and Hope." In Mananzan et al., *Women Resisting Violence,* 141–46.

Adams, Carol J., and Marie M. Fortune, eds. *Violence against Women and Children: A Christian Theological Sourcebook.* New York: Continuum, 1998.

Ahlgren, Gillian T. W. *Teresa of Avila and the Politics of Sanctity.* Ithaca, N.Y.: Cornell University Press, 1996.

Anderson, Sherry R., and Patricia Hopkins. *The Feminine Face of God.* New York: Bantam, 1991.

Aquino, Maria Pilar. *Our Cry for Life: Feminist Theology from Latin America.* Maryknoll, N.Y.: Orbis, 1993.

————, Daisy L. Machado, and Jeanette Rodriquez, eds. *A Reader in Latina Feminist Theology: Religion and Justice.* Austin: University of Texas Press, 2002.

Bakhtin, Mikhail. *Rabelais and His World.* Trans. H. Iswolsky. Cambridge: MIT Press, 1968.

Bednarowski, Mary Farrell. *The Religious Imagination of American Women.* Bloomington: Indiana University Press, 1999.

Bernauer, James W., ed. *Amor Mundi: Explorations in the Faith and Thought of Hannah Arendt.* Dordrecht, Netherlands: Martinus Nijhoff, 1987.

Berneking, Nancy J., and Pamela Carter Joern, eds. *Re-Membering and Re-Imagining.* Cleveland: Pilgrim, 1995.

Berry, Thomas. "The Spirituality of the Earth." In Charles Birch et al., eds., *Liberating Life: Contemporary Approaches to Ecological Theology,* 151–58. Maryknoll, N.Y.: Orbis, 1991.

Bielecki, Tessa. *Holy Daring: An Outrageous Gift to Modern Spirituality from Saint Teresa, the Grand Wild Woman of Avila.* Rockport, Mass.: Element, 1994.

————. *Teresa of Avila: Mystical Writings.* New York: Crossroad, 1994.

Bilinkoff, Jodi. *The Avila of Saint Teresa: Religious Reform in a Sixteenth-Century City.* Ithaca, N.Y.: Cornell University Press, 1989.

Black, Georgina Dopico. *Perfect Wives, Other Women: Adultery and Inquisition in Early Modern Spain.* Durham, N.C.: Duke University Press, 2001.

Borreson, K. E. *The Image of God: Gender Models in the Judaeo-Christian Tradition.* Minneapolis: Fortress Press, 1995.

Bouyer, Louis. *Women Mystics: Hadewijch of Antwerp, Teresa of Avila, Thérèse of Lisieux, Elizabeth of the Trinity, Edith Stein.* San Francisco: Ignatius, 1993.

Bowie, Fiona, ed. *Beguine Spirituality: Mystical Writings of Mechthild of Magdeburg, Beatrice of Nazareth, and Hadewijch of Brabant.* Trans. Oliver Davies. New York: Crossroad, 1990.

Brock, Rita Nakashima. *Journeys by Heart: A Christology of Erotic Power.* New York: Crossroad, 1988.

————, and Susan Thistlethwaite. *Casting Stones: Prostitution and Liberation in Asia and the United States*. Minneapolis: Fortress Press, 1996.

Bynum, Caroline Walker. *Fragmentation and Redemption: Essays on Gender and the Human Body in Medieval Religion*. New York: Zone, 1991.

————. *Holy Feast and Holy Fast: The Religious Significance of Food to Medieval Women*. Berkeley: University of California Press, 1988.

————. *Jesus as Mother: Studies in the Spirituality of the High Middle Ages*. Berkeley: University of California Press, 1984.

Cady, Susan, Marian Ronan, and Hal Taussig. *Sophia: The Future of Feminist Spirituality*. San Francisco: Harper & Row, 1986.

Cannon, Katie Geneva. *Katie's Canon: Womanism and the Soul of the Black Community*. New York: Continuum, 1995.

————, Beverly W. Harrison, et al. *God's Fierce Whimsy: Christian Feminism and Theological Education*. Cleveland: Pilgrim, 1995.

Carr, Anne E. *Transforming Grace: Christian Tradition and Women's Experience*. San Francisco: Harper & Row, 1988.

————, and Elisabeth Schüssler Fiorenza, eds. *The Special Nature of Women?* London: SCM, 1991.

Cartwright, John H. "The Religious Ethics of Howard Thurman." *Annual of the Society of Christian Ethics* (1985): 79–99.

Chatterjee, Margaret. *The Concept of Spirituality*. Bombay: Allied, 1989.

Chittick, William C. *The Sufi Path of Love: The Spiritual Teachings of Rumi*. Albany: State University of New York Press, 1983.

Chopp, Rebecca S., and Sheila Greeve Davaney, eds. *Horizons in Feminist Theology: Identity, Tradition, and Norms*. Minneapolis: Fortress Press, 1997.

Christ, Carol P., and Judith Plaskow, eds. *Womanspirit Rising: A Feminist Reader in Religion*. San Francisco: Harper & Row, 1979.

Conn, Joann Wolski, ed. *Women's Spirituality: Resources for Christian Development*. 2nd ed. New York: Paulist, 1996.

Cousins, Ewert H. *Christ of the Twenty-First Century*. Rockport, Mass.: Element, 1992.

————. Preface to Series, *World Spirituality: An Encyclopedic History of the Religious Quest*, xi–xiv. New York: Crossroad, 1987–.

————. "Spirituality: A Resource for Theology." *Catholic Theological Society of America Proceedings* 35 (1980): 124–37.

Cowans, Jon. *Early Modern Spain: A Documentary History*. Philadelphia: University of Pennsylvania Press, 2003.

Craigheid, Meinrad. "Immanent Mother." In Giles, ed., *The Feminist Mystic*, 71–83.

Cunningham, Lawrence S. *Thomas Merton and the Monastic Vision*. Grand Rapids: Eerdmans, 1999.

Daly, Mary. *Beyond God the Father: Toward a Philosophy of Women's Liberation*. 2nd ed. Boston: Beacon, 1993.

————. *The Church and the Second Sex*. 2nd ed. Boston: Beacon, 1985.

————. *Gyn/ecology: The Metaethics of Radical Feminism*. Boston: Beacon, 1978.

————. *Outercourse: The Bedazzling Voyage*. San Francisco: HarperSanFrancisco, 1992.

————. *Pure Lust: Elemental Feminist Philosophy*. Boston: Beacon, 1984.

Dastus, Aloo J., and Usha H. Mehta. *Gandhi's Contribution to the Emancipation of Women*. Bombay: Popular Prakashan, 1991.

Davies, Gareth Alban. "St. Teresa and the Jewish Question." In Margaret A. Rees, ed., *Teresa de Jesus and Her World*. Leeds: Trinity and All Saints College, 1981.

Day, Dorothy. *The Long Loneliness*. San Francisco: Harper & Row, 1981.

Des Pres, Terrence. *The Survivor: An Anatomy of Life in the Death Camps*. New York: Oxford University Press, 1976.

Donnelly, Dorothy H. "The Sexual Mystic: Embodied Spirituality." In Giles, ed., *The Feminist Mystic*, 120–41.

Donnelly, Jack. *Universal Human Rights in Theory and Practice*. Ithaca, N.Y.: Cornell University Press, 1989.

Donohue-White, Patricia. "Reading Divine Maternity in Julian of Norwich." *Spiritus: A Journal of Christian Spirituality* 5/1 (2005).

Doohan, Leonard. *The Contemporary Challenge of John of the Cross: An Introduction to His Life and Teaching*. Washington, D.C.: Institute of Carmelite Studies, 1995.

Dubay, Thomas. *Fire Within: St. Teresa of Avila, St. John of the Cross, and the Gospel on Prayer*. San Francisco: Ignatius, 1989.

Egan, Harvey. "Christian Apophatic and Kataphatic Mysticisms." *Theological Studies* 39 (1978): 399–426.

Egido, Teofanes. "The Historical Setting of St. Teresa's Life." *Carmelite Studies* 1 (1980): 122–82.

Eigo, Francis A., ed. *A Discipleship of Equals: Towards a Christian Feminist Spirituality*. Villanova, Pa.: Villanova University Press, 1988.

Esser, Annette, et al., eds. *Re-Visioning Our Sources: Women's Spirituality in European Perspective*. Kampen, The Netherlands: Kok Pharos, 1997.

Fabella, Virginia, and Mercy Amba Oduyoye, eds. *With Passion and Compassion: Third World Women Doing Theology*. Maryknoll, N.Y.: Orbis, 1989.

Finke, Laurie A. "Mystical Bodies and the Dialogics of Vision." In Wiethaus, ed., *Maps of Flesh and Light*, 28–44.

FitzGerald, Constance. "A Discipleship of Equals: Voices from Tradition—Teresa of Avila and John of the Cross." In Eigo, ed., *A Discipleship of Equals*, 63–97.

———. "Impasse and Dark Night." In Conn, ed., *Women's Spirituality*, 410–35.

———. "Transformation in Wisdom: The Subversive Character and Educative Power of Sophia in Contemplation." In Kevin Culligan and Regis Jordan, eds., *Carmel and Contemplation: Transforming Human Consciousness*, 281–358. Carmelite Studies 8. Washington, D.C.: Institute of Carmelite Studies, 2000.

———. "The Transformative Influence of Wisdom in John of the Cross." In Conn, ed., *Women's Spirituality*, 436–51.

Finnegan, Mary Jeremy. *Women of Helfta: Scholars and Mystics*. Athens: University of Georgia Press, 1991.

Fischer, Kathleen. *Women at the Well: Feminist Perspectives on Spiritual Direction*. New York: Paulist, 1998.

Fischer, Louis, ed. *The Essential Gandhi: His Life, Work, and Ideas*. New York: Vintage, 1962.

Flinders, Carol Lee. *At the Root of this Longing: Reconciling a Spiritual Hunger and a Feminist Thirst*. San Francisco: HarperSanFrancisco, 1998.

———. *Enduring Grace: Living Portraits of Seven Women Mystics*. San Francisco: HarperSanFrancisco, 1993.

Forman, Robert K. C. "A New Methodology for the Study of Religion: A Proposal." In Steven L. Chase, ed., *Doors of Understanding: Conversations on Global Spirituality in Honor of Ewert Cousins*, 29–48. Quincy, Ill.: Franciscan, 1997.

———. *The Problem of Pure Consciousness: Mysticism and Philosophy*. New York: Oxford University Press, 1990.

Frohlich, Mary. *The Intersubjectivity of the Mystic: a Study of Teresa of Avila's Interior Castle*. Atlanta: Scholars, 1993.

Fulkerson, Mary McClintock. *Changing the Subject: Women's Discourses and Feminist Theology*. Minneapolis: Fortress Press, 1994.

Furlong, Monica, ed. *Mirror to the Church: Reflections on Sexism*. London: SPCK, 1988.

———. *Visions and Longings: Medieval Women Mystics*. Boston: Shambhala, 1996.

Gatta, Julia. *Three Spiritual Directors for Our Time: Julian of Norwich, The Cloud of Unknowing, Walter Hilton*. Cambridge, Mass.: Cowley, 1986.

Giles, Mary E., ed. *The Feminist Mystic and Other Essays on Women and Spirituality*. New York: Crossroad, 1982.

———. *Women in the Inquisition: Spain and the New World*. Baltimore: Johns Hopkins University Press, 1999.

Gillis, Melissa J. "A Call for the Feminization of Human Rights." *Church & Society* 88/4 (March/April 1998): 80–91.

Gimbutas, Marija. *The Language of the Goddess*. San Francisco: Harper & Row, 1989.

———. *The Living Goddesses*. Berkeley: University of California Press, 1999.

Gottlieb, Lynn. *She Who Dwells Within: A Feminist Vision of a Renewed Judaism*. San Francisco: HarperSanFrancisco, 1995.

Grant, Jacquelyn. *White Women's Christ and Black Women's Jesus: Feminist Christology and Womanist Response*. Atlanta: Scholars, 1989.

Green, Arthur. "Introduction." In *Jewish Spirituality: From the Bible through the Middle Ages*, xi–xvi. World Spirituality: An Encyclopedic History of the Religious Quest. New York: Crossroad, 1988.

Green, Deidre. *Gold in the Crucible: Teresa of Avila and the Western Mystical Tradition*. Longmead, England: Element, 1989.

Gross, Francis L. *The Making of a Mystic: Seasons in the Life of Teresa of Avila*. Albany: State University of New York Press, 1993.

Hampson, Daphne. *Theology and Feminism*. Oxford: Blackwell, 1990.

Hardy, Richard P. "'Nursing': A Sanjuanist Image." *Science et Esprit* 28 (1976): 297–307.

Harvey, Andrew, and Anne Baring. *The Divine Feminine: Exploring the Feminine Face of God around the World*. Berkeley: Conari, 1996.

Hayes, Diana L. *Hagar's Daughters: Womanist Ways of Being in the World*. New York: Paulist, 1985.

Heschel, Abraham Joshua. *The Prophets*. 2 vols. New York: Harper & Row, 1955.

Hegy, Pierre, ed. *Feminist Voices in Spirituality*. Lewiston, N.Y.: Edwin Mellen, 1996.

Heyward, Carter. *Our Passion for Justice: Images of Power, Sexuality, and Liberation*. New York: Pilgrim, 1984.

————, and Ellen C. Davis. *Speaking of Christ: A Lesbian Feminist Voice*. New York: Pilgrim, 1989.

Hogan, Linda. *From Women's Experience to Feminist Theology*. Sheffield, England: Sheffield Academic, 1995.

Hollywood, Amy. *The Soul as Virgin Wife: Mechthild of Magdeburg, Marguerite Porete, and Meister Eckhart*. Notre Dame, Ind.: University of Notre Dame Press, 1995.

Howells, Edward. *John of the Cross and Teresa of Avila: Mystical Knowing and Selfhood*. New York: Crossroad, 2002.

Idel, Moshe. "Reification of Language in Jewish Mysticism." In Steven T. Katz, ed., *Mysticism and Language*, 42–79. New York: Oxford University Press, 1992.

————, and Bernard McGinn, eds. *Mystical Union and Monotheistic Faith: An Ecumenical Dialogue*. New York: Macmillan, 1989.

Irigaray, Luce. *Between East and West: From Singularity to Community*. Trans. Stephen Pluhacek. New York: Columbia University Press, 2002.

————. *Elemental Passions*. Trans. Joanne Collie and Judith Still. London: Athlone, 1992.

————. *Sexes and Genealogies*. Trans. Gillian C. Gill. New York: Columbia University Press, 1993.

————. *Speculum of the Other Woman*. Trans. Gillian C. Gill. Ithaca, N.Y.: Cornell University Press, 1974.

————. *Thinking the Difference*. Trans. Karin Montin. New York: Routledge, 1994.

Isasi-Díaz, Ada María. *En la Lucha/In the Struggle: Elaborating a Mujerista Theology*. Minneapolis: Fortress Press, 1993.

Jantzen, Grace M. *Becoming Divine: Towards a Feminist Philosophy of Religion*. Bloomington: Indiana University Press, 1999.

————. *Julian of Norwich: Mystic and Theologian*. New York: Paulist, 2000.

————. *Power, Gender, and Christian Mysticism*. Cambridge: Cambridge University Press, 1995.

Jayawardena, Kumari, and Malathi de Alwis, eds. *Embodied Violence: Communalising Women's Sexuality in South Asia*. London: Zed, 1996.

Johnson, Elizabeth A. *Friends of God and Prophets: A Feminist Theological Reading of the Communion of Saints*. New York: Continuum, 1998.

————. *She Who Is: The Mystery of God in Feminist Theological Discourse*. New York: Crossroad, 1993.

————. *Truly Our Sister: A Theology of Mary in the Communion of Saints*. New York: Continuum, 2003.

Jones, Serene. *Feminist Theory and Christian Theology: Cartographies of Grace*. Guides to Theological Inquiry. Minneapolis: Fortress Press, 2000.

Katz, Steven T. *Mysticism and Philosophical Analysis*. New York: Oxford University Press, 1978.

Kellenbach, Katharina von. *Anti-Judaism in Feminist Religious Writings*. American Academy of Religion Cultural Criticism 1. Atlanta: Scholars, 1994.

Kelly, C. F. *The Book of the Poor in Spirit by a Friend of God*. New York: Harper & Brothers, 1954.

Kim, C. W. Maggie, et al. *Transfigurations: Theology and the French Feminists*. Minneapolis: Fortress Press, 1993.

King, Ursula, ed. *Feminist Theology from the Third World: A Reader*. Maryknoll, N.Y.: Orbis, 1994.

———. *Religion and Gender*. Oxford: Blackwell, 1995.

———. "Spirituality for Life." In Mananzan et al., *Women Resisting Violence*, 147–60.

———. *Women and Spirituality: Voices of Protest and Promise*. 2nd ed. University Park: Pennsylvania State University Press, 1993.

Kinsley, David. *Hindu Goddesses: Visions of the Divine Feminine in the Hindu Religious Tradition*. Berkeley: University of California Press, 1988.

Kraemer, Ross Shepard, and Mary Rose D'Angelo, eds. *Women and Christian Origins*. New York: Oxford University Press, 1999.

Küng, Hans, and Jürgen Moltmann, eds. *The Ethics of World Religions and Human Rights*. Philadelphia: Trinity Press International, 1992.

LaCugna, Catherine Mowry, ed. *Freeing Theology: The Essentials of Theology in a Feminist Perspective*. New York: HarperCollins, 1993.

Lanzetta, Beverly, J. "Contemplative Ethics: Intimacy, *Amor Mundi*, and Dignification in Julian of Norwich and Teresa of Avila." *Spiritus: A Journal of Christian Spirituality* 5/1 (2005).

———. "Julian and Teresa as Cartographers of the Soul: A Contemplative Feminist Hermeneutic." Paper delivered at American Academy of Religion Annual Meeting, Atlanta. November 2003.

———. "The Soul of Woman and the Dark Night of the Feminine in St. Teresa of Avila." Paper delivered at American Academy of Religion Western Region (WESCOR), University of California, Davis. March 2003.

Lerner, Gerda. *The Creation of Feminist Consciousness: From the Middle Ages to Eighteen-seventy*. New York: Oxford University Press, 1993.

Loades, Ann L., ed. *Feminist Theology: A Reader*. London: SPCK, 1990.

Louth, Andrew. *Theology and Spirituality*. Oxford: S.L.G., 1976.

MacKinnon, Catharine A. *Feminism Unmodified: Discourses on Life and Law*. Cambridge: Harvard University Press, 1988.

Mananzan, Mary John, Mercy Amba Oduyoye, et al., eds. *Women Resisting Violence: Spirituality for Life*. Maryknoll, N.Y.: Orbis, 1996.

Mayeski, Marie Anne. *Women: Models of Liberation*. New York: Sheed and Ward, 1988.

McAvoy, Liz Herbert. "'The Moders Service': Motherhood as Matrix in Julian of Norwich." *Mystics Quarterly* 24/4 (1998): 181–97.

McEntire, Sandra J. *Julian of Norwich: A Book of Essays*. New York: Garland, 1998.

McEwan, Dorothea and Lisa Isherwood. *Introducing Feminist Theology*. Sheffield: Sheffield Academic, 1993.

McFague, Sallie. *Metaphorical Theology: Models of God in Religious Language*. Philadelphia: Fortress Press, 1982.

———. *Models of God: Theology for an Ecological, Nuclear Age.* Philadelphia: Fortress Press, 1987.

———. *The Body of God: An Ecological Theology.* Minneapolis: Fortress Press, 1993.

McGinn, Bernard. *The Flowering of Mysticism: Men and Women in the New Mysticism (1200-1350).* The Presence of God: A History of Western Mysticism. New York: Crossroad, 1998.

———. *The Foundations of Mysticism: Origins to the Fifth Century.* The Presence of God: A History of Western Mysticism. New York: Crossroad, 1992.

———. *Meister Eckhart and the Beguine Mystics.* New York: Continuum, 1994.

McKee, Chat. "Feminism: A Vision of Love." *Women of Power* (Summer 1985): 5.

McNamara, Jo Ann. "The Rhetoric of Orthodoxy: Clerical Authority and Female Innovation in the Struggle with Heresy." In Wiethaus, ed., *Maps of Flesh and Light*, 9–27.

Meadow, Mary Jo, and Carole A. Rayburn, eds. *A Time to Weep and a Time to Sing.* Minneapolis: Winston, 1985.

Meehan, Brenda. *Holy Women of Russia: The Lives of Five Orthodox Women Offer Spiritual Guidance for Today.* San Francisco: HarperSanFrancisco, 1993.

Merton, Thomas. "*Hagia Sophia.*" In Thomas P. McDonnell, ed., *A Thomas Merton Reader.* New York: Doubleday, 1989.

———. *Introductions East and West: The Foreign Prefaces of Thomas Merton.* Ed. Robert E. Daggy. Greensboro, N.C.: Unicorn, 1981.

———. *The Monastic Journey.* Ed. Brother Patrick Hart. Garden City, N.Y.: Doubleday, 1978.

———. *Spiritual Direction and Meditation.* Collegeville, Minn.: Liturgical, 1960.

Mohave, John Giles. *Hadewijch and Her Sisters: Other Ways of Loving and Knowing.* Albany: State University of New York Press, 1993.

Mood, John J. L. *Rilke on Love and Other Difficulties: Translations and Consideration of Rainer Maria Rilke.* New York: Norton, 1975.

Nasr, Seyyed Hossein. "Introduction." In *Islamic Spirituality: Foundations*, xv–xxix. World Spirituality: An Encyclopedic History of the Religious Quest. New York: Crossroad, 1991.

Newman, Barbara. *From Virile Woman to WomanChrist: Studies in Medieval Religion and Literature.* Philadelphia: University of Pennsylvania Press, 1995.

———. *Gods and the Goddesses: Vision, Poetry, and Belief in the Middle Ages.* Philadelphia: University of Pennsylvania Press, 2003.

———. "Henry Suso and the Medieval Devotion to Christ the Goddess." *Spiritus* 2 (2002): 1–14.

———. *Sister of Wisdom: St. Hildegard's Theology of the Feminine.* Berkeley: University of California Press, 1987.

———, ed. *Voice of the Living Light: Hildegard of Bingen and Her World.* Berkeley: University of California Press, 1998.

Newsom, Carol A., and Sharon H. Ringe, eds. *The Women's Bible Commentary.* Louisville, Ky.: Westminster John Knox, 1992.

Nhat Hanh, Thich. *Love in Action: Writings on Nonviolent Social Change.* Berkeley: Parallax, 1993.

Ochs, Carol. *Women and Spirituality*. New York: Rowman and Littlefield, 1997.

Oduyoye, Mercy Amba. *Daughters of Anowa: African Women and Patriarchy*. Maryknoll, N.Y.: Orbis, 1995.

———. *Introducing African Women's Theology*. Introductions in Feminist Theology. Cleveland: Pilgrim, 2001.

O'Halloran, Maura. *Pure Heart, Enlightened Mind: The Zen Journal and Letters of Maura "Soshin" O'Halloran*. New York: Riverhead, 1994.

Panikkar, Raimundo. *Blessed Simplicity: The Monk as Universal Archetype*. New York: Seabury, 1982.

Patrick, Anne E. *Liberating Conscience: Feminist Explorations in Catholic Moral Theology*. New York: Continuum, 1996.

Peers, E. Allison. *A Handbook to the Life and Times of St. Teresa and St. John of the Cross*. London: Burns & Oates, 1954.

———. *Mother of Carmel: A Portrait of St. Teresa of Jesus*. London: SPCK, 1945.

———. *Studies of the Spanish Mystics*. 2nd ed. London: SPCK, 1951.

Pelikan, Jaroslav. *Mary through the Centuries: Her Place in the History of Culture*. New Haven: Yale University Press, 1996.

Peperzak, Adriaan T., Simon Critchley, and Robert Bernasconi, eds. *Emmanuel Levinas: Basic Philosophical Writings*. Bloomington: Indiana University Press, 1996.

Pérez-Romero, Antonio. *Subversion and Liberation in the Writings of St. Teresa of Avila*. Atlanta: Rodopi, 1996.

Petroff, Elizabeth Alvilda. *Body and Soul: Essays on Medieval Women and Mysticism*. New York: Oxford University Press, 1994.

Pieris, Aloysius. "The Catholic Theology of Human Rights and the Covenant Theology of Human Responsibility." In Fernando F. Segovia, ed., *Toward a New Heaven and a New Earth: Essays in Honor of Elizabeth Schüssler Fiorenza*, 334–50. Maryknoll, N.Y.: Orbis, 2003.

Plaskow, Judith. *Standing Again at Sinai: Judaism from a Feminist Perspective*. San Francisco: HarperSanFrancisco, 1990.

———, and Carol P. Christ, eds. *Weaving the Vision: New Patterns in Feminist Spirituality*. San Francisco: HarperSanFrancisco, 1989.

Pobee, John S. "Africa's Search for Religious Human Rights through Returning to Wells of Living Water." In van der Vyver and Witte, eds., *Religious Human Rights*, 391–416.

Pollard, Alton B., III. *Mysticism and Social Change: The Social Witness of Howard Thurman*. Martin Luther King, Jr. Memorial Studies in Religion, Culture, and Social Development. Ed. Mozella G. Mitchell. New York: Peter Lang, 1992.

Priest, Ann-Marie. "Becoming Nothing: Mystical Annihilation as Feminine Being." Paper delivered to Studium, St. Benedict's Monastery. March 2001.

———. "Women as God, God as Women: Mysticism, Negative Theology and Luce Irigaray." *The Journal of Religion* 83 (2003): 1–23.

Pushpa Joshi, ed. *Gandhi on Women: Collection of Mahatma Gandhi's Writings and Speeches on Women*. Ahmedabad, India: Navajivan, 1988.

Rankka, Kristine M. *Women and the Value of Suffering: An Aw(e)ful Rowing Toward God*. Collegeville, Minn.: Liturgical, 1998.

Raphael, Melissa. *Thealogy and Embodiment: The Post-Patriarchal Reconstruction of Female Sacrality.* Sheffield, England: Sheffield Academic, 1996.

Ruether, Rosemary Radford. *New Woman, New Earth: Sexist Ideologies and Human Liberation.* Boston: Beacon, 1995 [1975].

————. *Sexism and God-Talk: Toward a Feminist Theology.* Boston: Beacon, 1983.

————. *Women and Redemption: A Theological History.* Minneapolis: Fortress Press, 1998.

————. *Women-Church: Theology & Practice of Feminist Liturgical Communities.* San Francisco: Harper & Row, 1986.

Russell, Letty M. "Spirituality, Struggle, and Cultural Violence." In Mananzan et al., *Women Resisting Violence,* 20–26.

————, ed. *Feminist Interpretation of the Bible.* Philadelphia: Westminster, 1985.

Schäfer, Peter. "Daughter, Sister, Bride, and Mother: Images of the Femininity of God in the Early Kabbala." *Journal of the American Academy of Religion* 68 (2000): 221–42.

————. *Mirror of Her Beauty: Feminine Images of God from the Bible to the Early Kabbalah.* Princeton, N.J.: Princeton University Press, 2002.

Schneiders, Sandra M. *Beyond Patching: Faith and Feminism in the Catholic Church.* New York: Paulist, 1991.

————. *Finding the Treasure: Locating Catholic Religious Life in a New Ecclesial and Cultural Context.* New York: Paulist, 2000.

————. "Spirituality in the Academy." *Theological Studies* 50 (1989): 676–97.

————. *Women and the Word.* New York: Paulist, 1986.

Scholem, Gershom. "*Shekhinah*: The Feminine Element in Divinity." In Gershom Scholem, *On the Mystical Shape of the Godhead: Basic Concepts in Kabbalah.* Trans. Joachim Neugroschel. Ed. Jonathan Chipman. New York: Schoken, 1991.

Schüssler Fiorenza, Elisabeth. *In Memory of Her: A Feminist Theological Reconstruction of Christian Origins.* New York: Crossroad, 1994 [1983].

————, ed. *Searching the Scriptures.* Vol. 1: *A Feminist Introduction.* Vol. 2: *A Feminist Commentary.* New York: Crossroad, 1993, 1998.

————. "Ties that Bind: Domestic Violence against Women." In Mananzan et al., *Women Resisting Violence,* 39–55.

Seelaus, Vilma. "The Feminine in Prayer in the Interior Castle." *Mystics Quarterly* 13 (1987): 203–14.

Segovia, Fernando F., ed. *Toward a New Heaven and a New Earth: Essays in Honor of Elizabeth Schüssler Fiorenza.* Maryknoll, N.Y.: Orbis, 2003.

Seifert, Ruth. "War and Rape: A Preliminary Analysis." In Alexandria Stiglmayer, ed., *Mass Rape: The War against Women in Bosnia-Herzegovina,* 54–72. Trans. Marion Faber. Lincoln: University of Nebraska Press, 1994.

Sells, Michael A. *Mystical Languages of Unsaying.* Chicago: University of Chicago Press, 1994.

Sivaraman, Krishna, "Introduction," in *Hindu Spirituality, Vedas through Vedanta,* xv–xl. World Spirituality: An Encyclopedic History of the Religious Quest, vol. 6. New York: Crossroad, 1989.

Slade, Carole. "St. Teresa of Avila as a Social Reformer." In Janet K. Ruffing, ed., *Mysticism and Social Transformation*, 91–103. Syracuse, N.Y.: Syracuse University Press, 2001.

Sobrino, Jon. *Spirituality of Liberation: Toward Political Holiness.* Trans. Robert R. Barr. Maryknoll, N.Y.: Orbis, 1988.

Soelle, Dorothee. *The Silent Cry: Mysticism and Resistance.* Trans. Martin and Barbara Rumscheidt. Minneapolis: Fortress Press, 2001.

—————. *The Strength of the Weak: Toward a Christian Feminist Identity.* Trans. Robert and Rita Kimber. Philadelphia: Westminster, 1984.

—————. *The Window of Vulnerability: A Political Spirituality.* Minneapolis: Fortress Press, 1990.

Stiglmayer, Alexandra, ed. *Mass Rape: The War against Women in Bosnia-Herzegovina.* Trans. Marion Faber. Lincoln: University of Nebraska Press, 1994.

Sumrall, Amber Coverdale, and Patrice Vecchione, eds. *Storming Heaven's Gate: An Anthology of Spiritual Writings by Women.* New York: Plume, 1997.

Sur, Carolyn Worman. *The Feminine Images of God in the Visions of Saint Hildegard of Bingen's Scivias.* Lewiston, N.Y.: Edwin Mellen, 1993.

Surtz, Ronald E. *Writing Women in Late Medieval and Early Modern Spain: the Mothers of Saint Teresa of Avila.* Philadelphia: University of Pennsylvania Press, 1995.

Swietlicki, Catherine. *Spanish Christian Cabala: The Works of Luis de Leon, Santa Teresa de Jesus, and San Juan de la Cruz.* Columbia: University of Missouri Press, 1986.

Symeon the New Theologian, "Love Songs to God." In Martin Buber, *Ecstatic Confessions: The Heart of Mysticism*, 36–42. San Francisco: Harper & Row, 1985.

Tamez, Elsa. *Bible of the Oppressed.* Maryknoll, N.Y.: Orbis, 1982.

Tarnas, Richard. *The Passion of the Western Mind.* New York: Harmony, 1991.

Teasdale, Wayne. "Spirituality as a Primary Resource in Promoting Peace." *Source Point* (Spring 2003). Online: http://www.source-point.org.

Townes, Emilie M., ed. *A Troubling in My Soul: Womanist Perspectives on Evil and Suffering.* Maryknoll, N.Y.: Orbis, 1995.

Traer, Robert. "Faith in Human Rights." *Church & Society* 88/4 (March/April 1998): 46–58.

Trible, Phyllis. *Texts of Terror: Literary-Feminist Readings of Biblical Narratives.* Overtures to Biblical Theology. Philadelphia: Fortress Press, 1984.

van der Vyver, Johan D., and John Witte Jr., eds. *Religious Human Rights in Global Perspective: Legal Perspectives.* The Hague: Martinus Nijhoff, 1996.

Villa-Vicencio, Charles. "Identity, Difference and Belonging: Religious and Cultural Rights." In van der Vyver and Witte, eds., *Religious Human Rights*, 515-37.

Vinje, Patricia Mary. *An Understanding of Love according to the Anchoress Julian of Norwich.* Salzburg, Austria: Institut fur angliktik und amerikanistik universitat, 1983.

Weaver, Mary Jo. *Cloister and Community: Life within a Carmelite Monastery.* Bloomington: Indiana University Press, 2002

Weber, Alison. *Teresa of Avila and the Rhetoric of Femininity.* Princeton, N.J.: Princeton University Press, 1990.

Weems, Renita J. *Battered Love: Marriage, Sex, and Violence in the Hebrew Prophets.* Overtures to Biblical Theology. Minneapolis: Fortress Press, 1995.

West, Traci C. *Wounds of the Spirit: Black Women, Violence and Resistance Ethics.* New York: New York University Press, 1999.

Whitford, Margaret, ed. *The Irigaray Reader.* Oxford: Blackwell, 1991.

Wiethaus, Ulrike, ed. *Maps of Flesh and Light: The Religious Experience of Medieval Women Mystics.* Syracuse, N.Y.: Syracuse University Press, 1993.

Williams, Delores S. *Sisters in the Wilderness: The Challenge of Womanist God-Talk.* Maryknoll, N.Y.: Orbis, 1993.

Williams, Rowan. *Teresa of Avila.* New York: Continuum, 2000.

Winter, Miriam Therese. *WomanWisdom: A Feminist Lectionary and Psalter—Women of the Hebrew Scriptures, Part One.* New York: Crossroad, 1991.

Witte, John, Jr. "A Dickensian Era of Religious Rights: An Update on *Religious Human Rights in Global Perspective." William and Mary Law Review* 42 (2001): 707–70.

Wood, James E., Jr. "An Apologia for Religious Human Rights." In van der Vyver and Witte, eds., *Religious Human Rights,* 455–85.

Wright, Wendy M. "The Feminine Dimension of Contemplation." In Giles, ed., *The Feminist Mystic,* 103–19.

Young, Iris. *Justice and the Politics of Difference.* Princeton, N.J.: Princeton University Press, 1990.

Zum Brunn, Emilie, and Georgette Epiney-Burgard. *Women Mystics in Medieval Europe.* New York: Paragon, 1989.

Index